Lecture Notes in Computer Science 11372

Commenced Publication in 1973
Founding and Former Series Editors:
Gerhard Goos, Juris Hartmanis, and Jan van Leeuwen

More information about this series at http://www.springer.com/series/7408

José Júlio Alferes · Moa Johansson (Eds.)

Practical Aspects of Declarative Languages

21th International Symposium, PADL 2019
Lisbon, Portugal, January 14–15, 2019
Proceedings

 Springer

Editors
José Júlio Alferes
Universidade Nova de Lisboa
Lisbon, Portugal

Moa Johansson (iD)
Chalmers University of Technology
Gothenburg, Sweden

ISSN 0302-9743   ISSN 1611-3349 (electronic)
Lecture Notes in Computer Science
ISBN 978-3-030-05997-2   ISBN 978-3-030-05998-9 (eBook)
https://doi.org/10.1007/978-3-030-05998-9

Library of Congress Control Number: 2018964133

LNCS Sublibrary: SL2 – Programming and Software Engineering

This Springer imprint is published by the registered company Springer Nature Switzerland AG
The registered company address is: Gewerbestrasse 11, 6330 Cham, Switzerland

Preface

This volume contains the papers presented at the 21st Symposium on Practical Aspects of Declarative Languages (PADL 2019), held during January 14–15, 2019, in Lisbon, Portugal. The symposium was co-located with the 46th ACM SIGPLAN Symposium on Principles of Programming Languages (POPL 2019).

PADL is a well-established forum for researchers and practitioners to present original work emphasizing novel applications and implementation techniques for all forms of declarative concepts, including, but not limited to, logic, constraint, and functional languages.

Declarative languages build on sound theoretical bases to provide attractive frameworks for application development. These languages have been successfully applied to many different real-world situations, ranging from database management to active networks, software engineering, natural language processing, ontologies, and decision support systems.

New developments in theory and implementation have opened up new application areas. At the same time, applications of declarative languages to novel problems raise numerous interesting research issues. Well-known questions include designing for scalability, language extensions for application deployment, and programming environments. Thus, applications drive the progress in the theory and implementation of declarative systems and benefit from this progress.

Originally established as a workshop (PADL 1999 in San Antonio, Texas), the PADL series developed into a regular annual symposium; previous editions took place in San Antonio, Texas (1999), Boston, Massachusetts (2000), Las Vegas, Nevada (2001), Portland, Oregon (2002), New Orleans, Louisiana (2003), Dallas, Texas (2004), Long Beach, California (2005), Charleston, South Carolina (2006), Nice, France (2007), San Francisco, California (2008), Savannah, Georgia (2009), Madrid, Spain (2010), Austin, Texas (2012), Rome, Italy (2013), and San Diego, California (2014), Portland, Oregon (2015), St. Petersburg, Florida (2016), and Paris, France (2017), and Los Angeles, California (2018).

This year, the Program Committee received 35 submissions. Each submission was reviewed by three Program Committee members, and 14 papers were accepted, based only on the merit of each submission and regardless of scheduling or space constraints.

We would like to express thanks to the Association of Logic Programming (ALP) and the Association for Computing Machinery (ACM) for their support of the symposium, and Springer for the longstanding, successful cooperation with the PADL series. We are very grateful to the 29 members of the PADL 2018 Program Committee and external reviewers for their invaluable work and for the precious help in selecting the two best papers. The chairs of POPL 2019 were also of great help in steering the organizational details of the event.

We are happy to note that the conference was successfully managed with the help of EasyChair.

January 2018   José Júlio Alferes
                                                               Moa Johansson

Organization

Program Committee

Erika Abraham	RWTH Aachen University, Germany
Jose Julio Alferes	Universidade NOVA de Lisboa, Portugal
Marcello Balduccini	Saint Joseph's University, USA
Lars Bergstrom	Mozilla Research
Edwin Brady	University of St. Andrews, UK
Manuel Carro	Technical University of Madrid (UPM) and IMDEA Software Institute, Spain
Stefania Costantini	University of L'Aquila, Italy
Ornela Dardha	University of Glasgow, UK
Esra Erdem	Sabanci University, Turkey
Wolfgang Faber	Alpen-Adria-Universität Klagenfurt, Austria
Marco Gavanelli	University of Ferrara, Italy
Martin Gebser	University of Potsdam, Germany
Alex Gerdes	University of Gothenburg, Sweden
Jurriaan Hage	Utrecht University, The Netherlands
Kevin Hamlen	The University of Texas at Dallas, USA
Moa Johansson	Chalmers University of Technology, Sweden
Ekaterina Komendantskaya	Heriot-Watt University, UK
Ramana Kumar	DeepMind
Nicola Leone	University of Calabria, Italy
Geoffrey Mainland	Drexel University, USA
Marco Maratea	DIBRIS, University of Genoa, Italy
Emilia Oikarinen	University of Helsinki, Finland
Axel Polleres	Vienna University of Economics and Business, Austria
Enrico Pontelli	New Mexico State University, USA
Ricardo Rocha	University of Porto, Portugal
Konstantin Schekotihin	Alpen-Adria Universität Klagenfurt, Austria
Meera Sridhar	University of North Carolina Charlotte, USA
Paul Tarau	University of North Texas, USA
Lukasz Ziarek	SUNY Buffalo, USA

Additional Reviewers

Alviano, Mario
Côrte-Real, Joana
Dodaro, Carmine
Farka, Frantisek
Kaminski, Roland
Leofante, Francesco

Obermeier, Philipp
Ogris, Paul
Perri, Simona
Son, Tran Cao
Wanko, Philipp

Contents

Strong Equivalence and Program's Structure in Arguing Essential Equivalence Between First-Order Logic Programs

Yuliya Lierler[✉]

University of Nebraska at Omaha, Omaha, USA
ylierler@unomaha.edu

Abstract. Answer set programming is a prominent declarative programming paradigm used in formulating combinatorial search problems and implementing distinct knowledge representation formalisms. It is common that several related and yet substantially different answer set programs exist for a given problem. Sometimes these encodings may display significantly different performance. Uncovering *precise formal* links between these programs is often important and yet far from trivial. This paper claims the correctness of a number of interesting program rewritings. Notably, they assume *programs with variables* and such important language features as choice, disjunction, and aggregates.

1 Introduction

Answer set programming (ASP) is a prominent knowledge representation paradigm with roots in logic programming [2]. It is frequently used for addressing combinatorial search problems. It has also been used to provide implementations and/or translational semantics to other knowledge representation formalisms such as action languages including language $\mathscr{AL}$ [13, Sect. 8]. In ASP, when a software engineer tackles a problem domain it is a common practice to first develop *a/some* solution/encoding to a problem and then rewrite this solution/encoding iteratively using, for example, a projection technique to gain a better performing encoding [3]. These common processes bring a question to light: What are the formal means to argue the correctness of renewed formulations of the original encoding to a problem or, in other words, to argue that these distinct formulations are essentially the same—in a sense that they capture solutions to the same problem.

It has been long recognized that studying various notions of equivalence between programs under the answer set semantics is of crucial importance. Researchers proposed and studied strong equivalence [18,19], uniform equivalence [4], relativized strong and uniform equivalences [23]. Also, equivalences relative to specified signatures [6,15] were considered. In most of the cases the

© Springer Nature Switzerland AG 2019
J. J. Alferes and M. Johansson (Eds.): PADL 2019, LNCS 11372, pp. 1–18, 2019.
https://doi.org/10.1007/978-3-030-05998-9_1

programs considered for studying the distinct forms of equivalence are propositional. Works [5,7,15,19,22] are exceptions. These authors consider programs with variables (or, first-order programs). Yet, it is first-order programs that ASP knowledge engineers develop. Thus, theories on equivalence between programs with variables are especially important as they can lead to more direct arguments about properties of programs used in practice. On the one hand, this work can be seen as a continuation of work by Eiter et al. [5], where we consider common program rewritings using a more complex dialect of logic programs. On the other hand, it grounds the concept of program's synonymity studied by Pearce and Valverde [22] in a number of practical examples. Namely, we illustrate how formal results on strong equivalence developed earlier and in this work help us to construct precise claims about programs in practice.

In this paper, we systematically study some common rewritings on first-order programs utilized by ASP practitioners. As a running and motivating example that grounds general theoretical presentation of this work into specific context, we consider two formalizations of a planning module given in [13, Sect. 9]. Namely,

1. a *Plan-choice* formalization that utilizes choice rules and aggregate expressions,
2. a *Plan-disj* formalization that utilizes disjunctive rules.

Such a planning module is meant to be augmented with an ASP representation of a dynamic system description expressed in action language $\mathscr{AL}$. In [13], Gelfond and Kahl formally state in Proposition 9.1.1 that the answer sets of program *Plan-disj* augmented with a given system description encode all the "histories/plans" of a specified length in the transition system captured by the system description. Although both *Plan-choice* and *Plan-disj* programs *intuitively* encode the same knowledge the exact connection between them is not immediate. In fact, these programs (i) do not share the same signature; (ii) use distinct syntactic constructs such as choice, disjunction, aggregates in the specification of a problem. Here, we establish a one-to-one correspondence between the answer sets of these programs on their properties. Thus, the aforementioned formal claim about *Plan-disj* translates into the same claim for *Plan-choice*. It is due to remark that although in [13], Gelfond and Kahl use the word "module" when formalizing a planning domain they utilize this term only informally to refer to a collection of rules responsible for formalizing "planning".

In this paper we use a dialect of ASP language called RASPL-1 [17]. Notably, this language combines choice, aggregate, and disjunction constructs. Its semantics is given in terms of the SM operator, which exemplifies the approach to the semantics of first-order programs that bypasses grounding. Relying on SM-based semantics allows us to refer to earlier work that study the formal properties of first-order programs [9,10] using this operator. We state a sequence of formal results on programs rewritings and/or programs' properties. Some discussed rewritings are well known and frequently used in practice. Often, their correctness is an immediate consequence of well known properties about logic programs (e.g., relation between intuitionistically provable first-order formulas and strongly equivalent programs viewed as such formulas). Other discussed rewritings are far less straightforward and require elaborations on previous theoretical findings about the operator SM. It is well known that propositional head-cycle-free disjunctive programs [1] can be rewritten to nondisjunctive programs by means of simple syntactic transformation. Here we not only generalize this result to the case of first-order programs, but also illustrate that at times we can remove disjunction from parts of a program even though the program is not head-cycle-free. This result is relevant to local shifting and component-wise shifting discussed in [5] and [16] respectively. We also generalize so called Completion Lemma and Lemma on Explicit Definitions stated in [8,11] for the case of propositional theories and propositional logic programs. These generalizations are applicable to first-order programs.

Summary. We view this paper as an important step towards bringing theories about program's equivalence to providing practical solutions in the realm of ASP as it is used by knowledge engineers. A portfolio of formal results on program rewritings stated in this paper can serve as a solid theoretical basis for

- a software system that may automatically produce new variants of logic programs (some of these encodings will often exhibit better performance) by utilizing studied rewritings;
- a proof technique for arguing the correctness of a logic program. This proof technique assumes the existence of a "gold standard" logic program formalizing a problem at hand, in a sense that this gold standard is trusted to produce correct results. A proper portfolio of known program rewritings and their properties equips ASP practitioners with powerful tools to argue that another encoding is essentially the same to the gold standard.

Paper Outline. We start this paper by presenting the *Plan-choice* and *Plan-disj* programs. We then introduce a logic program language called RASPL-1 [17]. The semantics of this language is given in terms of the SM operator. We then proceed to the statement of a sequence of formal results on program's rewritings.

2   Running Example and Observations

This section presents two ASP formalizations of a domain independent *planning module* given in [13, Sect. 9]. Such planning module is meant to be augmented with a logic program encoding a system description expressed in action language $\mathscr{A}\mathscr{L}$ that represents a domain of interest (in Sect. 8 of their book [13], Gelfond and Kahl present a sample Blocks World domain representation). Two formalizations of a planning module are stated here almost verbatim. Predicate names o and *sthHpd* intuitively stand for *occurs* and *something_happend*, respectively. We eliminate classical negation symbol by (i) utilizing auxiliary predicates non_o in place of ¬o; and (ii) introducing rule ← $o(A, I), non\_o(A, I)$. This is a standard practice and ASP systems perform the same procedure when processing classical negation symbol ¬ occurring in programs (in other words, symbol ¬ is treated as a syntactic sugar).

Let $SG(I)$ abbreviate $step(I)$, $not\ goal(I)$, $I \neq n$, where n is some integer specifying a limit on a length of an allowed plan. The first formalization called *Plan-choice* follows:

$$success \leftarrow goal(I),\ step(I).$$

$$\leftarrow not\ success.$$

$$\leftarrow o(A, I), non\_o(A, I) \tag{1}$$

$$non\_o(A, I) \leftarrow action(A),\ step(I),\ not\ o(A, I) \tag{2}$$

$$\{o(A, I)\} \leftarrow action(A),\ SG(I) \tag{3}$$

$$\leftarrow 2 \leq \#count\{A : o(A, I)\},\ SG(I). \tag{4}$$

$$\leftarrow not\ 1 \leq \#count\{A : o(A, I)\},\ SG(I) \tag{5}$$

One more remark is in order. In [13], Gelfond and Kahl list only a single rule

$$1\{o(A, I) : action(A)\}1 \leftarrow SG(I)$$

in place of rules (3–5). Note that this single rule is an abbreviation for rules (3–5) [12].

The second formalization that we call a *Plan-disj* encoding is obtained from *Plan-choice* by replacing rules (3–5) with the following:

$$o(A, I) \mid non\_o(A, I) \leftarrow action(A),\ SG(I) \tag{6}$$

$$\leftarrow o(A, I),\ o(A', I),\ action(A),\ action(A'),\ A \neq A' \tag{7}$$

$$sthHpd(I) \leftarrow o(A, I) \tag{8}$$

$$\leftarrow not\ sthHpd(I),\ SG(I). \tag{9}$$

It is important to note several facts about the considered planning module encodings. These planning modules are meant to be used with logic programs that capture (i) a domain of interest originally stated as a system description in the action language $\mathscr{AL}$; (ii) a specification of an initial configuration; (iii) a specification of a goal configuration. The process of encoding (i–iii) as a logic program, which we call a *Plan-instance* encoding, follows a strict procedure. As a consequence, some important properties hold about any *Plan-instance*. To state these it is convenient to recall a notion of a simple rule and define a "terminal" predicate.

A *signature* is a set of function and predicate symbols/constants. A function symbol of arity 0 is an *object constant*. A *term* is an object constant, an object variable, or an expression of the form $f(t_1, \ldots, t_m)$, where f is a function symbol of arity m and each t_i is a term. An *atom* is an expression of the form $p(t_1, \ldots, t_n)$ or $t_1 = t_2$, where p is an n-ary predicate symbol and each t_i is a term. A *simple body* has the form $a_1, \ldots, a_m, not\ a_{m+1}, \ldots, not\ a_n$ where a_i is an atom and n is possible 0. Expression $a_1, \ldots, a_m$ forms the positive part of a body. A *simple rule* has a form $h_1 \mid \cdots \mid h_k \leftarrow Body$ or $\{h_1\} \leftarrow Body$ where h_i is an atom and $Body$ is a simple body. We now state a recursive definition of a terminal predicate with respect to a program. Let i be a nonnegative integer. A predicate that occurs only in rules whose body is empty is called *0-terminal*. We call a predicate $i + 1$-*terminal* when it occurs only in the heads of simple rules (left hand side of an arrow), furthermore (i) in these rules all predicates occurring in their positive parts of the bodies must be at most i-*terminal* and (ii) at least one of these rules is such that some predicate occurring in its positive part of the body is i-*terminal*. We call any x-terminal predicate *terminal*. For example, in program

$$block(b0).\ block(b1).$$
$$loc(X) \leftarrow block(X). \qquad loc(table).$$

block is a 0-terminal predicate, *loc* is a 1-terminal predicate; and both predicates are terminal.

We are now ready to state important *Facts* about any possible *Plan-instance* and, consequently, about the considered planning modules

1. Predicate *o* never occurs in the heads of rules in *Plan-instance*.
2. Predicates *action* and *step* are terminal in *Plan-instance* as well as in *Plan-instance* augmented by either *Plan-choice* or *Plan-disj*.
3. By Facts 1 and 2, predicate *o* is terminal in *Plan-instance* augmented by either *Plan-choice* or *Plan-disj*.
4. Predicate *sthHpd* never occurs in the heads of the rules in *Plan-instance*.

In the remainder of the paper we will ground considered theoretical results by illustrating how they formally support the following *Observations*:

1. In the presence of rule (2) it is safe to add a rule

$$non\_o(A, I) \leftarrow not\ o(A, I),\ action(A),\ SG(I) \qquad (10)$$

   into an arbitrary program. By "safe to add/replace" we understand that the resulting program has the same answer sets as the original one.
2. It is safe to replace rule (4) with rule

$$\leftarrow o(A, I),\ o(A', I),\ SG(I),\ A \neq A' \qquad (11)$$

   within an arbitrary program.
3. In the presence of rules (1) and (2), it is safe to replace rule (3) with rule

$$o(A, I) \leftarrow not\ non\_o(A, I),\ action(A),\ SG(I) \qquad (12)$$

   within an arbitrary program.
4. Given the syntactic features of the *Plan-choice* encoding and any *Plan-instance* encoding, it is safe to replace rule (3) with rule (6). The argument utilizes *Observations* 1 and 3. Fact 4 forms an essential syntactic feature.
5. Given the syntactic features of the *Plan-choice* encoding and any *Plan-instance* encoding, it is safe to replace rule (4) with rule (7). The argument utilizes *Observation* 2, i.e., it is safe to replace rule (4) with rule (11). An essential syntactic feature relies on Fact 1, and the facts that (i) rule (3) is the only one in *Plan-choice*, where predicate *o* occurs in the head; and (ii) rule (7) differs from (11) only in atoms that are part of the body of (3).

6. By Fact 4 and the fact that *sthHpd* does not occur in any other rule but (9) in *Plan-disj*, the answer sets of the program obtained by replacing rule (5) with rules (8) and (9) are in one-to-one correspondence with the answer sets of the program *Plan-disj* extended with *Plan-instance*.

Essential Equivalence Between Two Planning Modules: These *Observations* are sufficient to claim that the answer sets of the *Plan-choice* and *Plan-disj* programs (extended with any *Plan-instance*) are in one-to-one correspondence. We can capture the simple relation between the answer sets of these programs by observing that dropping the atoms whose predicate symbol is *sthHpd* from an answer set of the *Plan-disj* program results in an answer set of the *Plan-choice* program.

3   Preliminaries: RASPL-1 Logic Programs, Operator SM, Strong Equivalence

We now review a logic programming language RASPL-1 [17]. This language is sufficient to capture choice, aggregate, and disjunction constructs (as used in *Plan-choice* and *Plan-disj*). There are distinct and not entirely compatible semantics for aggregate expressions in the literature. We refer the interested reader to the discussion by Lee et al. in [17] on the roots of semantics of aggregates considered in RASPL-1.

An *aggregate expression* is an expression of the form

$$b \leq \#count\{\mathbf{x} : L_1, \ldots, L_k\} \tag{13}$$

($k \geq 1$), where b is a positive integer (*bound*), $\mathbf{x}$ is a list of variables (possibly empty), and each L_i is an atom possibly preceded by *not*. This expression states that there are at least b values of $\mathbf{x}$ such that conditions $L_1, \ldots, L_k$ hold.

A *body* is an expression of the form

$$e_1, \ldots, e_m, not\ e_{m+1}, \ldots, not\ e_n \tag{14}$$

($n \geq m \geq 0$) where each e_i is an aggregate expression or an atom. A rule is an expression of either of the forms

$$a_1 \mid \cdots \mid a_l \leftarrow Body \tag{15}$$

$$\{a_1\} \leftarrow Body \tag{16}$$

($l \geq 0$) where each a_i is an atom, and *Body* is the body in the form (14). When $l = 0$, we identify the head of (15) with symbol $\perp$ and call such a rule a *denial*. When $l = 1$, we call rule (15) a *defining* rule. We call rule (16) a *choice* rule. A *(logic) program* is a set of *rules*. An atom of the form $not\ t_1 = t_2$ is abbreviated by $t_1 \neq t_2$.

It is easy to see that rules in the *Plan-choice* and *Plan-disj* encodings are in the RASPL-1 language.

3.1 Operator SM

Typically, the semantics of logic programs with variables is given by stating that these rules are an abbreviation for a possibly infinite set of propositional rules. Then the semantics of propositional programs is considered. The SM operator introduced by Ferraris et al. in [9] gives a definition for the semantics of first-order programs bypassing grounding. It is an operator that takes a first-order sentence F and a tuple $\mathbf{p}$ of predicate symbols and produces the second order sentence that we denote by $\mathrm{SM}_\mathbf{p}[F]$.

We now review the operator SM. The symbols $\bot, \wedge, \vee, \rightarrow, \forall$, and $\exists$ are viewed as primitives. The formulas $\neg F$ and $\top$ are abbreviations for $F \rightarrow \bot$ and $\bot \rightarrow \bot$, respectively. If p and q are predicate symbols of arity n then $p \le q$ is an abbreviation for the formula $\forall \mathbf{x}(p(\mathbf{x}) \rightarrow q(\mathbf{x}))$, where $\mathbf{x}$ is a tuple of variables of length n. If $\mathbf{p}$ and $\mathbf{q}$ are tuples $p_1, \dots, p_n$ and $q_1, \dots, q_n$ of predicate symbols then $\mathbf{p} \le \mathbf{q}$ is an abbreviation for the conjunction $(p_1 \le q_1) \wedge \cdots \wedge (p_n \le q_n)$, and $\mathbf{p} < \mathbf{q}$ is an abbreviation for $(\mathbf{p} \le \mathbf{q}) \wedge \neg(\mathbf{q} \le \mathbf{p})$. We apply the same notation to tuples of predicate variables in second-order logic formulas. If $\mathbf{p}$ is a tuple of predicate symbols $p_1, \dots, p_n$ (not including equality), and F is a first-order sentence then $\mathrm{SM}_\mathbf{p}[F]$ denotes the second-order sentence

$$F \wedge \neg \exists \mathbf{u}(\mathbf{u} < \mathbf{p}) \wedge F^*(\mathbf{u}),$$

where $\mathbf{u}$ is a tuple of distinct predicate variables $u_1, \dots, u_n$, and $F^*(\mathbf{u})$ is defined recursively:

- $p_i(\mathbf{t})^*$ is $u_i(\mathbf{t})$ for any tuple $\mathbf{t}$ of terms;
- F^* is F for any atomic formula F that does not contain members of $\mathbf{p}$;[1]
- $(F \wedge G)^*$ is $F^* \wedge G^*$;
- $(F \vee G)^*$ is $F^* \vee G^*$;
- $(F \rightarrow G)^*$ is $(F^* \rightarrow G^*) \wedge (F \rightarrow G)$;
- $(\forall x F)^*$ is $\forall x F^*$;
- $(\exists x F)^*$ is $\exists x F^*$.

Note that if $\mathbf{p}$ is the empty tuple then $\mathrm{SM}_\mathbf{p}[F]$ is equivalent to F. For intuitions regarding the definition of the SM operator we direct the reader to [9, Sects. 2.3, 2.4].

By $\sigma(F)$ we denote the set of all function and predicate constants occurring in first-order formula F (not including equality). We will call this the *signature of F*. An interpretation I over $\sigma(F)$ is a $\mathbf{p}$-*stable model* of F if it satisfies $\mathrm{SM}_\mathbf{p}[F]$, where $\mathbf{p}$ is a tuple of predicates from $\sigma(F)$. We note that a $\mathbf{p}$-stable model of F is also a model of F.

By $\pi(F)$ we denote the set of all predicate constants (excluding equality) occurring in a formula F. Let F be a first-order sentence that contains at least

---

[1] This includes equality statements and the formula $\bot$.

one object constant. We call an Herbrand interpretation of $\sigma(F)$ that is a $\pi(F)$-stable model of F *an answer set.*[2] Theorem 1 from [9] illustrates in which sense this definition can be seen as a generalization of a classical definition of an answer set (via grounding and reduct) for typical logic programs whose syntax is more restricted than syntax of programs considered here.

3.2 Semantics of Logic Programs

From this point on, we view logic program rules as alternative notation for particular types of first-order sentences. We now define a procedure that turns every aggregate, every rule, and every program into a formula of first-order logic, called its *FOL representation.* First, we identify the logical connectives $\wedge$, $\vee$, and $\neg$ with their counterparts used in logic programs, namely, the comma, the disjunction symbol $|$, and connective *not*. This allows us to treat $L_1, \ldots, L_k$ in (13) as a conjunction of literals. The FOL representation of an aggregate expressions of the form $b \leq \#count\{\mathbf{x} : F(\mathbf{x})\}$ follows

$$\exists \mathbf{x^1} \cdots \mathbf{x^b} \Big[\bigwedge_{1 \leq i \leq b} F(\mathbf{x^i}) \wedge \bigwedge_{1 \leq i < j \leq b} \neg(x^i = x^j) \Big], \tag{17}$$

where $\mathbf{x^1} \cdots \mathbf{x^b}$ are lists of new variables of the same length as $\mathbf{x}$. The FOL representations of logic rules of the form (15) and (16) are formulas

$$\widetilde{\forall}(Body \rightarrow a_1 \vee \cdots \vee a_l) \quad \text{and} \quad \widetilde{\forall}(\neg\neg a_1 \wedge Body \rightarrow a_1),$$

where each aggregate expression in *Body* is replaced by its FOL representation. Symbol $\widetilde{\forall}$ denotes universal closure.

For example, expression $SG(I)$ stands for formula $step(I) \wedge \neg goal(I) \wedge \neg I = n$ and rules (3) and (5) in the *Plan-choice* encoding have the FOL representation:

$$\widetilde{\forall}\big(\neg\neg o(A, I) \wedge SG(I) \wedge action(A) \rightarrow o(A, I)\big) \tag{18}$$

$$\forall I\big(\neg \exists A[o(A, I)] \wedge SG(I) \rightarrow \bot\big) \tag{19}$$

The FOL representation of rule (4) is the universal closure of the following implication

$$(\exists AA'\big(o(A, I) \wedge o(A', I) \wedge \neg A = A'\big) \wedge SG(I)) \rightarrow \bot.$$

We define a concept of an answer set for logic programs that contain at least one object constant. This is inessential restriction as typical logic programs without object constants are in a sense trivial. In such programs, whose semantics is

---

[2] An Herbrand interpretation of a signature σ (containing at least one object constant) is such that its universe is the set of all ground terms of σ, and every ground term represents itself. An Herbrand interpretation can be identified with the set of ground atoms (not containing equality) to which it assigns the value true.

given via grounding, rules with variables are eliminated during grounding. Let Π be a logic program with at least one object constant. (In the sequel we often omit expression "with at least one object constant".) By $\widehat{\Pi}$ we denote its FOL representation. (Similarly, for a body $Body$ or a rule R, by $\widehat{Body}$ or $\widehat{R}$ we denote their FOL representations.) An *answer set* of Π is an answer set of its FOL representation $\widehat{\Pi}$. In other words, an *answer set* of Π is an Herbrand interpretation of $\widehat{\Pi}$ that is a $\pi(\widehat{\Pi})$-stable model of $\widehat{\Pi}$, i.e., a model of

$$\text{SM}_{\pi(\widehat{\Pi})}[\widehat{\Pi}]. \tag{20}$$

Sometimes, it is convenient to identify a logic program Π with its semantic counterpart (20) so that formal results stated in terms of SM operator immediately translate into the results for logic programs.

3.3   Review: Strong Equivalence

We restate the definition of strong equivalence given in [9] and recall some of its properties. First-order formulas F and G are *strongly equivalent* if for any formula H, any occurrence of F in H, and any tuple $\mathbf{p}$ of distinct predicate constants, $\text{SM}_{\mathbf{p}}[H]$ is equivalent to $\text{SM}_{\mathbf{p}}[H']$, where H' is obtained from H by replacing F by G. Trivially, any strongly equivalent formulas are such that their stable models coincide (relative to any tuple of predicate constants). In [19], Ferraris et al. show that first-order formulas F and G are strongly equivalent if they are equivalent in **SQHT** $^=$ logic—an intermediate logic between classical and intuitionistic logics. We recall that every formula provable in the natural deduction system without the law of the excluded middle ($F \vee \neg F$) is a theorem in intuitionistic logic. Also, every formula provable using natural deduction, where the axiom of the law of the excluded middle ($F \vee \neg F$) is replaced by the weak law of the excluded middle ($\neg F \vee \neg\neg F$), is a theorem of **SQHT** $^=$.

The definition of strong equivalence between first-order formulas paves the way to a definition of strong equivalence for logic programs. A logic program Π_1 is *strongly equivalent* to logic program Π_2 when for any program Π,

$$\text{SM}_{\pi(\widehat{\Pi \cup \Pi_1})}[\widehat{\Pi \cup \Pi_1}] \text{ is equivalent to } \text{SM}_{\pi(\widehat{\Pi \cup \Pi_2})}[\widehat{\Pi \cup \Pi_2}].$$

It immediately follows that logic programs Π_1 and Π_2 are *strongly equivalent* if first-order formulas $\widehat{\Pi}_1$ and $\widehat{\Pi}_2$ are equivalent in logic of **SQHT** $^=$.

We now review an important result about properties of denials.

Theorem 1 (Theorem 3 [9]). *For any first-order formulas F and G and arbitrary tuple $\mathbf{p}$ of predicate constants, $SM_{\mathbf{p}}[F \wedge \neg G]$ is equivalent to $SM_{\mathbf{p}}[F] \wedge \neg G$.*

As a consequence, $\mathbf{p}$-stable models of $F \wedge \neg G$ can be characterized as the $\mathbf{p}$-stable models of F that satisfy first-order logic formula $\neg G$. Consider any denial $\leftarrow Body$. Its FOL representation has the form $\widetilde{\forall}(Body \rightarrow \bot)$ that is intuitionistically equivalent to formula $\neg \widetilde{\exists} Body$. Thus, Theorem 1 tells us that given any denial of a program it is safe to compute answer sets of a program without this denial and a posteriori verify that the FOL representation of a denial is satisfied.

Corollary 1. *Two denials are strongly equivalent if their FOL representations are classically equivalent.*

This corollary is also an immediate consequence of the Replacement Theorem for intuitionistic logic [21, Sect. 13.1] stated below.

Replacement Theorem. If F is a first-order formula containing a subformula G and F' is the result of replacing that subformula by G' then $\widetilde{\forall}(G \leftrightarrow G')$ intuitionistically implies $F \leftrightarrow F'$.

4   Rewritings

4.1   Rewritings via Pure Strong Equivalence

Strong equivalence can be used to argue the correctness of some program rewritings practiced by ASP software engineers. Here we state several theorems about strong equivalence between programs. *Observations* 1, 2, and 3 are consequences of these results.

We say that body *Body* subsumes body *Body'* when *Body'* has the form *Body, Body''* (note that an order of expressions in a body is immaterial). We say that a rule R subsumes rule R' when heads of R and R' coincide while body of R subsumes body of R'. For example, rule (2) subsumes rule (10).

Subsumption Rewriting: Let $\mathbf{R}'$ denote a set of rules subsumed by rule R. It is easy to see that formulas $\widehat{R}$ and $\widehat{R} \wedge \widehat{\mathbf{R}'}$ are intuitionistically equivalent. Thus, program composed of rule R and program $\{R\} \cup \mathbf{R}'$ are strongly equivalent. It immediately follows that *Observation* 1 holds. Indeed, rule (2) is strongly equivalent to the set of rules composed of itself and (10). Indeed, rule (2) subsumes rule (10).

Removing Aggregates: The following theorem is an immediate consequence of the Replacement Theorem for intuitionistic logic.

Proposition 1. *Program*

$$H \leftarrow b \leq \#count\{\mathbf{x} : F(\mathbf{x})\}, \ G \tag{21}$$

is strongly equivalent to program

$$H \leftarrow \underset{1 \leq i \leq b}{,} F(\mathbf{x^i}) \underset{1 \leq i < j \leq b}{,} x^i \neq x^j, \ G \tag{22}$$

where G and H have no occurrences of variables in $\mathbf{x^i}$ ($1 \leq i \leq b$).

Proposition 1 shows us that *Observation* 2 is a special case of a more general fact. Indeed, take rules (4) and (11) to be the instances of rules (21) and (22) respectively.

We note that the Replacement Theorem for intuitionistic logic also allows us to immediately conclude the following.

Corollary 2. *Program* $H \leftarrow G$ *is strongly equivalent to program* $H \leftarrow G'$ *when* $\forall(\widehat{G} \leftrightarrow \widehat{G'})$.

Proposition 1 is a special case of this corollary. We could use Corollary 2 to illustrate the correctness of *Observation* 2. Yet, the utility of Proposition 1 is that it can guide syntactic analysis of a program with a goal of equivalent rewriting (for instance, for the sake of performance or clarity). In contrast, Corollary 2 equips us with a general semantic condition that can be utilized in proving the syntactic properties of programs in spirit of Proposition 1.

   Replacing Choice Rule by Defining Rule: Theorem 2 shows us that *Observation* 3 is an instance of a more general fact.

Theorem 2. *Program*

$$\leftarrow p(\mathbf{x}),\ q(\mathbf{x}) \tag{23}$$

$$q(\mathbf{x}) \leftarrow not\ p(\mathbf{x}), F_1 \tag{24}$$

$$\{p(\mathbf{x})\} \leftarrow F_1,\ F_2 \tag{25}$$

is strongly equivalent to program composed of rules (23), (24) *and rule*

$$p(\mathbf{x}) \leftarrow not\ q(\mathbf{x}),\ F_1,\ F_2 \tag{26}$$

Indeed, we can derive the former program (its FOL representation) from the latter intuitionistically; and we can derive the later from the former in logic **SQHT$^=$**. For the second direction, De Morgan's law $\neg(F \wedge G) \to \neg F \vee \neg G$ (provable in logic **SQHT$^=$**, but not valid intuitionistically) is essential.

   To illustrate the correctness of *Observation* 3 by Theorem 2: (i) take rules (1), (2), (3) be the instances of rules (23), (24), (25) respectively, and (ii) rule (12) be the instance of rule (26).

4.2   Useful Rewritings Using Structure

In this section, we study rewritings on a program that rely on its structure. We review the concept of a dependency graph used in posing structural conditions on rewritings.

Review: Predicate Dependency Graph. We present the concept of the predicate dependency graph of a formula following the lines of [10]. An occurrence of a predicate constant, or any other subexpression, in a formula is called *positive* if the number of implications containing that occurrence in the antecedent is even, and *strictly positive* if that number is 0. We say that an occurrence of a predicate constant is *negated* if it belongs to a subformula of the form $\neg F$ (an abbreviation for $F \to \bot$), and *nonnegated* otherwise.

   For instance, in formula (18), predicate constant o has a strictly positive occurrence in the consequence of the implication; whereas the same symbol o has a negated positive occurrence in the antecedent

$$\neg\neg o(A, I) \wedge step(I) \wedge \neg goal(I) \wedge \neg I = n \wedge action(A) \tag{27}$$

of (18). Predicate symbol *action* has a strictly positive non-negated occurrence in (27). The occurrence of predicate symbol *goal* is negated and not positive in (27). The occurrence of predicate symbol *goal* is negated and positive in (18).

An *FOL rule* of a first-order formula F is a strictly positive occurrence of an implication in F. For instance, in a conjunction of two formulas (18) and (19) the FOL rules are as follows

$$\neg\neg o(A, I) \wedge SG(I) \wedge action(A) \rightarrow o(A, I) \tag{28}$$
$$\neg\exists A[o(A, I)] \wedge SG(I) \rightarrow \bot. \tag{29}$$

For any first-order formula F, the *(predicate) dependency graph* of F relative to the tuple $\mathbf{p}$ of predicate symbols (excluding =) is the directed graph that (i) has all predicates in $\mathbf{p}$ as its vertices, and (ii) has an edge from p to q if for some FOL rule $G \rightarrow H$ of F

- p has a strictly positive occurrence in H, and
- q has a positive nonnegated occurrence in G.

We denote such a graph by $DG_{\mathbf{p}}[F]$. For instance, the dependence graph of a conjunction of formulas (18) and (19) relative to all its predicate symbols contains four vertices, namely, o, *action*, *step*, and *goal*, and two edges: one from vertex o to vertex *action* and the other one from o to *step*. Indeed, consider the only two FOL rules (28) and (29) stemming from this conjunction. Predicate constant o has a strictly positive occurrence in the consequent $o(A, I)$ of the implication (28), whereas *action* and *step* are the only predicate constants in the antecedent $\neg\neg o(A, I) \wedge SG(I) \wedge action(A)$ of (28) that have positive and nonnegated occurrence in this antecedent. It is easy to see that a FOL rule of the form $G \rightarrow \bot$, e.g., FOL rule (29), does not contribute edges to any dependency graph.

For any logic program Π, the *dependency graph* of Π, denoted $DG[\Pi]$, is a directed graph of $\widehat{\Pi}$ relative to the predicates occurring in Π. For example, let Π be composed of two rules (3) and (5). The conjunction of formulas (18) and (19) forms its FOL representation.

Shifting. We call a logic program *disjunctive* if all its rules have the form (15), where *Body* only contains atoms possibly preceded by *not*. We say that a disjunctive program is *normal* when it does not contain disjunction connective |. In [14], Gelfond et al. defined a mapping from a propositional disjunctive program Π to a propositional normal program by replacing each rule (15) with $l > 1$ in Π by l new rules

$$a_i \leftarrow Body, \ not \ a_1, \ldots not \ a_{i-1}, not \ a_{i+1}, \ldots not \ a_l.$$

They showed that every answer set of the constructed program is also an answer set of Π. Although the converse does not hold in general, in [1] Ben-Eliyahu and Dechter showed that the converse holds if Π is "head-cycle-free". In [20], Linke et al. illustrated how this property holds about programs with nested expressions that capture choice rules, for instance. Here we generalize these findings further. First, we show that shifting is applicable to first-order programs (that also allow choice rules and aggregates in addition to disjunction). Second, we illustrate that under certain syntactic/structural conditions on a program we may apply shifting "locally" to some rules with disjunction and not others.

For an atom a, by a^0 we denote its predicate constant. For example $o(A, I)^0 = o$. Let R be a rule of the form (15) with $l > 1$. By $shift_{\mathbf{p}}(R)$ (where $\mathbf{p}$ is a tuple of distinct predicates excluding $=$) we denote the rule

$$\Big|_{1 \leq i \leq l,\, a_i^0 \in \mathbf{p}} \quad a_i \leftarrow Body \quad , \quad \underset{1 \leq j \leq l,\, a_j^0 \notin \mathbf{p}}{not\ a_j}. \tag{30}$$

Let C be the set of strongly connected components in the dependency graph of Π. By $shift(R)$ we denote the new rules $shift_s(R)$ for every $s \in C$ where s has a predicate symbol that occurs in the head of R. Consider a sample program Π_{samp} composed of two rules with disjunction

$$a \mid b \mid c \leftarrow \qquad\qquad d \mid c \leftarrow$$

and three defining rules

$$a \leftarrow b \qquad b \leftarrow a \qquad e(1). \tag{31}$$

The strongly connected components of program Π_{samp} are $\{\{a, b\}, \{c\}, \{d\}, \{e(1)\}\}$. Expression $shift(a \mid b \mid c \leftarrow)$ denotes rules $a \mid b \leftarrow not\ c$ and $c \leftarrow not\ a, not\ b$.

Theorem 3. *Let Π be a logic program, $\mathbf{R}$ be a set of rules in Π of the form* (15) *with $l > 1$. A program constructed from Π by replacing each rule $R \in \mathbf{R}$ with $shift(R)$ has the same answer sets as Π.*

This theorem tells us, for example, that the answer sets of the sample program Π_{samp} coincide with the answer sets of three distinct programs composed of rules in (31) and rules in any of the following columns:

$a \mid b \leftarrow not\ c$	$a \mid b \leftarrow not\ c$	$a \mid b \mid c \leftarrow$
$c \leftarrow not\ a, not\ b$	$c \leftarrow not\ a, not\ b$	
$d \leftarrow not\ c$	$d \mid c \leftarrow$	$d \leftarrow not\ c$
$c \leftarrow not\ d$		$c \leftarrow not\ d$

To obtain the rules in the first column take $\mathbf{R}$ to consist of the first two rules of Π_{samp}. To obtain the second column take $\mathbf{R}$ to consist of the first rule of Π_{samp}. To obtain the last column take $\mathbf{R}$ to consist of the second rule of Π_{samp}.

We now use Theorem 3 to argue the correctness of *Observation* 4. Let *Plan-choice'* denote a program constructed from the *Plan-choice* encoding by replacing (3) with (6). Let *Plan-choice''* denote a program constructed from the *Plan-choice*, by (i) replacing (3) with (12) and (ii) adding rule (10). Theorem 3 tells us that programs *Plan-choice'* and *Plan-choice''* have the same answer sets. Indeed,

1. take **R** to consist of rule (6) and
2. recall Facts 1, 2, and 3. Given any *Plan-instance* intended to use with *Plan-choice* a program obtained from the union of *Plan-instance* and *Plan-choice'* is such that *o* is terminal. It is easy to see that any terminal predicate in a program occurs only in the singleton strongly connected components of a program's dependency graph.

Due to *Observations* 1 and 3, the *Plan-choice* encoding has the same answer sets as *Plan-choice''* and consequently the same answer sets as *Plan-choice'*. This argument accounts for the proof of *Observation* 4.

Completion. We now proceed at stating formal results about first-order formulas and their stable models. The fact that we identify logic programs with their FOL representations translates these results to the case of the RASPL-1 programs.

About a first-order formula F we say that it is in *Clark normal form* [9] relative to the tuple/set **p** of predicate symbols if it is a conjunction of formulas of the form

$$\forall \mathbf{x}(G \rightarrow p(\mathbf{x})) \tag{32}$$

one for each predicate $p \in \mathbf{p}$, where $\mathbf{x}$ is a tuple of distinct object variables. We refer the reader to Sect. 6.1 in [9] for the description of the intuitionistically equivalent transformations that can convert a first-order formula, which is a FOL representation for a RASPL-1 program (without disjunction and denials), into Clark normal form.

The *completion* of a formula F in Clark normal form relative to predicate symbols **p**, denoted by $Comp_{\mathbf{p}}[F]$, is obtained from F by replacing each conjunctive term of the form (32) with $\forall \mathbf{x}(G \leftrightarrow p(\mathbf{x}))$.

The following Corollary is an immediate consequence of Theorem 10 in [9], Theorem 1, and the fact that formula of the form $\widetilde{\forall}(Body \rightarrow \bot)$ is intuitionistically equivalent to formula $\neg\widetilde{\exists}Body$.

Corollary 3. *For any formula $G \wedge H$ such that (i) formula G is in Clark normal form relative to* **p** *and H is a conjunction of formulas of the form $\widetilde{\forall}(K \rightarrow \bot)$, the implication*

$$SM_{\mathbf{p}}[G \wedge H] \rightarrow Comp_{\mathbf{p}}[G] \wedge H$$

is logically valid.

To illustrate the utility of this result we now construct an argument for the correctness of *Observation* 5. This argument finds one more formal result of use:

Proposition 2. *For a program Π, a first-order formula F such that every answer set of Π satisfies F, and any two denials R and R' such that $F \rightarrow (\widehat{R} \leftrightarrow \widehat{R'})$, the answer sets of programs $\Pi \cup \{R\}$ and $\Pi \cup \{R'\}$ coincide.*

Consider the *Plan-choice* encoding without denial (4) extended with any *Plan-instance*. We can partition it into two parts: one that contains the denials, denoted by Π_H, and the remainder, denoted by Π_G. Recall Fact 1. Following the steps described by Ferraris et al. in [9, Sect. 6.1], formula $\widehat{\Pi_G}$ turned into Clark normal form relative to the predicate symbols occurring in $\Pi_H \cup \Pi_G$ contains implication (18). The completion of this formula contains equivalence

$$\widetilde{\forall}\big(\neg\neg o(A, I) \land SG(I) \land action(A) \leftrightarrow o(A, I)\big). \tag{33}$$

By Corollary 3 it follows that any answer set of $\Pi_H \cup \Pi_G$ satisfies formula (33). It is easy to see that an interpretation satisfies (33) and the FOL representation of (11) if and only if it satisfies (33) and the FOL representation of denial (7). Thus, by Proposition 2 program $\Pi_H \cup \Pi_G$ extended with (11) and program $\Pi_H \cup \Pi_G$ extended with (7) have the same answer sets. Recall *Observation 2* claiming that it is safe to replace denial (4) with denial (11) within an arbitrary program. It follows that program $\Pi_H \cup \Pi_G$ extended with (7) have the same answer sets $\Pi_H \cup \Pi_G$ extended with (4). This concludes the argument for the claim of *Observation 5*.

We now state the last formal results of this paper. The Completion Lemma stated next is essential in proving the Lemma on Explicit Definitions. *Observation 6* follows immediately from the latter lemma.

Theorem 4 (Completion Lemma). *Let F be a first-order formula and $\mathbf{q}$ be a set of predicate constants that do not have positive, nonnegated occurrences in any FOL rule of F. Let $\mathbf{p}$ be a set of predicates in F disjoint from $\mathbf{q}$. Let D be a formula in Clark normal form relative to $\mathbf{q}$ so that in every conjunctive term (32) of D no occurrence of an element in $\mathbf{q}$ occurs in G as positive and nonnegated. Formula $SM_{\mathbf{pq}}[F \land D]$ is equivalent to formulas*

$$SM_{\mathbf{pq}}[F \land D] \land Comp[D], \tag{34}$$

$$SM_{\mathbf{p}}[F] \land Comp[D], \text{ and} \tag{35}$$

$$SM_{\mathbf{pq}}\Big[F \land \bigwedge_{q \in \{\mathbf{q}\}} \forall \mathbf{x}(\neg\neg q(\mathbf{x}) \rightarrow q(\mathbf{x}))\Big] \land Comp[D]. \tag{36}$$

For an interpretation I over signature Σ, by $I_{|\sigma}$ we denote the interpretation over $\sigma \subseteq \Sigma$ constructed from I so that every function or predicate symbol in σ is assigned the same value in both I and $I_{|\sigma}$. We call formula G in (32) a *definition* of $p(\mathbf{x})$.

Theorem 5 (Lemma on Explicit Definitions). *Let F be a first-order formula, $\mathbf{q}$ be a set of predicate constants that do not occur in F, and $\mathbf{p}$ be an arbitrary set of predicate constants in F. Let D be a formula in Clark normal form relative to $\mathbf{q}$ so that in every conjunctive term (32) of D there is no occurrence of an element in $\mathbf{q}$ in G.*

Then

i $M \mapsto M_{|\sigma(F)}$ is a 1-1 correspondence between the models of $SM_{\mathbf{pq}}[F \land D]$ and the models $SM_{\mathbf{p}}[F]$, and *ii* $SM_{\mathbf{pq}}[F \wedge D]$ *and* $SM_{\mathbf{pq}}[F^{\mathbf{q}} \wedge D]$ *are equivalent, where we understand* $F^{\mathbf{q}}$ *as a formula obtained from* F *by replacing occurrences of the definitions of* $q(\mathbf{x})$ *in* D *with* $q(\mathbf{x})$.

We note that Splitting Theorem from [10], Theorem 2 and Theorem 11 from [9] provide sufficient grounds to carry out the argument for Theorem 4. The proof of item (i) in Theorem 5 relies on Theorem 4 and the fact that the completion of considered formula D in Theorem 5 corresponds to so called explicit definitions in classical logic. The proof of item (ii) utilizes the Replacement Theorem for intuitionistic logic.

It is easy to see that program composed of a single rule

$$p(\mathbf{y}) \leftarrow 1 \leq \#count\{\mathbf{x} : F(\mathbf{x}, \mathbf{y})\}$$

and program $p(\mathbf{y}) \leftarrow F(\mathbf{x}, \mathbf{y})$ are strongly equivalent. Thus, we can identify rule (8) in the *Plan-disj* encoding with the rule

$$sthHpd(I) \leftarrow 1 \leq \#count\{A : o(A, I)\}. \tag{37}$$

Using this fact and Theorem 5 allows us to support *Observation* 6. Take F to be the FOL representation of *Plan-choice* encoding extended with any *Plan-instance* and D be the FOL representation of (37), $\mathbf{q}$ be composed of a single predicate *sthHpd* and $\mathbf{p}$ be composed of all the predicates in *Plan-choice* and *Plan-instance*.

Conclusions. This paper lifts several important theoretical results for propositional programs to the case of first-order logic programs. These new formal findings allow us to argue a number of first-order program rewritings to be safe. We illustrate the usefulness of these findings by utilizing them in constructing an argument which shows that the sample programs *Plan-choice* and *Plan-disj* are essentially the same. We believe that these results provide a strong building block for a portfolio of safe rewritings that can be used in creating an automatic tool for carrying these rewritings during program performance optimization phase discussed in Introduction.

Acknowledgements. We are grateful to Vladimir Lifschitz and Miroslaw Truszczynski for valuable discussions on the subject of this paper. Yuliya Lierler was partially supported by the NSF 1707371 grant.

References

1. Ben-Eliyahu, R., Dechter, R.: Propositional semantics for disjunctive logic programs. Ann. Math. Artif. Intell. **12**, 53–87 (1994)
2. Brewka, G., Eiter, T., Truszczyński, M.: Answer set programming at a glance. Commun. ACM **54**(12), 92–103 (2011)

3. Buddenhagen, M., Lierler, Y.: Performance tuning in answer set programming. In: Calimeri, F., Ianni, G., Truszczynski, M. (eds.) LPNMR 2015. LNCS (LNAI), vol. 9345, pp. 186–198. Springer, Cham (2015). https://doi.org/10.1007/978-3-319-23264-5_17

4. Eiter, T., Fink, M.: Uniform equivalence of logic programs under the stable model semantics. In: Palamidessi, C. (ed.) ICLP 2003. LNCS, vol. 2916, pp. 224–238. Springer, Heidelberg (2003). https://doi.org/10.1007/978-3-540-24599-5_16

5. Eiter, T., Fink, M., Tompits, H., Traxler, P., Woltran, S.: Replacements in non-ground answer-set programming. In: Proceedings of International Conference on Principles of Knowledge Representation and Reasoning (KR) (2006)

6. Eiter, T., Tompits, H., Woltran, S.: On solution correspondences in answer-set programming. In: Proceedings of International Joint Conference on Artificial Intelligence (IJCAI), pp. 97–102 (2005)

7. Eiter, T., Traxler, P., Woltran, S.: An implementation for recognizing rule replacements in non-ground answer-set programs. In: Fisher, M., van der Hoek, W., Konev, B., Lisitsa, A. (eds.) JELIA 2006. LNCS (LNAI), vol. 4160, pp. 477–480. Springer, Heidelberg (2006). https://doi.org/10.1007/11853886_41

8. Ferraris, P.: Answer sets for propositional theories. In: Baral, C., Greco, G., Leone, N., Terracina, G. (eds.) LPNMR 2005. LNCS (LNAI), vol. 3662, pp. 119–131. Springer, Heidelberg (2005). https://doi.org/10.1007/11546207_10

9. Ferraris, P., Lee, J., Lifschitz, V.: Stable models and circumscription. Artif. Intell. **175**, 236–263 (2011)

10. Ferraris, P., Lee, J., Lifschitz, V., Palla, R.: Symmetric splitting in the general theory of stable models. In: Proceedings of International Joint Conference on Artificial Intelligence (IJCAI), pp. 797–803. IJCAI press (2009)

11. Ferraris, P., Lifschitz, V.: Weight constraints as nested expressions. Theory Pract. Log. Program. **5**, 45–74 (2005)

12. Gebser, M., Harrison, A., Kaminski, R., Lifschitz, V., Schaub, T.: Abstract gringo. Theory Pract. Log. Program. **15**, 449–463 (2015). https://doi.org/10.1017/S1471068415000150. http://journals.cambridge.org/article_S1471068415000150

13. Gelfond, M., Kahl, Y.: Knowledge Representation, Reasoning, and the Design of Intelligent Agents: The Answer-Set Programming Approach. Cambridge University Press, Cambridge (2014)

14. Gelfond, M., Lifschitz, V., Przymusińska, H., Truszczyński, M.: Disjunctive defaults. In: Allen, J., Fikes, R., Sandewall, E. (eds.) Proceedings of International Conference on Principles of Knowledge Representation and Reasoning (KR), pp. 230–237 (1991)

15. Harrison, A., Lierler, Y.: First-order modular logic programs and their conservative extensions. In: Theory and Practice of Logic programming, 32nd International Conference on Logic Programming (ICLP) Special Issue (2016)

16. Janhunen, T., Oikarinen, E., Tompits, H., Woltran, S.: Modularity aspects of disjunctive stable models. In: Procedings of International Conference on Logic Programming and Nonmonotonic Reasoning (LPNMR), pp. 175–187 (2007)

17. Lee, J., Lifschitz, V., Palla, R.: A reductive semantics for counting and choice in answer set programming. In: Proceedings of the AAAI Conference on Artificial Intelligence (AAAI), pp. 472–479 (2008)

18. Lifschitz, V., Pearce, D., Valverde, A.: Strongly equivalent logic programs. ACM Trans. Comput. Log. **2**, 526–541 (2001)

19. Lifschitz, V., Pearce, D., Valverde, A.: A characterization of strong equivalence for logic programs with variables. In: Baral, C., Brewka, G., Schlipf, J. (eds.) LPNMR 2007. LNCS (LNAI), vol. 4483, pp. 188–200. Springer, Heidelberg (2007). https://doi.org/10.1007/978-3-540-72200-7_17

20. Linke, T., Tompits, H., Woltran, S.: On acyclic and head-cycle free nested logic programs. In: Demoen, B., Lifschitz, V. (eds.) ICLP 2004. LNCS, vol. 3132, pp. 225–239. Springer, Heidelberg (2004). https://doi.org/10.1007/978-3-540-27775-0_16

21. Mints, G.: A Short Introduction to Intuitionistic Logic. Springer, New York (2000)

22. Pearce, D., Valverde, A.: Synonymous theories and knowledge representations in answer set programming. J. Comput. Syst. Sci. **78**(1), 86–104 (2012). https://doi.org/10.1016/j.jcss.2011.02.013. http://www.sciencedirect.com/science/article/pii/S0022000011000420, jCSS Knowledge Representation and Reasoning

23. Woltran, S.: Characterizations for relativized notions of equivalence in answer set programming. In: Alferes, J.J., Leite, J. (eds.) JELIA 2004. LNCS (LNAI), vol. 3229, pp. 161–173. Springer, Heidelberg (2004). https://doi.org/10.1007/978-3-540-30227-8_16

Automatic Program Rewriting
in Non-Ground Answer Set Programs

Nicholas Hippen[✉] and Yuliya Lierler

University of Nebraska Omaha, Omaha, USA
{nhippen,ylierler}@unomaha.edu

Abstract. Answer set programming is a popular constraint programming paradigm that has seen wide use across various industry applications. However, logic programs under answer set semantics often require careful design and nontrivial expertise from a programmer to obtain satisfactory solving times. In order to reduce this burden on a software engineer we propose an automated rewriting technique for non-ground logic programs that we implement in a system PROJECTOR. We conduct rigorous experimental analysis, which shows that applying system PROJECTOR to a logic program can improve its performance, even after significant human-performed optimizations.

1 Introduction

Answer set programming (ASP) [4] is a leading knowledge representation/declarative programming paradigm. ASP seeks to provide techniques and tools to quickly and reliably design robust software solutions for complex knowledge-intensive applications. It reduces the programming task to modeling an application domain as a set of logic rules, and leaves all computational concerns to automated reasoning. Many efficient implementations of automated reasoning tools for ASP that include grounders and solvers are available. See [19] for a brief survey of grounders – e.g., LPARSE, GRINGO, IDLV– and solvers – e.g., SMODELS, DLV, CLASP. Thanks to these implementations, ASP has been successfully used in scientific and industrial applications. Examples include decision support systems for space shuttle flight controllers [1] and team building and scheduling [21].

These successful applications notwithstanding, ASP faces challenges. Practice shows that to achieve a required level of performance it is *crucial* to select the *right combination* of a representation and a processing tool. Unfortunately, at present this fundamental task is still not well understood, and it typically requires substantial expertise and effort, and there is still no guarantee of success. Gebser et al. in [14] presented a set of "rules-of-thumb" used by their expert team in tuning ASP solutions. These rules include suggestions on program rewritings that often result in substantial performance gains. Buddenhagen

We are grateful to Michael Dingess, Brian Hodges, Daniel Houston, Roland Kaminski, Liu Liu, Miroslaw Truszczynski, Stefan Woltran for the fruitful discussions.

© Springer Nature Switzerland AG 2019
J. J. Alferes and M. Johansson (Eds.): PADL 2019, LNCS 11372, pp. 19–36, 2019.
https://doi.org/10.1007/978-3-030-05998-9_2

and Lierler in [5] studied the impact of the rewritings on an ASP-based natural language parser called ASPCCG [20]. They reported orders of magnitude in gains in memory and time consumption as a result of some program transformations they executed manually. One of the rewriting techniques used in that application a number of times was so called "projection". In this paper, we present a system that performs various forms of projection automatically. We then extensively study the effects of automatic projection. In particular, we revisit several versions of an ASP-based natural language parser ASPCCG and evaluate the effects of different variants of projection on their performance. We also consider several benchmarks from the Fifth Answer Set Programming Competition.

Related Work. The possible impact of program rewritings on its performance is well understood. Many answer set solvers start their computation by performing propositional program simplifications based on answer set preserving rewritings, see, for instance, [18, Sect. 6.1] and [15]. It is important to note that solvers will perform their preprocessing on ground programs. Tool SIMPLIFY[1] [10,11] implements two program simplification techniques for non-ground disjunctive programs, namely, rule subsumption (dropping a rule in presence of another "subsuming" rule) and shifting (replacing a rule with disjunction in its head by rules without disjunction, when possible). System LPOPT[2] [2,3] decomposes rules of an ASP program, in the following way. Given a rule to rewrite, LPOPT may replace it with several new ones with a guarantee that the number of distinct variables occurring in each of these rules is less than that of the original. This is done by constructing a graph problem based on a given rule. A general-purpose library called *htd*[3] is used to find a solution to such graph problem. A resulting solution is then used by LPOPT to compose logic rules to replace the given one. In this work we continue the efforts undertaken by LPOPT, and propose a system called PROJECTOR. Unlike LPOPT, PROJECTOR develops its own rewriting strategies rooted in ideas underlying projection technique – a database optimization technique – commonly used by ASP practitioners in optimizing their encodings as well as ASP grounders [7,12].

Paper Outline. We start by presenting the notions of α and β-projection in Sect. 2. We continue into describing an algorithm called `Projection` for performing the rewritings of logic programs based on the ideas of α and β-projection. We then present the details behind system PROJECTOR that implements the `Projection` procedure. We conclude with the section on experimental analysis.

2   Projections in Theory

In this section we present two methods for program rewritings, namely α and β-projecting. We start by presenting some preliminary terminology and notation. We then proceed towards defining α and β-projecting for arbitrary logic rules.

---

[1] http://www.kr.tuwien.ac.at/research/systems/eq/simpl/index.html.
[2] http://dbai.tuwien.ac.at/research/project/lpopt/.
[3] https://github.com/mabseher/htd.

Preliminaries. We consider a vocabulary of function and predicate symbols associated with an arity (nonnegative integer). A function symbol of arity 0 is called a constant. A *term* is either a constant, a variable, or an expression of the form $f(t_1, \ldots, t_k)$ where f is a function symbol of arity $k > 0$ and t_i is a term. An *atom* has the form $p(t_1, \ldots, t_k)$ where p is a predicate symbol of arity k and t_i is a term. For instance, an atom $p(q(A), B, C, 1)$ is such that

- symbols A, B, C are variables (we use the convention customary in logic programming and denote variables by identifiers starting with a capital letter),
- 1 is a constant (a function symbol of arity 0),
- q is a function symbol of arity 1, and
- p is a predicate symbol of arity 4.

A *rule* is an expression of the form

$$a_0 \leftarrow a_1, \ldots, a_m, not\ a_{m+1}, \ldots, not\ a_n. \tag{1}$$

where $n \geq m \geq 0$, a_0 is either an atom or symbol $\bot$, and $a_1, \ldots, a_n$ are atoms. The atom a_0 is the *head* of the rule and $a_1, \ldots, a_m, not\ a_{m+1}, \ldots, not\ a_n$ is the *body*. At times we use letter $\mathbb{B}$ to denote a body of a rule. We call atoms and expressions of the form $not\ a$ (where a is an atom) *literals*. It is often convenient to identify the body of a rule with the set of the literals occurring in it. For example, we may identify the body of rule (1) with the set $\{a_1, \ldots, a_m, not\ a_{m+1}, \ldots, not\ a_n\}$. To literals $a_1, \ldots, a_m$ we refer as positive, whereas to literals $not\ a_{m+1}, \ldots, not\ a_n$ we refer as negative. We say that a *rule* is *positive* when its body consists only of positive literals. For example, the rule below is positive

$$p(A, D) \leftarrow q(A, B, C), r(A, D). \tag{2}$$

For a set L of literals, we say that a variable V is *unsafe* in L, if V does not occur in a positive literal in L. For instance, B is the only unsafe variable in $\{p(A),\ not\ q(A, B)\}$. We call a *rule safe* when no variable in this rule is an unsafe variable in its body. Rule (2) is safe. Rules $p(A).$ and $\bot \leftarrow p(A),\ not\ q(A, B).$ exemplify unsafe rules. In answer set programming, rules are required to be safe by the grounders [6].

α-Projecting for Positive Rules. Given a literal l by $vars[l]$ we denote the set of variables occurring in l. For example, $vars[p(f(A), B, C, 1)] = \{A, B, C\}$. Also, for a set L of literals $vars[L]$ denotes the set of all variables occurring in the elements of L. For instance, $vars[\{p(f(A), B, C, 1), r(A, D)\}] = \{A, B, C, D\}$.

For a rule ρ and a set V of variables, by $\alpha(\rho, V)$ we denote the set of all literals in the body of ρ such that they contain *some* variable in V. Let ρ_1 be a rule (2). Then,

$$\alpha(\rho_1, \{B\}) = \{q(A, B, C)\}$$
$$\alpha(\rho_1, \{B, C\}) = \{q(A, B, C)\}$$

For a literal l and a set V of variables, we say that l is V-free when no variable in V occurs in l. Symbol $\bot$ is V-free for any set V.

For a set V of variables and a positive rule ρ of the form $a \leftarrow \mathbb{B}$ where a is V-free, the process of α-*projecting* V out of this rule will result in replacing it by two rules:

1. a rule
$$q(\mathbf{t}) \leftarrow \alpha(\rho, V).$$

   so that
   - q is a fresh predicate symbol with respect to original program, and
   - $\mathbf{t}$ is composed of the variables that occur in $\alpha(\rho, V)$, but not in V (in other words, $\mathbf{t} = vars[\alpha(\rho, V)] \setminus V$; here we abuse the notation and associate a set of elements with a tuple. Let us assume a lexicographical order as a default order of elements in a constructed tuple — we will use this convention in the remainder of the paper);
2. a rule
$$a \leftarrow (\mathbb{B} \setminus \alpha(\rho, V)) \cup \{q(\mathbf{t})\}.$$

For instance, the result of α-projecting variable B (here we identify a variable with a singleton set composed of it) from ρ_1 follows:

$$q'(A, C) \leftarrow q(A, B, C).$$
$$p(A, D) \leftarrow q'(A, C), r(A, D).$$

The result of α-projecting variables $\{B, C\}$ from ρ_1 follows:

$$q'(A) \leftarrow q(A, B, C).$$
$$p(A, D) \leftarrow q'(A), r(A, D). \tag{3}$$

An Order of Projecting. We associate projections with a positive integer n – an *order* – where n is the cardinality of $\alpha(\rho, V)$. For instance, the result of projecting variable B or variables $\{B, C\}$ from ρ_1 are projections of order 1. In other words, these are projections that affect only variables that occur in a single literal in a body of a rule. Let ρ_2 be a rule

$$p(A, D, F) \leftarrow q(A, B, C), r(B, D), s(D, E), u(C), w(F). \tag{4}$$

Then, $\alpha(\rho_2, \{B\}) = \{q(A, B, C), r(B, D)\}$. The result of α-projecting variable B from ρ_2 follows. This is an example of projection of order 2.

$$qr'(A, C, D) \leftarrow q(A, B, C), r(B, D). \tag{5}$$
$$p(A, D, F) \leftarrow qr'(A, C, D), s(D, E), u(C), w(F). \tag{6}$$

On Grounders GRINGO **and** IDLV. In practice, grounders GRINGO and IDLV implement instances of projection of order 1. For instance, given a program with rule ρ_1, IDLV rewrites this rule and replaces it with rules listed in (3). System GRINGO is capable to do the same rewriting when anonymous variables are used. For example, if a rule ρ_1 is stated as

$$p(A, D) \leftarrow q(A, \_, \_), r(A, D).$$

then GRINGO will replace it with rules listed in (3), where B and C are substituted by anonymous variable symbol _.

α-**Projecting for Arbitrary Rules.** We now generalize α-projecting to arbitrary rules. The reader may observe that the definitions become more complex. The complexity is due to the necessity of producing safe rules as a result of projecting. Recall that rules are required to be safe by the grounders.

For a set L of literals, L^u denotes the set of all unsafe variables in L. For function $\alpha(\rho, V)$, we define function $V\uparrow$ as follows

$$V\uparrow 0 = V$$

and for $i = 0, 1, 2, \ldots$

$$V\uparrow i + 1 = V\uparrow i \cup \alpha(\rho, V\uparrow i)^u.$$

For instance, consider extending rule (2) as follows

$$p(A, D) \leftarrow q(A, B, C), r(A, D), t(E), not\ s(B, E).$$

By ρ_3 we denote this rule. Then,

$$\alpha(\rho_3, \{B\}) = \{q(A, B, C), not\ s(B, E)\}$$
$$\{q(A, B, C), not\ s(B, E)\}^u = \{E\}$$
$$\{B\}\uparrow 0 = \{B\}$$
$$\{B\}\uparrow 1 = \{B, E\}$$
$$\{B\}\uparrow \omega = \{B, E\}$$
$$\alpha(\rho_3, \{B\}\uparrow \omega) = \{q(A, B, C), not\ s(B, E), t(E)\}.$$

For a set V of variables and a rule ρ of the form $a \leftarrow \mathbb{B}$ where a is V-free, the process of α-*projecting* V out of this rule will result in replacing it by two rules:

1. a rule

$$q(\mathbf{t}) \leftarrow \alpha(\rho, V\uparrow \omega)$$

   so that q is a fresh predicate symbol with respect to original program and tuple $\mathbf{t}$ is composed of the variables that occur in $\alpha(\rho, V\uparrow \omega)$, but not in V;
2. a rule

$$a \leftarrow (\mathbb{B} \setminus \alpha(\rho, V\uparrow \omega)) \cup \{q(\mathbf{t})\}. \tag{7}$$

It is easy to see that for a positive rule, $\alpha(\rho, V\uparrow \omega) = \alpha(\rho, V)$. Thus, the presented definition of α-projecting for an arbitrary rule is a generalization of this concept for positive rules. The result of α-projecting B from ρ_3 follows:

$$qst'(A, C, E) \leftarrow q(A, B, C), t(E), not\ s(B, E).$$
$$p(A, D) \leftarrow r(A, D), qst'(A, C, E).$$

β-**Projecting.** For a rule ρ and a set V of variables, by $\beta(\rho, V{\uparrow}\omega)$ we denote the set of all literals in the body of ρ such that *all* their variables are contained in $vars[\alpha(\rho, V{\uparrow}\omega)]$.

For example,

$$\beta(\rho_2, \{B\}{\uparrow}\omega) = \{q(A, B, C), r(B, D), u(C)\}$$
$$\beta(\rho_3, \{B\}{\uparrow}\omega) = \alpha(\rho_3, \{B\}{\uparrow}\omega)$$

It is easy to see that $\alpha(\rho, V{\uparrow}\omega) \subseteq \beta(\rho, V{\uparrow}\omega)$.

For a set V of variables and a rule ρ of the form $a \leftarrow \mathbb{B}$ where a is V-free, the process of β-*projecting* V out of this rule will result in replacing it by two rules:

1. a rule

$$q(\mathbf{t}) \leftarrow \beta(\rho, V{\uparrow}\omega)$$

   so that q is a fresh predicate symbol with respect to original program and tuple $\mathbf{t}$ is composed of the variables that occur in $\beta(\rho, V{\uparrow}\omega)$, but not in V;
2. a rule (7).

For instance, the result of β-projecting variable B from rule ρ_2 consists of a rule

$$qr'(A, C, D) \leftarrow q(A, B, C), r(B, D), u(C). \tag{8}$$

and rule (6). Note that rules (5) and (8) differ only in one atom in the body, namely, $u(C)$. The result of β-projecting variable B from rule ρ_3 coincides with that of α-projecting B from ρ_3.

In the sequel, it is convenient for us to refer to the first rule produced in α and β-projecting as α and β-rules respectively. For instance, rule (5) is the α-rule of α-projecting variable B from ρ_2. The second rule produced in α and β-projecting we call a *replacement* rule.

3   Projections in Practice

In this section we describe an algorithm, which carries out program rewritings utilizing α and β-projection. We implement this algorithm in a system called PROJECTOR[4]. We conclude this section by providing technical details on the PROJECTOR implementation.

Algorithm 1 presents procedure `Projection`. As an input it takes a rule ρ, a projection type τ (that can take values α or β), and a positive integer n that specifies the order of projecting. Algorithm `Projection` performs projection iteratively. It picks a set of variables for projecting and computes the respective τ and replacement rules. It then attempts to repeat the same procedure on the replacement rule. Procedure `Projection` starts by defining V as the set of variables on which the τ-projecting of order n or less may be applied (line 2).

---

[4]   https://www.unomaha.edu/college-of-information-science-and-technology/natural-language-processing-and-knowledge-representation-lab/software/projector.php.

Next, $\mathbb{R}$ is initialized as an empty set that will in the future hold rules added by projection. Lines 5–11 handle variable selection so that set W computed in these lines contains variables to project on. This selection process targets to perform projections of smaller orders first. Also, this process groups any variables that can be projected together without introducing new literals into the τ-rule. Then, the τ-rule is computed (line 12). If the set of variables occurring in the body of the computed τ-rule *is different* from the set of variables occurring in the body of ρ, we add the τ-rule to $\mathbb{R}$ (line 14), update rule ρ with the replacement rule for τ-projection (line 15), and remove all of the variables we projected so far from V (line 16). *Otherwise*, we remove v from V to eliminate consideration of projecting it again. We repeat this process until set V is empty (lines 4–21).

Recall that ρ_2 is rule (4). To illustrate Algorithm 1, we present the execution of $\text{Projection}(\rho_2, \beta, 2)$ as a table in Fig. 1. The first and second rows of the table state the values of variables $V, \mathbb{R}, \rho$ at line 4 during the first and second iterations of the while-loop respectively. The last row presents the values of these variables at line 22.

While-Loop Iterations	Variables	Values
1	V	$\{B, C, E\}$
	$\mathbb{R}$	$\emptyset$
	ρ	ρ_2
2	V	$\{B, C\}$
	$\mathbb{R}$	$\{s'(D) \leftarrow s(D, E).\}$
	ρ	$p(A, D, F) \leftarrow q(A, B, C), r(B, D), u(C), w(F), s'(D).$
Return	V	$\emptyset$
	$\mathbb{R}$	$\{s'(D) \leftarrow s(D, E).$
		$qr'(A, D) \leftarrow q(A, B, C), r(B, D), u(C), s'(D).\}$
	ρ	$p(A, D, F) \leftarrow w(F), s'(D), qr'(A, D).$

Fig. 1. Algorithm 1 illustration with $\rho = \rho_2$, $\tau = \beta$, and $n = 2$.

It is due to note that procedure Projection is nondeterministic due to line 5. In case of our illustration on $\text{Projection}(\rho_2, \beta, 2)$ there are two possibilities to consider. In both cases the procedure will return rules of the form

$$s'(D) \leftarrow s(D, E).$$
$$p(A, D, F) \leftarrow w(F), s'(D), proj_{bc}(A, D).$$

whereas it will differ on the other rules presented in the table below.

possibility 1	possibility 2
$proj_c(A, B) \leftarrow q(A, B, C), u(C).$	$proj_{bc}(A, D) \leftarrow q(A, B, C), r(B, D),$
$proj_{bc}(A, D) \leftarrow proj_c(A, B), r(B, D), s'(D).$	$\qquad\qquad u(C), s'(D).$

Algorithm 1: *Projection*

Input   : ρ: rule of the form $a \leftarrow \mathbb{B}$
            τ: projection type α or β
            n: positive integer (order of projection)
Output: a pair where the first element is the rewritten rule and the second
            element is the set of τ rules produced

1   **Function Projection(ρ, τ, n):**
2      $V \leftarrow \{v \mid$
         v is a variable in ρ that doesn't occur in its head and $|\alpha(\rho, \{v\}\uparrow\omega)| \leq n\}$;
3      $\mathbb{R} \leftarrow \emptyset$;
4   **while** $V \neq \emptyset$ **do**
5          $v \leftarrow$ a variable in V such that there is no variable v' in V where
            $|\alpha(\rho, \{v\}\uparrow\omega)| > |\alpha(\rho, \{v'\}\uparrow\omega)|$;
6          $W \leftarrow \{v\}$;
7   **foreach** w *in* V *different from* v **do**
8   **if** $\alpha(\rho, \{w\}\uparrow\omega) \subseteq \tau(\rho, \{v\}\uparrow\omega)$ **then**
9                $W \leftarrow W \cup \{w\}$;
10   **end**
11   **end**
12         $s \leftarrow$ the τ rule of τ projecting W from ρ;
13   **if** *the set of variables occurring in the body of s is different from the set*
           of variables in the body of ρ **then**
14           $\mathbb{R} \leftarrow \mathbb{R} \cup \{s\}$;
15           $\rho \leftarrow$ the replacement rule of τ projecting process;
16   Delete all elements in W from V;
17   **end**
18   **else**
19   Delete v from V;
20   **end**
21   **end**
22   **return** $(\rho, \mathbb{R})$;
23 **End Function**

Implementation Details. System CLINGO version 5.3.0 is an answer set programming tool chain that incorporates grounder GRINGO [13,17] and solver CLASP [16]. Our implementation of PROJECTOR utilizes PYCLINGO, a sub-system of CLINGO that provides users with various system enhancements through the scripting language Python. One such enhancement allows us to intervene in the workings of CLINGO. The PROJECTOR system uses PYCLINGO to parse a logic program and turn it into a respective abstract syntax tree. At this point, the PROJECTOR subroutines take over by analyzing the parsed program and modifying its "normal" rules according with the described procedures. (By "normal" we refer to the rules of the form discussed in this paper. Yet, the language of CLINGO offers its users more sophisticated constructs in its rule, for example, aggregates. The PROJECTOR ignores such rules.) Once program rewritings are performed on the level of the abstract syntax tree representation of the program the control is given back to PYCLINGO that continues with grounding and then solving. The PYCLINGO interface allows us to guarantee that the system PROJECTOR is applicable to all programs supported by CLINGO version 5.3.0.

System PROJECTOR can be controlled with various flags that determine which type of projection to perform. At the url of the system given at Footnote 4, the flags are described in detail. It is important to note that the flag `--random` allows a user to specify a seed that is used to carry out the nondeterministic decision of line 5 in the `Projection` algorithm.

4 Experimental Analysis

In our experiments we utilize the application called ASPCCG described in [20] and three benchmarks, namely, *Stable Marriage, Permutation Pattern Matching, and Knight Tour with Holes* stemming from the Fifth Answer Set programming Competition [9]. In ASPCCG, the authors formulate the task of parsing natural language, namely, recovering the internal structure of sentences, as a planning problem in answer set programming. The three other mentioned benchmarks were used by the authors of the system LPOPT [3] to report on its performance.

Results on ASPCCG. Our choice of the ASPCCG application, is due to the fact that a prior extensive experimental analysis was performed on it in [5]. We now restate some of these earlier findings relevant to our analysis. System ASPCCG version 0.1 (ASPCCG-0.1) and ASPCCG version 0.2 (ASPCCG-0.2) vary only in how specifications of the planning problem are stated, while the constraints of the problem remain the same. Yet, the performance of ASPCCG-0.1 and ASPCCG-0.2 differs significantly for longer sentences. The way from ASPCCG-0.1 to ASPCCG-0.2 comprised 20 encodings, and along that way, grounding size and solving time were the primary measures directing the changes in the encodings. Rewriting suggestions by Gebser et al. [14] guided the ASPCCG encodings tuning. These suggestions include such "hints on modeling" as

Keep the grounding compact:

(i) If possible, use aggregates; (ii) Try to avoid combinatorial blow-up; (iii) Project out unused variables; (iv) But don't remove too many inferences!

In our experiments we consider three encodings out of the mentioned 20:

– the ENC1 encoding that constitutes ASPCCG-0.1,
– the ENC7 encoding that constitutes one of the improved encodings on a path from ASPCCG-0.1 to ASPCCG-0.2, and
– the ENC19 encoding that constitutes ASPCCG-0.2.

Lierler and Schüller [20] describe the procedure of acquiring instances of the problem using CCGbank[5], a corpus of parsed sentences from real world sources. In [5], the authors report on the performance of answer set solver CLASP v 2.0.2 on a set of 30 randomly selected problem instances from CCGbank that were used in performance tuning by Lierler and Schüller. In Fig. 2, we reproduce their findings for ENC1, ENC7, and ENC19. The second column presents the total number of timeouts/memory outs (3000 sec. timeout), the third column presents the average solving time (in seconds; on instances that did not timeout/memoryout), and the last column reports a number n so that n and 10^5 are factors relating to the average number of ground rules reported by CLASP v 2.0.2. These numbers were obtained in experiments using a Xeon X5355 @ 2.66GHz CPU. The presented table illustrates that the selected ENC1, ENC7, and ENC19 encodings differ substantially. It is interesting to note that on the way from ENC1 to ENC7 a software engineer applied projection technique once and from ENC7 to ENC19 three times. In order to conduct extensive analysis on the impact of solver's configuration on ASPCCG, Buddenhagen and Lierler [5] separated CCGbank instances (sentences) by word count into five word intervals restricting attention to sentences having between 6 and 25 words. They then randomly selected an equal number of sentences from each class when creating different sets of instances. In our experiments, we utilize the set of 60 instances that they call held-out set. We present the results for the hardest 20 instances in this set based on the performance of PYCLINGO (using the default configuration of GRINGO) on ENC19. In all figures the instances are given on the x-axis sorted by the performance of PYCLINGO on ENC19. We benchmarked α and β projections using the greatest possible order for each case. We also provide the results for the LPOPT system. In the figures, we present data on runtimes (time spent in grounding and solving) and size of ground programs (number of ground rules reported by PYCLINGO). In all figures, ENC1, ENC7, and ENC19 present numbers associated with PYCLINGO (using the default configuration of GRINGO) on the respective encoding. We used an Intel® Core™ i5-4250U CPU @ 1.30GHz CPU.

Encoding	# timeout/memout	solving in sec	factor w.r.t. grounding
ENC1	6	301	14
ENC7	5	138	4
ENC19	2	128	8

Fig. 2. ASPCCG performance

Figure 3 presents the total runtime in seconds for ENC1 for three distinct variants of β-projection. The numbers 123, 456, and 789 are the seeds passed on to the system with the --random flag. We observe that a seed may affect the performance of the system significantly. In the remainder, we present the results

---

[5] http://groups.inf.ed.ac.uk/ccg/ccgbank.html.

for the 123 seed only, to keep the graphs readable. (The choice of this seed is arbitrary.) We use the same seed for presenting the results on α projection. System LPOPT also displays nondeterministic behavior, where the flag -s is used to specify a seed. We present the results on LPOPT using the seed 123.

Figure 4 compares the runtime of all considered systems, namely, PYCLINGO, α-PROJECTOR, β-PROJECTOR, and LPOPT. Neither α nor β-projection show any significant performance loss across the experimented instances. In nearly all instances, PROJECTOR outperforms PYCLINGO. Of the 20 displayed instances, 16 show improvement for β-projection over α-projection. Besides the effects of randomness, we attribute the difference in the performance of α and β-projection to the additional literals of β-rule (in comparison to α-rule) that act as "guards"[6]. These guards impose further limits on the domains of variables occurring in them so that a grounding procedure implemented in PYCLINGO benefits from these additional restrictions. Figure 5 presents the data on sizes of ground programs for the same systems and instances. For these instances, β-projection results in a reduction of grounding size compared to α-projection for all instances. This can again be attributed to the guards added by β-projection. This is not surprising, as no new variables are introduced into the β-rule when compared to its α-rule counterpart, so the additional guard literals can only restrict the grounding size. It is also obvious that there is a strong correlation between the reduction in grounding size and improvement of runtime.

Figure 6 compares the runtime of all considered systems on the ENC7 encoding. Here we again note that β-projection is generally superior to α-projection, yet we cannot claim that β-projection improves on the original encoding ENC7. Figure 7 illustrates that both α and β-projection produce ground programs that are larger than these produced by PYCLINGO given the original encoding. This once more illustrates the strong correlation between the reduction in grounding size and improvement of runtime.

Figure 8 compares the runtime of all considered systems on ENC19. Figure 9 presents the data on sizes of ground programs. These graphs illustrate similar behavior of the systems as in the case of the ENC7 encoding.

Figure 10 presents the runtimes for PYCLINGO on ENC1, ENC7, and ENC19 together with the runtime of β-PROJECTOR on ENC1. It shows that β-projection can be used to supplement human efforts in performance tuning, as the runtime of β-PROJECTOR on ENC1 is comparable to that of PYCLINGO on ENC7. Recall that ENC7 was obtained from ENC1 using 7 iterations by a human and substantial experimental analysis between these iterations (see [5] for details).

So far the presented experiments illustrate that the rule decomposition method implemented in LPOPT is superior to both α and β-projection techniques introduced here. The encodings of ASPCCG contain rules with aggregate expressions. System LPOPT is capable to perform its decomposition method also

---

[6] The term *guards* was suggested by Miroslaw Truszczynski.

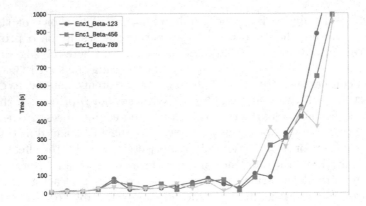

Fig. 3. ENC1: Runtime of β-PROJECTOR with different random seeds

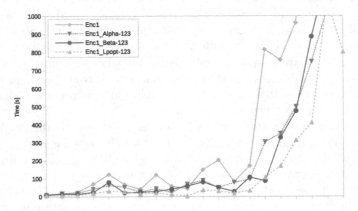

Fig. 4. ENC1: Runtime

within these expressions, whereas PROJECTOR ignores the aggregates. It is a direction of future research to expand the capabilities of PROJECTOR to handle aggregates. Then, a more fair comparison on the ASPCCG domain can be made between the systems.

Results on Stable Marriage and More. Figures 11 and 12 present the runtimes of β-projection and LPOPT with three distinct seeds on Stable Marriage and Permutation Pattern Matching domains. *No aggregates* were used in the benchmarked encodings of these problems. It is apparent that the LPOPT system is truly sensitive to a provided seed. System PROJECTOR exhibits comparable performance between its variants.

In case of Stable Marriage, β-projection always outperforms PYCLINGO on the original encoding. In case of LPOPT, two of its variants exhibit substantially worse behavior than PYCLINGO. In case of Permutation Pattern Matching, it is safe to say that in general program rewriting techniques implemented in LPOPT and PROJECTOR are of benefits (Fig. 12).

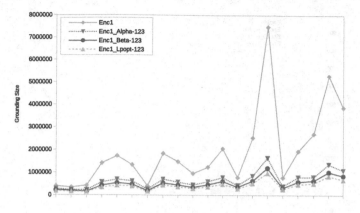

Fig. 5. ENC1: Grounding size

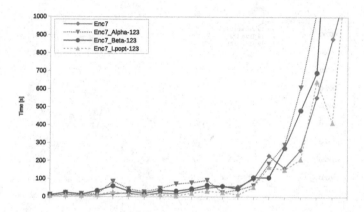

Fig. 6. ENC7: Runtime

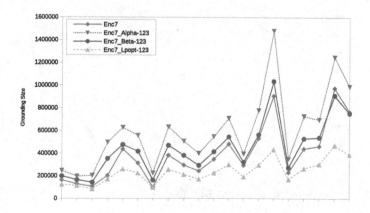

Fig. 7. ENC7: Grounding size

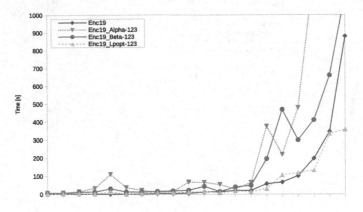

Fig. 8. ENC19: Runtime

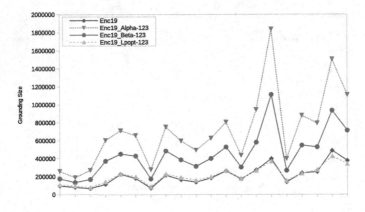

Fig. 9. ENC19: Grounding size

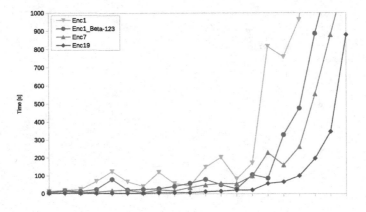

Fig. 10. ENC1, ENC7, ENC19: Runtime

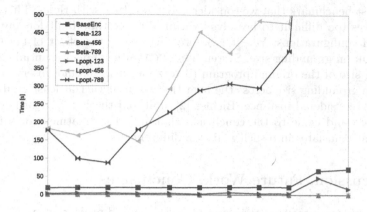

Fig. 11. Stable marriage: runtime

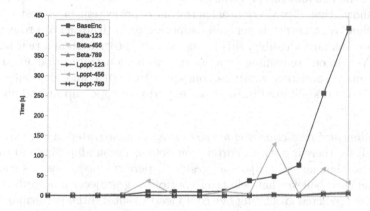

Fig. 12. Permutation pattern matching: runtime

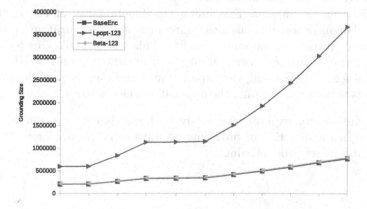

Fig. 13. Knight tour with holes: grounding size

The last benchmark that we consider is Knight Tour with Holes. This benchmark proves too difficult to be solved within 300 sec time limit for any of the considered configurations. Yet, it is interesting to see the effect of LPOPT and PROJECTOR on grounding size. System PROJECTOR has no substantial effect on grounding size of the original program (if to zoom in we would observe a slight increase in grounding size across the board). System LPOPT at least doubles the size of any considered instance. Bichler [2] analyzed the behavior of LPOPT on this domain and came to the conclusion that it is the treatment of safety by LPOPT that translates into such a drastic difference.

5   Discussion, Future Work, Conclusions

In this work we introduce the concepts of α and β-projection and state an algorithm called `Projection` that performs these projections iteratively. We then implement the `Projection` procedure in system PROJECTOR. Our experimental analysis shows that β-projection outperforms α-projection in almost all cases. We also show that LPOPT is generally superior to both forms of projection on the ASPCCG domain. Possibly, this is due to the LPOPT system's rich language support. Yet, in our remaining experiments we demonstrated that PROJECTOR generates more consistent runtimes compared to LPOPT and also outperforms LPOPT. The results collected through our experiments open up several directions of future work:

- *Grounding size prediction and heuristics.* As demonstrated in our experimental analysis, there is a strong correlation between grounding size and runtime. It is clear that not all projections result in performance gains. As such, it is reasonable to believe that selectively performing projection according to the resulting predicted grounding size could lead to substantial performance gain. Recent work on LPOPT has shown that a heuristic approach to performing decompositions can lead to performance gains   [8]. Similar approaches to PROJECTOR may also be beneficial.
- *Improve language support.* Expanding the functionality of PROJECTOR to include language features such as aggregates and optimization statements may enable further performance benefits. This will also allow us to perform a more fair comparison between LPOPT and PROJECTOR on more domains.
- *Data collection.* Expanding the experimental analysis to more domains will enable us to better understand the implications behind the use of PROJECTOR.

In conclusion, our experimental analysis shows that system PROJECTOR is a solid step in the direction of providing an automated means for performance tuning in answer set programming.

References

1. Balduccini, M., Gelfond, M., Nogueira, M.: Answer set based design of knowledge systems. Ann. Math. Artif. Intell. **47**(1–2), 183–219 (2006)
2. Bichler, M.: Optimizing non-ground answer set programs via rule decomposition. Bachelor thesis. TU Wien (2015)
3. Bichler, M., Morak, M., Woltran, S.: lpopt: a rule optimization tool for answer set programming. In: Proceedings of International Symposium on Logic-Based Program Synthesis and Transformation (2016)
4. Brewka, G., Eiter, T., Truszczynski, M.: Answer set programming at a glance. Commun. ACM **54**(12), 92–103 (2011)
5. Buddenhagen, M., Lierler, Y.: Performance tuning in answer set programming. In: Proceedings of the Thirteenth International Conference on Logic Programming and Nonmonotonic Reasoning (LPNMR) (2015)
6. Calimeri, F., Cozza, S., Ianni, G., Leone, N.: Computable functions in ASP: theory and implementation. In: Proceedings of International Conference on Logic Programming (ICLP), pp. 407–424 (2008)
7. Calimeri, F., Fusca, D., Perri, S., Zangari, J.: I-DLV: the new intelligent grounder of DLV. Intelligenza Artificiale **11**(1), 5–20 (2017)
8. Calimeri, F., Fuscà, D., Perri, S., Zangari, J.: Optimizing answer set computation via heuristic-based decomposition. In: Calimeri, F., Hamlen, K., Leone, N. (eds.) PADL 2018. LNCS, vol. 10702, pp. 135–151. Springer, Cham (2018). https://doi.org/10.1007/978-3-319-73305-0_9
9. Calimeri, F., Gebser, M., Maratea, M., Ricca, F.: Design and results of the fifth answer set programming competition. Artif. Intell. **231**, 151–181 (2016). https://doi.org/10.1016/j.artint.2015.09.008. http://www.sciencedirect.com/science/article/pii/S0004370215001447
10. Eiter, T., Fink, M., Tompits, H., Traxler, P., Woltran, S.: Replacements in non-ground answer-set programming. In: Proceedings of International Conference on Principles of Knowledge Representation and Reasoning (KR) (2006)
11. Eiter, T., Traxler, P., Woltran, S.: An implementation for recognizing rule replacements in non-ground answer-set programs. In: Fisher, M., van der Hoek, W., Konev, B., Lisitsa, A. (eds.) JELIA 2006. LNCS (LNAI), vol. 4160, pp. 477–480. Springer, Heidelberg (2006). https://doi.org/10.1007/11853886_41
12. Faber, W., Leone, N., Mateis, C., Pfeifer, G.: Using database optimization techniques for nonmonotonic reasoning, pp. 135–139 (1999)
13. Gebser, M., Kaminski, R., Kaufmann, B., Ostrowski, M., Schaub, T., Thiele, S.: A user's guide to gringo, clasp, clingo, and iclingo (2010). http://potassco.sourceforge.net
14. Gebser, M., Kaminski, R., Kaufmann, B., Schaub, T.: Challenges in answer set solving. In: Balduccini, M., Son, T.C. (eds.) Logic Programming, Knowledge Representation, and Nonmonotonic Reasoning. LNCS (LNAI), vol. 6565, pp. 74–90. Springer, Heidelberg (2011). https://doi.org/10.1007/978-3-642-20832-4_6
15. Gebser, M., Kaufmann, B., Neumann, A., Schaub, T.: Advanced preprocessing for answer set solving. In: Proceedings of the 2008 Conference on ECAI 2008: 18th European Conference on Artificial Intelligence, pp. 15–19. IOS Press, Amsterdam (2008). http://dl.acm.org/citation.cfm?id=1567281.1567290
16. Gebser, M., Kaufmann, B., Schaub, T.: Conflict-driven answer set solving: from theory to practice. Artif. Intell. **187**, 52–89 (2012)

17. Gebser, M., Schaub, T., Thiele, S.: GrinGo: a new grounder for answer set programming. In: Baral, C., Brewka, G., Schlipf, J. (eds.) LPNMR 2007. LNCS (LNAI), vol. 4483, pp. 266–271. Springer, Heidelberg (2007). https://doi.org/10.1007/978-3-540-72200-7_24
18. Lierler, Y.: SAT-based Answer Set Programming. Ph.D. thesis, University of Texas at Austin (2010)
19. Lierler, Y., Maratea, M., Ricca, F.: Systems, engineering environments, and competitions. AI Mag. **37**(3), 45–52 (2016)
20. Lierler, Y., Schüller, P.: Parsing combinatory categorial grammar via planning in answer set programming. In: Erdem, E., Lee, J., Lierler, Y., Pearce, D. (eds.) Correct Reasoning. LNCS, vol. 7265, pp. 436–453. Springer, Heidelberg (2012). https://doi.org/10.1007/978-3-642-30743-0_30
21. Ricca, F., et al.: Team-building with answer set programming in the Gioia-Tauro seaport. Theory Pract. Logic Program. **12**(3), 361–381 (2012)

Personalized Course Schedule Planning Using Answer Set Programming

Muhammed Kerem Kahraman and Esra Erdem[(⊠)]

Faculty of Engineering and Natural Sciences, Sabanci University, Istanbul, Turkey
{kkerem,esraerdem}@sabanciuniv.edu

Abstract. Course scheduling or timetabling is a well-known problem that is generally studied from the perspective of schools; the goal is to schedule the courses, considering, e.g., the expected number of students, the sizes of the available classrooms, time conflicts between courses of the same category. We study a complementary problem to help the students during the course registration periods; the goal is to plan personalized course schedules for students, considering, e.g., their preferences over sections, instructors, distribution of the courses. We present a declarative method to compute personalized course schedules, and an application of this method using answer set programming, and discuss promising results of some preliminary user evaluations via surveys.

Keywords: Course scheduling · Answer set programming
Declarative problem solving

1 Introduction

Students spend a lot of time during registration periods to plan their course schedules, even when they know more or less which courses to take. They need to decide which courses and their sections to register for, considering their instructors and times, times between classes, total number of courses per day, free time, etc. For instance, some students have to take a specific section due to its time since they may want to catch the shuttle from their home. Some students may prefer to take some sections because their friends are registering for that section, or they like its instructor better. Some students may want to stay on campus and prefer a schedule that distributes the courses and their sections in such a way; some may prefer otherwise, to have more free bulk time.

We have defined this problem more precisely, guided by students' constraints and preferences, and developed a declarative solution using Answer Set Programming (ASP) [8,9,14,15,17] (based on answer sets [11,13]) utilizing its constructs, like aggregates, hard/weak constraints, optimization statements.

Based on this declarative solution, we have developed a software system (called SUCHEDULER) that extracts the relevant information from the published course schedule on the web, interacts with the user to determine their preferences and constraints, utilizes both types of information for decision making using ASP,

© Springer Nature Switzerland AG 2019
J. J. Alferes and M. Johansson (Eds.): PADL 2019, LNCS 11372, pp. 37–45, 2019.
https://doi.org/10.1007/978-3-030-05998-9_3

and presents several personalized course schedule plans for the user. If there is a conflict between the requests of the user (e.g., some sections may have a time conflict), SUCHEDULER provides an explanation.

We have performed both objective (e.g., in terms of computation time) and subjective experiments (e.g., user evaluations in terms of surveys); the results are promising.

2 Problem Description

Some courses have multiple sections, and supplementary sessions, like recitations, laboratory sessions, and/or discussion sessions. Once the students decide for their courses, they also have to choose their sections, recitations, discussion sessions, and/or laboratory sessions; we call this problem *course schedule planning*. It takes as input

- a complete course schedule S (i.e., times, places, instructors of classes and their sections, recitations, discussion/laboratory session) published by a school, and
- a set C of courses (specified by their names) that the student plans to register.

As an output, it returns a schedule plan for the courses in C according to S, including

- exactly one section for every course $c \in C$,
- exactly one recitation for every course $c \in C$ that has some recitations,
- exactly one laboratory session for every course $c \in C$ that has some laboratory sessions, and
- exactly one discussion session for every course $c \in C$ that has some discussion sessions

such that there is no time and place conflict between any two courses (i.e., their sections and supplementary sessions).

While deciding for which sections, recitations, laboratory sessions, and/or discussion sessions to register for, students usually consider various criteria, such as the instructors and times, times between classes, total number of classes per day, free time, shuttle hours, etc. To be able to help each student during their registrations, we need to solve a further personalized version of the course schedule planning problem that also takes into account these criteria; we call this problem *personalized course schedule planning*.

To identify the most desired constraints/preferences considered by the students during registration, we have interviewed with 61 students at Sabanci University by a survey. Figure 1 shows a summary of the results of this survey. According to these results;

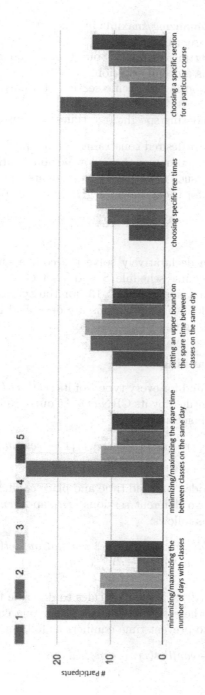

Fig. 1. A summary of the survey results, where each participant has evaluated how much useful each criterion is based on a Likert scale of 1 to 5 (1 being more useful, 5 being less useful).

- 45 students think that "minimizing/maximizing the number of days with classes" are useful criteria,
- 42 students think that "minimizing/maximizing the total spare time between classes on the same day" are useful criteria,
- 39 students think that "setting an upper bound on the spare time between classes on the same day" is a useful criterion,
- 36 students think that "choosing a specific section of a particular course" is a useful criterion, and
- 31 students think that "choosing specific free times" is a useful criterion.

After identifying these most desired constraints/preferences, we have formulated them in an elaboration tolerant way that allow personalization of the course schedule planning problem in such a way that the students can not only choose which criteria are important for them, but also give priorities to the criteria.

3   Method

Let us first describe how we declaratively solve the course schedule planning problem characterized by a course schedule S and a set C of courses, in ASP. We refer the reader to relevant sources [7,12,13] for the syntax and semantics of programs in ASP. In the following, programs are described in mathematical format instead of the input language of an ASP solver.

3.1   Course Schedule Planning

First, for every course $c \in C$ and for every type t of its sections/sessions, exactly one such section/session (identified by its CRN crn – Course Reference Number) is decided by the following choice rules:

$$1\{add(crn) \; : \; session(c, crn), crnType(crn, t)\}1 \leftarrow sessionType(c, t).$$

Then, hard constraints are added to avoid time and place conflicts. For instance, the time conflicts between two different sessions crn_1 and crn_2 that occur on the same day d are defined as follows:

$$conflict(crn_1, crn_2, d) \leftarrow add(crn_1), add(crn_2), not\ noConflict(crn_1, crn_2, d),$$
$$courseDay(crn_1, d), courseDay(crn_2, d). \quad (crn_1 < crn_2)$$

where $noConflict(crn_1, crn_2, d)$ is defined by rules to describe the sessions that do not conflict (i.e., one of them starts after the other one ends). After that, hard constraints are added to prevent time conflicts as follows:

$$\leftarrow conflict(crn_1, crn_2, d).$$

The answer sets for the ASP program whose parts are described above characterize course schedule plans.

3.2   Personalizing Course Schedule Planning

Now let us discuss how the students' desired constraints/preferences are formalized in ASP, to be able to solve the personalized course schedule planning problem. Consider, for instance, "minimizing the number of days with classes" is chosen as the most important criterion for a student. For that, first we identify the days with selected classes and then count them:

$$existsCourse(d) \leftarrow add(crn), courseDay(crn, d).$$
$$totalCourses(n) \leftarrow n = \#count\{d : existsCourse(d)\}.$$

After that, we minimize this number:

$$\#minimize\{n@1 \; : \; totalCourses(n)\}.$$

Note that the priority of this optimization is set to 1.

Suppose that, as a second criterion, the student specifies that "minimizing the total spare time between classes on the same day" is also important for her/him. For that, we identify all consecutive courses crn_1 and crn_2 (where crn_1 occurs before crn_2), define the spare time between them:

$$spareTime(crn_1, crn_2, start_2 - end_1, d) \leftarrow consecutiveCRN(crn_1, crn_2, d),$$
$$courseDate(crn_1, d, start_1, end_1), courseDate(crn_2, d, start_2, end_2).$$

and then minimize the total spare time between the classes selected by the student:

$$\#minimize\{diff@2, crn_1, crn_2, d \; : \; spareTime(crn_1, crn_2, diff, d)\}.$$

Note that the priority of this optimization is set to 2.

If the student would also prefer "choosing a specific section/session A of type T for a particular course M", the following weak constraint is generated by SUCHEDULER and added to the program above:

$$\leftsquigarrow session(M, crn), crnType(crn, T), section(crn, A), not \; add(crn).[1@3, crn]$$

3.3   Implementation of SUCHEDULER

The system SUCHEDULER is implemented in Python, utilizing various technologies (e.g., php, Java script, SQLite) for its user interface and information retrieval.

SUCHEDULER first extracts the relevant information from the published course schedule on the web, including the courses' names, CRNs, sections, recitations, labs, and discussion sessions, as well as their times, places, and instructors. It represents these course information in a database as a set of facts.

Via its interactive user interface (implemented, utilizing pull-down menus), SUCHEDULER allows the user to specify their preferences and constraints that are mentioned above.

After that, SUCHEDULER combines the ASP program for course schedule planning (described in Sect. 3.1), the ASP program obtained from the users' preferences/constraints (as described in Sect. 3.2), and the relevant part of the database (obtained by SQL queries), and tries to compute several answer sets using the ASP solver CLINGO [10]. If an answer set is found, then a course program is extracted from each answer set and presented to the user as a table. Otherwise, time conflicts are identified by turning the hard constraint about time conflicts into a weak constraint, and presented to the user as warnings.

4   Experimental Evaluations

We have performed two types of experimental evaluations: objective evaluations (e.g., over computation timings), and subjective evaluations (e.g., via user surveys).

To understand its computational performance in terms of CPU time, we have tried SUCHEDULER with the whole course schedule for Fall 2016 semester, published by Sabanci University on the web, over 972 courses: 259 of them have multiple sections, 72 of them have discussion sessions, 211 have recitations, and 27 of them have lab sessions. We have observed that course schedule plans are computed in less than a second on a regular laptop (with 2.7 GHz dual-core Intel Core i5 processor, 8GB RAM, and macOS Sierra).

To evaluate the coverage and the usefulness the functionalities of SUCHEDULER offered to students, we have interviewed with 21 students at Sabanci University by a survey. Figure 2 shows a summary of the results of this survey. According to these results;

– 20 students think that SUCHEDULER covers a quite comprehensive set of criteria for the students to express their constraints/preferences,
– 20 students think that being able to express their preferences is useful, and
– 8 students think that the time conflict warnings given by SUCHEDULER are useful.

We have also asked participants to provide us feedback as to how it can be further improved. Some of the participants have suggested showing also the types of the courses (e.g., core, area, elective) and the prerequisities of courses as further information. These suggestions will be adopted in the next versions of SUCHEDULER.

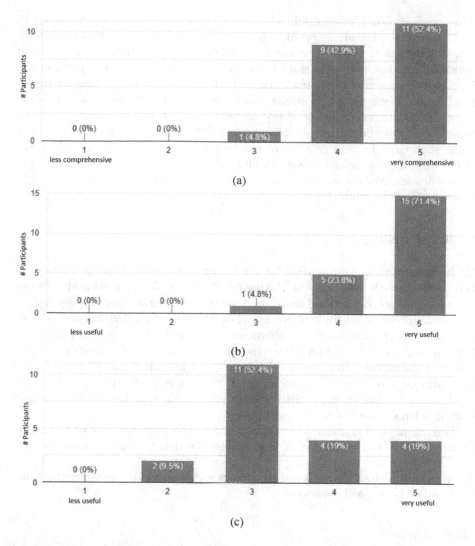

Fig. 2. A summary of the survey results: (a) how much comprehensive are the presented criteria? (b) how much useful is it to specify preferences? (c) how much useful are the warnings?

5   Related Work

One of the most closely related work is about course scheduling or timetabling, a widely studied problem in literature [4,16,18]. Some of the proposed solutions also use ASP [1,5,6]. Course timetabling is studied for the purpose of efficiently allocating the schools' resources (e.g., classrooms, lab spaces) to the courses offered at that school, considering constraints about the expected number of students, the sizes of the available classrooms, time conflicts between courses of the same category, etc. The personalized course schedule planning problem is studied after the course timetabling problem is solved: it takes the whole course schedule (i.e., the output of course timetabling problem), and aims to help each student decide an efficient course program according to her/his constraints/preferences.

Another most closely related work is about recommender systems for course enrollments. These systems consider prerequisites of courses and course loads of students, and act as virtual academic advisors [2,3] on possible course schedule plans (i.e., the output of personalized course schedule planning problem). In that sense, such virtual academic advisors can be used in conjunction with SUCHED-ULER: once a personalized course schedule plan is generated by SUCHEDULER, virtual academic advisors can be used for recommendations, e.g., considering the course load of the student.

6   Conclusion

We have developed an application for personalized course program generation, to help students with their decisions during registrations. We have utilized a declarative problem solving method based on Answer Set Programming, for generating personalized course schedule plans, based on the representation methodology of (i) generating possible candidate solutions, using choice rules, and (ii) eliminating the candidates that do not correspond to solutions, using constraints, and auxiliary definitions. To represent the students' constraints and preferences, we have utilized hard constraints and weak constraints, respectively. For optimizing the number of courses, days with courses, etc. we have utilized aggregates and optimization statements supported by ASP.

Our ongoing work includes improvements of the user interface of SUCHED-ULER as well as its functionalities, as suggested by the students via user surveys.

Acknowledgments. We thank the anonymous reviewers and the survey participants for useful comments and suggestions.

References

1. Aini, I.F., Saptawijaya, A., Aminah, S.: Bringing answer set programming to the next level: a real case on modeling course timetabling. In: Proceedings of ICACSIS, pp. 471–476 (2017)
2. Ajanovski, V.V.: A personal mobile academic adviser. In: Daniel, F., Papadopoulos, G.A., Thiran, P. (eds.) MobiWIS 2013. LNCS, vol. 8093, pp. 300–303. Springer, Heidelberg (2013). https://doi.org/10.1007/978-3-642-40276-0_25
3. Ajanovski, V.V.: Curriculum mapping as a tool for improving students satisfaction with the choice of courses. In: Proceedings of ITiCSE, pp. 76–77 (2017)
4. Asín Achá, R., Nieuwenhuis, R.: Curriculum-based course timetabling with sat and maxsat. Ann. Oper. Res. **218**(1), 71–91 (2014)
5. Banbara, M., et al.: teaspoon: solving the curriculum-based course timetabling problems with answer set programming. Ann. Oper. Res. (2018)

6. Banbara, M., Soh, T., Tamura, N., Inoue, K., Schaub, T.: Answer set programming as a modeling language for course timetabling. TPLP **13**(4–5), 783–798 (2013)
7. Baral, C.: Knowledge Representation, Reasoning, and Declarative Problem Solving. Cambridge University Press, New York (2003)
8. Brewka, G., Eiter, T., Truszczynski, M.: Answer set programming at a glance. ACM Communun. **54**(12), 92–103 (2011)
9. Brewka, G., Eiter, T., Truszczynski, M.: Answer set programming: an introduction to the special issue. AI Mag. **37**(3), 5–6 (2016)
10. Gebser, M., Kaufmann, B., Kaminski, R., Ostrowski, M., Schaub, T., Schneider, M.T.: Potassco: the potsdam answer set solving collection. AI Comm. **24**(2), 107–124 (2011)
11. Gelfond, M., Lifschitz, V.: The stable model semantics for logic programming. In: Proceedings of ICLP, pp. 1070–1080. MIT Press (1988)
12. Gelfond, M., Kahl, Y.: Knowledge Representation, Reasoning, and the Design of Intelligent Agents: The Answer-Set Programming Approach. Cambridge University Press, New York (2014)
13. Gelfond, M., Lifschitz, V.: Classical negation in logic programs and disjunctive databases. New Gener. Comput. **9**, 365–385 (1991)
14. Lifschitz, V.: Answer set programming and plan generation. AIJ **138**, 39–54 (2002)
15. Marek, V., Truszczyński, M.: Stable models and an alternative logic programming paradigm. In: Apt, K.R., Marek, V.W., Truszczynski, M., Warren, D.S. (eds.) The Logic Programming Paradigm. Artificial Intelligence, pp. 375–398. Springer, Heidelberg (1999). https://doi.org/10.1007/978-3-642-60085-2_17
16. McCollum, B.: A perspective on bridging the gap between theory and practice in university timetabling. In: Burke, E.K., Rudová, H. (eds.) PATAT 2006. LNCS, vol. 3867, pp. 3–23. Springer, Heidelberg (2007). https://doi.org/10.1007/978-3-540-77345-0_1
17. Niemelä, I.: Logic programs with stable model semantics as a constraint programming paradigm. Ann. Math. Artif. Intell. **25**, 241–273 (1999)
18. Schaerf, A.: A survey of automated timetabling. AI Rev. **13**(2), 87–127 (1999)

An ASP Based Approach to Answering Questions for Natural Language Text

Dhruva Pendharkar[✉] and Gopal Gupta[✉]

University of Texas at Dallas, Richardson, USA
dhruva.pendharkar@gmail.com, gupta@utdallas.edu

Abstract. An approach based on answer set programming (ASP) is proposed in this paper for representing knowledge generated from natural language text. Knowledge in the text is modeled using a Neo Davidsonian-like formalism, represented as an answer set program. Relevant common sense knowledge is additionally imported from resources such as WordNet and represented in ASP. The resulting knowledge-base can then be used to perform reasoning with the help of an ASP system. This approach can facilitate many natural language tasks such as automated question answering, text summarization, and automated question generation. ASP-based representation of techniques such as default reasoning, hierarchical knowledge organization, preferences over defaults, etc., are used to model common-sense reasoning methods required to accomplish these tasks. In this paper we describe the CASPR system that we have developed to automate the task of answering natural language questions given English text. CASPR can be regarded as a system that answers questions by "understanding" the text and has been tested on the SQuAD data set, with promising results.

Keywords: ASP · Common sense reasoning · NLP · KR

1 Introduction

The goal of AI is to build systems that can exhibit human-like intelligent behavior. Decision making and the ability to reason are important attributes of intelligent behavior. Hence, AI systems must be capable of performing automated reasoning as well as responding to changing environment (for example, changing knowledge). To exhibit such a behavior, an AI system needs to understand its environment as well interact with it to achieve certain goals. Classical logic based approaches have traditionally been used to build automated reasoning systems but have not lead to systems that can be called truly intelligent. Humans, arguably, do not use classical logic in their day to day reasoning tasks. They considerably simplify their burden of reasoning by using techniques such as defaults, exceptions, and preference patterns. Also, humans use non-monotonic reasoning and can deal with incomplete information [12,13]. All these features need to be built into an AI system, if we want to simulate human-like intelligence.

© Springer Nature Switzerland AG 2019
J. J. Alferes and M. Johansson (Eds.): PADL 2019, LNCS 11372, pp. 46–63, 2019.
https://doi.org/10.1007/978-3-030-05998-9_4

It has been shown that common-sense reasoning can be realized via a combination of (stable model semantics-based) negation as failure and classical negation [3,12] in ASP. ASP is a well-developed paradigm and has been applied to solving problem in planning, constraint satisfaction and optimization. There are comprehensive, well known implementations of ASP such as CLASP [11] and DLV [1]. Scalable implementations of ASP that support predicates (i.e., do not require grounding) and are query-driven, such as s(ASP) and s(CASP), have also been developed [2,16]. ASP is also well suited for representing knowledge and for modelling common-sense reasoning. Most of the knowledge resources available today are in the form of unstructured data, either in the form of written documents, or information present online.

In this paper we propose a system called CASPR (Commons-sense ASP Reasoning) to automatically convert textual knowledge into ASP programs, and use it to answer natural language questions translated into ASP queries. The problem of converting natural language text into ASP is challenging enough, however, even if we succeed in this translation task, the resulting knowledge is not enough to answer questions to the level that a human can. When humans read a passage, we automatically draw upon a large amount of common sense knowledge that we have acquired over the course of years in understanding the passage and in answering questions related to the passage. An automated QA system ought to do the same. CASPR, thus, resorts to resources such as WordNet [17], that encapsulate some of the common-sense knowledge, to augment the knowledge derived from the text. CASPR also allows users to add common sense knowledge—coded in ASP—manually as well.

CASPR runs on the s(ASP) answer set programming system. The s(ASP) system [16] is a query-driven predicate ASP system that is scalable, in that it can run answer set programs containing predicates with arbitrary terms. Since the s(ASP) system is query-driven, it does not require grounding, a crucial feature needed for building large-scale natural language-based KR applications using ASP. Proof of the query serves as a justification, allowing us to give the reasoning behind an answer to a question in CASPR.

Our research makes several contributions: (i) it shows that with the help of novel, query-driven systems such as s(ASP), it is possible to build practical NLP applications that rely on "text understanding"; and, (ii) traditional problems of Natural Language Understanding such as word sense disambiguation can be solved quite elegantly with ASP.

2   System Architecture

CASPR is composed of two main sub systems: the Knowledge Generation System and the Query Generation System. The architecture, as illustrated in Fig. 1, comprises of a common resource framework shared by both these systems consisting of NLP tools such as Stanford Core NLP Tools, WordNet API as well as modules for pre-processing input text.

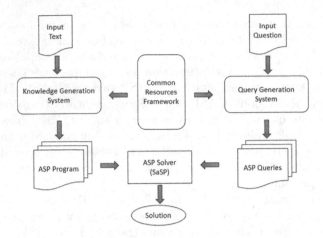

Fig. 1. System architecture

The Knowledge Generation System is mainly responsible for extracting knowledge from natural language text. For extracting the knowledge from text, this component uses Stanford NLP tools like the POS Tagger [22,23], Stanford Dependency Parser [5], and the Stanford NER Tagger [10] to gain more information about the input text. Apart from these resources it also taps into the vast information that is provided by WordNet [17] and extracts information from it, converting it into an answer set program. WordNet provides significant amount of common sense knowledge about nouns. For verbs, at present, there are very few digital resources available that are similar to WordNet. Common sense knowledge for verbs, thus, has to be modeled manually as an answer set program, and added to the common resource framework.

The Query Generation System automatically translates the question to an ASP query that can be executed against the ASP-coded knowledge-base generated from the textual passage augmented with common sense knowledge. Execution is performed using the s(ASP) system. The solution found represents an accurate answer to the question. The query obtained from the natural language question is a conjunction of multiple sub-goals. If the query fails, then some of the sub-goals are systematically removed and the query re-executed to find less accurate answers. These less accurate answers are reported too, along with the level of accuracy (likely, possible, guess).

3   Knowledge Representation

The Stanford Dependency Parser is used to parse the pre-processed text. A semantic graph is generated using the Stanford Typed Dependencies representation [8,9].

Example 1. *"NASA carried out the Apollo program."*
Following is the Stanford Dependency (SD) representation: nsubj(carried-2, NASA-1), root(ROOT-0,carried-2), compound:prt(carried-2,out-3), det (program-6,the-4), compound(program-6,Apollo-5), dobj(carried-2,program-6)

These dependencies map straightforwardly onto a directed graph representation in which words in the sentence are nodes in the graph and grammatical relations are edge labels. In English, most event mentions correspond to verbs and most verbs are triggers to events. Although this is true in most cases there are other word groups that can trigger events as well. The different verbs in the sentence thus define various events that take place in the sentence and how these events are connected to each other. Consider a more complex example.

Example 2. *"Miitomo, which Nintendo introduced globally in 2016, features the company's, Mii, avatar-system and lets the users communicate by exchanging personal information such as favorite movies."*

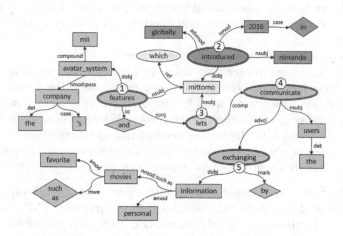

Fig. 2. Semantic graph representing event regions

Figure 2 shows how various words in the example passage are connected to each other in the sentence. The main verbs of the sentence are *"feature"* and *"let"* connected by a coordinating conjunction. The verbs in Fig. 2 represent the head of events in the sentence and are marked using event IDs. The various color regions denote the rough boundaries of these event regions. The semantic graph along with the event regions are used to create ASP facts and rules.

3.1   Predicate Generation

Knowledge is represented using a collection of pre-defined predicates, following the neo-Davidsonian approach [7]. Some of the predicates capture specialized concepts such as *abbreviation, start_time* etc., whereas others are more generic like *mod, event* and so on. The generic predicates that convey information are explicitly present in the text, whereas all others model implicit information. Note that it is important to keep this predicate representation as simple as possible, so that individual pieces of knowledge can be composed using common sense reasoning patterns. These reasoning patterns have to be kept very simple as well. Otherwise, we run the risk that we may have appropriate knowledge in our knowledge-base to answer the given question, but we fail in answering it because we are unable to compose that knowledge due to complexity of its representation. A summary of important predicates that have been used by CASPR is given below: We explain the event predicate in detail and summarize the rest (details can be found elsewhere [19,20]).

Event Predicate: The event predicate defines an event that happens in the sentence. The verb marks the head of the event predicate. The *event* predicate consists of the various actors (doers) and participants involved in the event with the signature:

event(event_id, trigger_verb, actor, participant)

where the *event_id* is an integer that uniquely identifies that event in the paragraph. The *trigger_verb* denoted in the event predicate is the *lemma*, i.e., the stem word, of the actual word used in the sentence. The actors in the event predicate are the subjects to the trigger_verb in the sentence. Subjects in the sentence can be found with the help of dependencies like *nsubj* and *nsubj:xsubj*. Just as actors can be obtained from the subject of the sentence, the participants can be determined from direct object dependency (*dobj*).

Example 3. *"The American_Football_Conference's (AFC) champion team, Denver_Broncos, defeated the National_Football_Conference's (NFC) champion team, Carolina_Panthers, by 24_10 to earn AFC third Super_Bowl title"*

event(1, defeat, denver_broncos, carolina_panthers)
event(2, earn, afc, title)

Here we can get richer information about the event by generating duplicate event predicates for each modifier for the actor as well as the participants involved in the event. To generate such event predicates, we use the *amod* or *nummod* dependencies for the actors and the participants and create compound atoms from the modifiers and their governors. Consider the following duplicate event predicate:

event(2, earn, afc, third_super_bowl_title)

Note that in absence of information, the default value for the actor and the participant field maybe null. A null value indicates that either the term is absent for the event or the system was not able to determine it.

Property Predicate: The property predicate elaborates on the properties of the modified noun or verb. The modifier in this case is generally a prepositional phrase in the sentence. A property predicate is coupled with an event and describes the modification only for that event.

Example 4. *"The game was played on February 7 2016, at Levis_Stadium, in the San_Francisco_Bay_Area, at Santa_Clara in California"*
  _property(2, play, on, 'february_7_2016')
  _property(2, play, at, levis_stadium)
  _property(2, play, in, san_francisco_bay_area)
  _property(2, play, at, santa_clara)
  _property(2, santa_clara, in, california)

Modifier Predicate: The modifier predicate is used to model the relationship between adjectives and the nouns they modify and between verbs and their modifying adverbs.

Example 5. *"The Amazon_rainforest, also known in English as Amazonia or the Amazon_Jungle, is a moist broadleafed forest that covers most of the Amazon_basin of South_America."*
  _mod(forest, broadleafed)
  _mod(forest, moist)
  _mod(know, also)

Possessive Predicate: The possessive predicate is used to model the genitive case in English. It is used to show possession or a possessive relation between two entities in the sentence.

Example 6. *"The American_Football_Conference's (AFC) champion team, Denver_Broncos, defeated the National_Football_Conference's (NFC) champion team, Carolina_Panthers, by 24_10 to earn AFC third Super_Bowl title"*
  _possess(american_football_conference, team)
  _possess(national_football_conference, team)
  _possess(american_football_conference, denver_broncos)
  _possess(national_football_conference, carolina_panthers)

Instance Predicate: The instance predicate models the concept of an instance. As an example, red is an instance of a color.

Example 7. *"Nikola_Tesla was a serbian-american inventor, electrical engineer, mechanical engineer, physicist, and futurist"*
  _is(nikola_tesla, inventor).
  _is(nikola_tesla, serbian_american_inventor).

In the above example we see that the verb (*is*) is associated with other concepts like engineer, physicist, and futurist using the conjunction. Thus, we can extend the definition of the instance predicate to also include these other facts:

_is(nikola_tesla, electrical_engineer),

_is(nikola_tesla, futurist),

....

Adding these facts makes the knowledge base richer which is now able to infer many other things about the passage. Another case, where we can generate the instance predicate is in cases where multi-word expressions like such as, or like are used to compare two concepts to be equivalent. Details are omitted due to lack of space.

Relation Predicate: The relation predicate is used to connect two concepts in events. This predicate is generated to model mainly two relations, dependent clauses and conjunctions.

Example 8. *"The American_Broadcasting_Company (ABC), stylized in the network's logo as ABC since 1957, is an American commercial broadcast television network"*

_relation(american_broadcasting_company, 1, _clause)

event(1, stylize, null, null)

The relation predicate is also used to model the conjunction relation between any two clauses. An example of such a predicate is given below.

Example 9. *"Water heats and transforms into steam within a boiler operating at a high pressure"*

_relation(2, 3, _conj)

event(2, heat, water, null)

event(3, transform, water, null)

Named Entity Predicate: CASPR uses the Named Entity Tagger [10] to get information about entities in the text. The Named Entity Tagger marks various classes like LOCATION, PERSON, ORGANIZATION, MONEY, PERCENT, TIME in the text. We make use of these tags to generate facts of the form *concept(instance)*. These facts together with the rules generated by the ontology help in reasoning about the text.

Special Predicates: Special predicates have been used in the system, to model concepts that are patterns and are understood by humans implicitly. As grammatical relations in the sentence do not convey the meaning of these concepts, they must be extracted explicitly. Some of them include abbreviations, time spans and so on. The more of these patterns are learned by the system the better it can reason like humans. Some of these patterns are discussed in this paper. Again, we omit details due to lack of space.

3.2   Common Sense Knowledge Generation

We make use of additional knowledge sources such as the WordNet to gain supplementary information (common sense knowledge) about the concepts in the input passage. CASPR uses the Hypernym relation from WordNet to build its ontology, coded as an answer set program. To generate ontology rules, we use standard knowledge patterns from answer-set programming like the preference pattern and the default reasoning pattern [6,12]. In general a concept is represented in our work using the following signature:

   concept(concept_instance, instance_sense)

For example: *lion(simba, noun_animal)*.

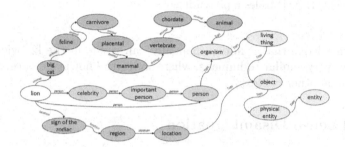

Fig. 3. Concept graph of Hypernym relation

Hypernyms can be used to infer various properties of and functions about concepts. Hypernyms make use of the generalization principle to transfer properties from more general concepts to their specific concepts. There are three steps required to do so (i) Identify the concepts from the passage and generate a hypernym graph; words may be used in multiple senses (e.g., the word *lion* has four commonly used senses); example graph for word lion highlighting 4 different senses is shown in Fig. 3. (ii) Aggregate the concepts into common base concepts. (iii) Generate hypernym rules. Figure 4 shows ASP rules generated by CASPR for one of the senses of the concept *lion*.

Adding Common Sense Knowledge Manually: Note that at the moment we are only using WordNet, however, other knowledge resources, such as YAGO [15], VerbNet [14], NELL [18], etc., can be incorporated as well to extract additional common sense knowledge. Doing so is relatively straightforward, as it mostly involves syntactic transformation to ASP syntax. Note that, currently, common sense knowledge about verbs is entered manually. An example of adding knowledge manually is the following:

The term Nikola_Tesla is similar to Tesla:

   _similar(tesla, nikola_tesla).

A team X can represent an organization Y, if Y possesses X:

   event(E, represent, X, Y) :- _possess(Y, X), organization(Y), team(X).

```
big_cat(X, noun_animal) :- lion(X, noun_animal)
feline(X, noun_animal) :- big_cat(X, noun_animal)
carnivore(X, noun_animal) :- feline(X, noun_animal)
placental(X, noun_animal) :- carnivore(X, noun_animal)
mammal(X, noun_animal) :- placental(X, noun_animal)
vertebrate(X, noun_animal) :- mammal(X, noun_animal)
chordate(X, noun_animal) :- vertebrate(X, noun_animal)
animal(X, noun_tops) :- chordate(X, noun_animal)
organism(X, noun_tops) :- animal(X, noun_tops)
living_thing(X, noun_tops) :- organism(X, noun_tops)
object(X, noun_tops) :- living_thing(X, noun_tops)
physical_entity(X, noun_tops) :- object(X, noun_tops)
entity(X, noun_tops) :- physical_entity(X, noun_tops)
```

Fig. 4. ASP Rules representing the animal branch of "lion"

Note that knowledge that is added manually can reside in the knowledge-base permanently (very similar to humans, where we learn knowledge once, and may use it later in another context).

4   Word Sense Disambiguation

Word sense disambiguation (WSD) is the task of selecting the best sense out of a collection of senses applicable to a concept. When queried from WordNet we get a list of senses for a specific concept ordered from the most used to the least used. WSD is a very common problem in NLP applications and has many statistical solutions that have been developed. We develop a method using negation as failure, classical negation and preferences that performs WSD correctly. Essentially, contextual knowledge is used to disambiguate the word sense, in a manner similar to what humans do. We explain it next.

Representation of Word Senses: Word senses are represented using two different logic patterns in our work. Using both these patterns together, senses are selected for the various concepts in the text which activate their hypernym relations. The pattern discussed in this section, tries to prove a sense for a concept. Its template can be given as follows

$c(X, s_i)$:- $c(X)$, $properties\_si(X)$, not -$c(X, s_i)$.

In the above template, we are trying to prove that "X is an instance_of concept c with sense s_i". Here every concept c has one or more senses denoted by s_i. The above rule states that X is an instance of the concept c with the sense s_i only if we can prove that X is some instance of concept c, X has all the properties required to be of sense s_i, and we cannot prove that X is definitely not an instance of concept c with sense s_i. Such rules are generated for every sense s_i of the concept in the order of senses from the most used sense to the least used sense. The first term given by '$c(X)$' is responsible to short circuit and fail the rule if the instance X does not belong to the class c. The second term, '$properties\_si(X)$', is the main predicate which tries to prove that X shows the properties of having sense s_i. It is this predicate that can be added either manually or using other sources to prove the sense. The third term of the body is a strong exception against the head of the rule, that fails the rule if an exception is found against the application of the sense.

According to WordNet, the concept *'tree'* has three senses, S = {*plant, diagram, person*}, ordered according to their frequency of use. Thus, using the above-mentioned template for the sense the three rules generated for the tree concept can be given as follows

$tree(X, plant)$:- $tree(X)$, $properties\_plant(X)$,
        not -$tree(X, plant)$.
$tree(X, diagram)$:- $tree(X)$, $properties\_diagram(X)$,
        not -$tree(X, diagram)$.
$tree(X, person)$:- $tree(X)$, $properties\_person(X)$,
        not -$tree(X, person)$.

Preference Patterns for Senses: We humans perform word sense disambiguation in our day to day life by taking cues from the context. Over a period of time we learn which senses are more common than others and develop a preference order. Consider a concept c having three senses s_1, s_2 and s_3 ordered according to the frequency of their use from the most used to the least used. We first assume the sense to be s_1, unless we know that s_1 is not the sense from some other source. Then we move on to the next sense s_2 unless we know that both s_1 and s_2 cannot be applicable. Then finally we choose s_3. This process of elimination of senses and choosing senses according to preferences can be modeled as the following ASP code template.

$c(X, s_p)$:- $c(X)$, not -$c(X, s_p)$,
      -$c(X, s_1)$, -$c(X, s_2)$, ..., -$c(X, s_{p-1})$,
      not $c(X, s_{p+1})$, not $c(X, s_{p+2})$, ..., not $c(X, s_n)$.

The above skeleton is applied for all the senses of concept c in order of preference. The above template represents the rule generated for the pth sense of the concept c such that $1 < p < n$, where n is the total number of senses of concept c. If $p = 1$ then the template omits the classical negation terms as follows

$c(X, s_1)$:- $c(X)$, not -$c(X, s_1)$, not $c(X, s_2)$,
      not $c(X, s_3)$, ..., not $c(X, s_n)$.

Similarly, if $p = n$, then the template omits the negation as failure terms:

$c(X, s_n)$:- $c(X)$, not -$c(X, s_n)$, -$c(X, s_1)$,
      -$c(X, s_2)$, ... -$c(X, s_{n-1})$.

We can apply this pattern to the 'tree' concept as an example. A tree can be a living object (plant), a diagram, or a person (Mr. Tree).

$tree(X, plant)$:- $tree(X)$, not -$tree(X, plant)$,
        not $tree(X, diagram)$, not $tree(X, person)$.
$tree(X, diagram)$:- $tree(X)$, not -$tree(X, diagram)$,
        -$tree(X, plant)$, not $tree(X, person)$.
$tree(X, person)$:- $tree(X)$, not -$tree(X, person)$,
        -$tree(X, plant)$, -$tree(X, diagram)$.

This pattern is responsible for assigning at least one sense for every concept in the text. This preference pattern along with the property pattern mentioned previously helps disambiguate word sense in a manner that humans do.

5   Query Generation from Natural Language Question

Once knowledge has been generated from the text and auxiliary sources, our next task is to translate the question we want to answer into an ASP query.

Since a question is also a sentence, it is processed in the same way that any other sentence would be, as mentioned before in this paper. This means that a semantic graph is generated for every question, and event regions are created within the question assigning event ids to different parts of the question. To generate an ASP query from the semantic graph the following steps are applied: (i) Question understanding (ii) Generation of query predicates (iii) Applying base constraints (iv) Combining constraints. Currently, this module is only built to deal with simple interrogative sentences but can be extended to deal with more complex questions.

Question Understanding: For analyzing questions, we obtain four kinds of information from the question, namely, the question word, the question type as mentioned in the previous section, the answer word or the focus of the question, and the answer type.

The question word is the Wh-word found in the question. In general, Wh-words can be found out by looking at the following POS Tags on the words: WDT, WP, WP$ and WRB. If none of the tags are found, then the questions may have a copula as its question word or a modal as its question word. The question type contains a set of predefined question types that help in further processing. These include WHAT, WHERE, WHO, WHICH, WHEN, HOW_-MANY, HOW_MUCH, HOW_LONG, HOW_FAR, and UNKNOWN. Once the main question word is found, we can use the word and its relations to determine the exact question type. The third type of information we try to extract is the answer word or the focus of the question. The answer word is the word in a question that tells us what kind of answer is expected from the question. Not all types of questions require an answer word, so in those cases this information is null. The fourth and the last information that we extract from the question is the answer type. The answer type depends on the question type. For most of the question types the required answer type is predefined. The answer types supported by the system are as follows SUBJECT, OBJECT, PLACE, PERSON, TIME, YEAR, DAY, MONTH, NUMBER and UNKNOWN. Table 1 shows expected answer types depending on question types. With the help of this basic analysis, we start generating the predicates for query generation.

Generating Query Predicates: Using the information that we gathered during Question Understanding, we start generating predicate facts for all the words in the question. We will use predicates mentioned previously in the paper as a reference. There are some changes that need to be made in a few predicates,

Table 1. Expected answer types for question types

Question type	Expected answer type
WHERE	PLACE
WHO	PERSON
WHEN	TIME
HOW_MANY	NUMBER [Non-neg integer]
HOW_MUCH	NUMBER
HOW_LONG	NUMBER [length]
HOW_FAR	NUMBER [distance]
WHAT	** variable **
WHICH	** variable **
UNKNOWN	UNKNOWN

e.g., event predicate, property predicate, etc. Others (possess, mod, and named entity predicates) are generated as discussed earlier.

Event Predicate: In case of questions, we do not know the event_id of the event in question so we replace it with a variable. The trigger_verb is in the question that triggers the predicate generation. The actor acts like the subject of the verb and the participant is the object or the modifier. The participants can be obtained from the direct object (*dobj*) relations of the verb. There are various ways in which we can obtain the actor or the subject in any event. Details are omitted due to lack of space, but we give an example.

Example 10. *Given the question "What company owns walt_disney?", the three possibilities for the event predicate are:*
  1. event(E1, own, X1, O1), _similar(walt_disney, O1).
  2. event(E1, own, _, O1), _property(E1, own, _by, X1),
     _similar(walt_disney, O1).
  3. event(E1, own, _, _), _relation(X1, E1, _clause),
     _similar(walt_disney, O1).

Property Predicate: Property predicates are generated from verbs and nouns that are modified by nominal phrases in the sentence. Here, like the event predicate, we are unaware of the event_id and hence it will be set as a variable. The modified_entity is the noun or the verb that triggered the predicate generation. The preposition here can either be obtained from the case relation or can be left blank (_). The modifier is the head of the nominal modifier that can be used to constraint the query. If the modifier is the answer word, then we replace the word with the answer tag (X_k).

Example 11. *Given "On what streets is the ABC's headquarter located?", we generate: _property(E2, locate, on, X2).*

Similar Predicate: The *similar* predicate models the concept of similarity between entities in which one entity is so like the other one that they can replace each other. The similar predicate thus models one of the principles of common-sense reasoning where we as humans make use of the similarity relationship while reasoning (referring to Albert Einstein as just Einstein). Some rules for the similar predicate are as follows:

    a. _similar(X, Y) :- _abbreviation(X, Y).
    b. _similar(X, Y) :- _abbreviation(Y, X).
    c. _similar(X, Y) :- _is(X, Y).
    d. _similar(X, Y) :- _similar(X, Z), _similar(Z, Y).

Generating Base Constraints: Base constraints are generated at the end after all the constraints from the question have been generated. These constraints refer to the constraint that depend on the answer type of the question. For the following cases we generate the base constraints as follows.

    TIME $\rightarrow$ time(X_k)
    DAY $\rightarrow$ day(T_k, X_k), time(T_k)
    MONTH $\rightarrow$ month(T_k, X_k), time(T_k)
    YEAR $\rightarrow$ year(T_k, X_k), time(T_k)
    PLACE $\rightarrow$ location(X_k) or location(X_k, noun_location)
    PERSON $\rightarrow$ person(X_k) or person(X_k, noun_person)

In case the answer type is UNKNOWN, we may expect the answer to be a specific concept represented by the answer word. In such cases the base constraint comes from the answer word itself.

    UNKNOWN $\rightarrow$ concept(X_k)
    e.g., company(X_k) or city(X_k)

Combining Constraints: After generation of the predicates from the question and the base constraints from answer type we combine all the constraints to create the final query. This can be best explained with an example.

Example 12. *For the question "When was Nikola Tesla born?", the following queries will be generated and automatically tried in order.*

    ?- event(E2, bear, S2, O2), _similar(nikola_tesla, S2),
        property(E2, bear, on, X2), time(X2).
    ?- event(E2, bear, _, O2), _property(E2, bear, _by, S2),
        _similar(nikola_tesla, S2), property(E2, bear, on, X2), time(X2).
    ?- event(E2, bear, _, _), _relation(S2, E2, _clause),
        similar(nikola_tesla, S2), property(E2, bear, on, X2), time(X2).
    ?- _start_date(S2, X2), _similar(nikola_tesla, S2), time(X2).

In this sentence, we have the special predicates _start_date applying the constraints of time-spans on the entity 'Nikola Tesla'.

Query Confidence Classes: To make any question answering system robust, so that it fails gracefully, we introduce the concept of *confidence classes* on the generated queries by relaxing constraints on the queries to make their execution more flexible. In the absence of an answer, the CASPR system starts removing constraints (sub-goals) in the query and relaxing it with the hope of executing it successfully and obtaining some answer. Currently, queries have been divided into 4 confidence classes:

Certain: These queries have all the constraints generated by our question processing module. If an answer is produced, it is a correct answer.

Likely: If a *certain* answer is not produced, all sub-goals that do not have variables are dropped.

Possible: If *likely* answer is not produced, then only the answer predicates and base constraints are included in the query (rest of the subgoals are dropped).

Guess: If possible answer is not produced, only base constraints are included in the query (rest of the subgoals are dropped).

As an example, suppose we ask the question: "When was Tesla born?", given a biographical passage about Tesla. If the query that is formulated succeeds, it will produce the certain answer (1856). However, if for some reason the query fails, in the worst case, we would just retrieve any year in the passage and *guess* it as an answer. *It should be noted that with enough knowledge, we are always guaranteed to produce the correct answer.*

Note also that there are many other ways of relaxing constraints in the query to obtain less precise answers. The above is just one reasonable scheme.

6 Evaluation Results

The SQuAD Dataset [21] contains more than 100,000 reading comprehensions along with questions and answers for those reading passages. SQuAD dataset uses the top 500+ articles from the English Wikipedia. These articles are then divided into paragraphs. We used the Dev Set v1.1 of the SQuAD Dataset to obtain comprehension passages for building a prototype for the proposed approach. This dataset has around 48 different articles with each article having around 50 paragraphs each. Out of the 48 different articles in the SQuAD dev set, 20 articles were chosen from different domains to help build the CASPR system (these 20 passages and associated questions can be found in [20]). Using the 20 different articles mentioned above, the ASP code was generated for one paragraph from each article. Then, ASP queries were generated for all the questions in the dataset for these paragraphs. The results show the percentage of questions for which the answer generated from the ASP solver was present in the list of answers specified for the question in the SQuAD dataset. The results are summarized in Table 2. Our results show that approximately 77.76% of the questions are correctly answered. This shows that most of the knowledge, if not all, has been captured successfully in the ASP program generated for the passage. The ASP queries generated for the questions are very similar to the original question and convey the same meaning.

Note that the two main reasons why a query may fail to produce an exact (certain) answer are: (i) CASPR fails to parse the question; or, (ii) common sense knowledge regarding concepts in the question is missing.

Table 2. Results for question answering

No	Article	Result	%	No	Article	Result	%
1	ABC Corp.	5/5	100	11	Kenya	5/5	100
2	Amazon rainforest	12/14	85.7	12	Martin Luther	2/5	40
3	Apollo	4/5	80	13	Nikola Tesla	6/7	85.7
4	Chloroplasts	4/5	80	14	Normans	4/5	80
5	Computational complexity	3/3	100	15	Oxygen	8/15	53.3
6	Ctenophora	9/12	75	16	Rhine	5/8	62.5
7	European Union Law	13/13	100	17	Southern California	3/5	60
8	Genghis Khan	3/5	60	18	Steam Engine	4/5	80
9	Geology	4/5	80	19	Super Bowl 50	25/29	86.2
10	Immune system	13/15	86.6	20	Warsaw	3/5	60
Total						135/171	78.95%
Average Result						77.76%	

Note that our system has shown excellent execution performance on the 171 questions on 20 passages tried thus far: 80% of the questions were answered in 2 to 3 ms, while the rest were answered in a few seconds.

7 Contributions, Related Work, Conclusions

The main contribution of this paper is an effective and efficient method for converting textual data into knowledge represented as an answer set program that can be processed on our query-driven s(ASP) ASP system. This includes developing a neo-davidsonian logic inspired generic calculus that helps represent knowledge, and using knowledge sources such as WordNet to acquire common sense knowledge about terms found in the text to create a custom ontology for the problem at hand. Yet another novelty is in showing how word sense disambiguation can be elegantly modeled using ASP. Our system is based on "understanding" the text in a manner similar to what humans do when they answer questions. Our system is scalable and shows good execution performance as the custom ontology is generated dynamically.

The paper also proposes a framework for converting natural language questions into ASP queries. These queries can be run on the query-driven s(ASP) system to compute answers. The query generation framework is made robust through broadening of queries by dropping constraints, thus increasing the possibility that the question will indeed be answered (even though in the worst case the answer may just be a guess). This approach to handling question answering is yet another novelty of the proposed system.

Wrt related work, Cyc [25] is one of the oldest AI project that attempts to model common sense reasoning. In Cyc, knowledge is presented in the form of a vast collection of ontologies that consist of implicit knowledge and rules about the world that represents common sense knowledge. Cyc uses a *community of agents* consisting of multiple reasoning agents that rely on more than 1000 heuristic modules to solve inference problems. Cyc, however, does not work with natural language, though recently some efforts have been started. A potential problem with Cyc is knowing which agent to apply, and which heuristic to use. For a common sense reasoning system to be successful, *it has to be modeled in a very simple way*. Otherwise, we may possess the individual pieces of knowledge to answer a given question, but may not be able to compose these pieces together to arrive at an answer. For this reason, CASPR represents knowledge using very few generic predicates and uses simple ASP-based reasoning patterns to compute answers. Our initial experiments suggest that our approach is effective.

Vo and Baral [24] have developed the NL2KR tool that allows natural language text to be translated to an answer set program. Several researchers have worked on applying ASP for NLP tasks and many of these efforts are reported in the first workshop on NLP and Automated Reasoning [4]. Our approach has many elements common with these efforts, however, our work is based on the query-driven s(ASP) predicate ASP engine, and thus is scalable and not constrained by limitations of grounding based implementations of ASP. The query-driven s(ASP) system is crucial to our success. We omit details of the comparison with other efforts due to lack of space.

There are many approaches to question answering based on machine learning (cf. SQuAD website [21]). However, they are not based on *actually understanding* the text and so can only answer questions related to data they are trained on. CASPR, in contrast, *understands* the knowledge contained in the text and has shown promising results for a subset of the SQuAD dataset.

A critical component of CASPR's success is the s(ASP) query-driven, predicate ASP system that leads to three major advantages for CASPR: (i) only parts of the knowledge base relevant to answering the question are explored during execution; (ii) justification for answers can be extracted from the justification tree produced by s(ASP); and, (iii) the question answering system is scalable, as no grounding of the program needs to be done as s(ASP) can execute predicates directly under the stable model semantics.

CASPR is a step toward building truly intelligent systems that mimic human reasoning. Future work includes (i) extending the system to handle more complex questions (e.g., causality questions), (ii) incorporating additional knowledge resources for importing more common sense knowledge, (iii) Generating justifications to a question's answer in a more human-readable way, (iv) Extending the system for other NLP tasks: text summarization, question generation, etc.

Acknowledgment. Authors thank NSF (Grant IIS 1718945) and members of their research group (Zhuo Chen, Farhad Shakerin, Elmer Salazar, Joaquin Arias, Sarat Varanasi, Kyle Marple).

References

1. Alviano, M., Faber, W., Leone, N., Perri, S., Pfeifer, G., Terracina, G.: The disjunctive datalog system DLV. In: de Moor, O., Gottlob, G., Furche, T., Sellers, A. (eds.) Datalog 2.0 2010. LNCS, vol. 6702, pp. 282–301. Springer, Heidelberg (2011). https://doi.org/10.1007/978-3-642-24206-9_17
2. Arias, J., Carro, M., Salazar, E., Marple, K., Gupta, G.: Constraint answer set programming without grounding. TPLP **18**(3–4), 337–354 (2018)
3. Baral, C.: Knowledge Representation Reasoning and Declarative Problem Solving. Cambridge university press, New York (2003)
4. Baral, C., Schüller, P. (eds.): Proceedings of 1st Workshop on NLP and Automated Reasoning 2013, vol. 1044 (2013). http://ceur-ws.org/Vol-1044
5. Chen, D., Manning, C.: A fast and accurate dependency parser using neural networks. In: Proceedings of 2014 EMNLP, pp. 740–750 (2014)
6. Chen, Z., Marple, K., Salazar, E., Gupta, G., Tamil, L.: A physician advisory system for CHF based on knowledge patterns. TPLP **16**(5–6), 604–618 (2016)
7. Davidson, D.: Inquiries into Truth and Interpretation. Oxford University Press, New York (1984)
8. De Marneffe, M.C., Dozat, T., et al.: Universal Stanford dependencies: a cross-linguistic typology. In: LREC, vol. 14, pp. 4585–4592 (2014)
9. De Marneffe, M.C., Manning, C.D.: Stanford typed dependencies manual. Technical report, Stanford University (2008)
10. Finkel, J.R., et al.: Incorporating non-local information into information extraction systems by Gibbs sampling. In: Proceedings of 43rd ACL, pp. 363–370 (2005)
11. Gebser, M., Kaminski, R., Kaufmann, B., Ostrowski, M., Schaub, T., Thiele, S.: Gringo, Clasp, Clingo, and Iclingo User Guide (2010)
12. Gelfond, M., Kahl, Y.: Knowledge Representation, Reasoning, and the Design of Intelligent Agents: The ASP Approach. Cambridge University Press, New York (2014)
13. Jonson-Laird, P.: How We Reason. Oxford University Press, New York (2009)
14. Kipper, K., et al.: Extending verbnet with novel verb classes. In: Proceedings of LREC 2006, Genoa, Italy, pp. 1027–1032 (2006)
15. Mahdisoltani, F., et al.: YAGO3: A knowledge base from multilingual Wikipedias. In: Proceedings of CIDR (2015)
16. Marple, K., Salazar, E., Gupta, G.: Computing stable models of normal logic programs without grounding. arXiv preprint arXiv:1709.00501 (2017)
17. Miller, G.A.: Wordnet: a Lexical database for English. Commun. ACM **38**(11), 39–41 (1995)
18. Mitchell, T.M., et al.: Never-ending language learning. In: Proceedings of Twenty-Ninth AAAI Conference on Artificial Intelligence, pp. 2302–2310 (2015)
19. Pendharkar, D.: An ASP-based Approach to Representing and Querying Textual Knowledge. M.S. Thesis, UT Dallas. http://utdallas.edu/~gupta/dpthesis.pdf
20. Pendharkar, D.: CASPR. https://github.com/DhruvaPendharkar/thesis-project
21. Rajpurkar, P., et al.: 100,000+ questions for machine comprehension of text. arXiv preprint arXiv:1606.05250 (2016)

22. Toutanova, K., et al.: Feature-rich part-of-speech tagging with a cyclic dependency network. In: Proceedings of 2003 NAACL, pp. 173–180 (2003)
23. Toutanova, K., Manning, C.D.: Enriching the knowledge sources used in a maximum entropy part-of-speech tagger. In: Proceedings of EMNLP 2000, pp. 63–70 (2000)
24. Vo, N.H., Mitra, A., Baral, C.: The NL2KR platform for building natural language translation systems. In: Proceedings of ACL 2015, pp. 899–908 (2015)
25. Wikipedia contributors: Cyc – Wikipedia. Accessed 17 May 2018. https://en. wikipedia.org/w/index.php?title=Cyc&oldid=841189903

Natural Language Generation
from Ontologies

Van Nguyen[✉], Tran Cao Son[✉], and Enrico Pontelli[✉]

New Mexico State University, Las Cruces, NM 88003, USA
{vnguyen,tson,epontell}@cs.nmsu.edu

Abstract. This paper addresses the problem of automatic generation of *natural language descriptions* for *ontology-described artifacts*. The original motivation for the work is the challenge of providing textual narratives of automatically generated scientific workflows (e.g., paragraphs that scientists can include in their publications). The paper presents two systems which generate descriptions of sets of atoms derived from a collection of ontologies. The first system, called `nlgPhylogeny`, demonstrates the feasibility of the task in the *Phylotastic* project, providing evolutionary biologists with narrative for automatically generated analysis workflows. `nlgPhylogeny` utilizes the fact that the *Grammatical Framework (GF)* is suitable for the natural language generation (NLG) task; the paper shows how elements of the ontologies in Phylotastic, such as web services and information artifacts, can be encoded in GF for the NLG task. The second system, called `nlgOntology`^{A}, is a generalization of `nlgPhylogeny`. It eliminates the requirement that a GF needs to be defined and proposes the use of *annotated ontologies* for NLG. Given a set of annotated ontologies, `nlgOntology`^{A} generates a GF suitable for the creation of natural language descriptions of sets of atoms derived from these ontologies. The paper describes the algorithms used in the development of `nlgPhylogeny` and `nlgOntology`^{A} and discusses potential applications of these systems.

Keywords: Natural language generation · Ontologies
Web service · Grammatical Framework · Attempto Controlled English

1 Introduction

In many application domains, where users are not proficient in computer programming, it is of the utmost importance to be able to communicate the results of a computation in an easily understandable way, e.g., using text rather than a complex data structure or mathematic formulae. The problem of generating *natural language explanations* has been explored in several research efforts. For example, the problem has been studied in the context of question-answering systems,[1] recommendation systems,[2] etc. With the proliferation of spoken dialogue

---

[1] http://coherentknowledge.com.

[2] http://gem.med.yale.edu/ergo/default.htm.

© Springer Nature Switzerland AG 2019
J. J. Alferes and M. Johansson (Eds.): PADL 2019, LNCS 11372, pp. 64–81, 2019.
https://doi.org/10.1007/978-3-030-05998-9_5

systems and conversational agents, verbal interfaces such as Amazon Echo and Google Home for human-robot-interaction, and the availability of text-to-speech programs, such as the TTSReader Extension,[3] the application arena of systems capable of generating natural language representations will continue growing. In this paper, we describe two systems for generating natural language descriptions of collections of atoms derived from a set of ontologies.

The first system, called `nlgPhylogeny`, is used to generate natural language descriptions of automatically generated workflows, obtained by composing web services. This is motivated by the needs of the *Phylotastic* project [1]; the project provides tools for the automated construction of workflows that allow evolutionary biologists, teachers, and students to extracts phylogenies relevant to given sets of species. The automated construction of workflows is justified by the existence of a large number of web services that perform parts of a desired analysis protocol, and the complexity of effectively interfacing the services (e.g., due to the lack of data format standardization). A typical Phylotastic workflow is composed of operations to collect list of species names (e.g., from a scientific paper), "clean" them to ensure that the proper scientific names are used, extract a subtree of a reference phylogeny that covers the desired species and visualize it. Phylotastic has been implemented using an *Answer Set Programming (ASP)* backend for reasoning about ontologies and for web service composition [6]. The web services are described by an ontology, the Phylotastic ontology (*PO*). *PO* is composed of two parts: an ontology that describes the artifacts manipulated by the services (e.g., alignments, phylogenetic trees, species names) [7] and an ontology to describe the operations performed by the services (the *WSO*).

Figure 2 displays a sample output of `nlgPhylogeny` given the workflow in Fig. 1. The workflow in this example is a plan generated by the ASP-based web service composition component of the Phylotastic project [6], and consists of a sequence of steps (green rectangles). The boxes before and after each green rectangle represent input(s) and output(s) of the service, respectively. As the inputs of one service might require some format different from the format of the previous outputs, data conversions might be necessary (the double arrows). Each step corresponds to a processing step on data provided by one of the preceding steps. Specifically, the workflow is composed of three steps:

- Extracting the set of organisms from the input text;
- Resolving the names of the identified organisms (e.g., correct spelling, identify proper scientific names); and
- Deriving the corresponding phylogenetic tree.

Figure 2 shows the description of the workflow as generated by `nlgPhylogeny`. Since the fact that to illustrate a workflow, an graphical version is approximately good enough, but to put the workflow in a biological paper, sometimes, authors would need to write some explanations for the workflow. We find that it would be helpful to generate the textural version as a complement to the graphical version, and provide them as a package. So, the authors are free to

---

[3] https://ttsreader.com.

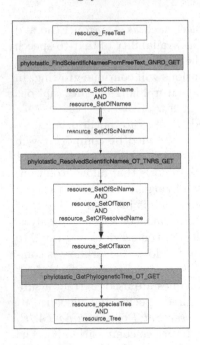

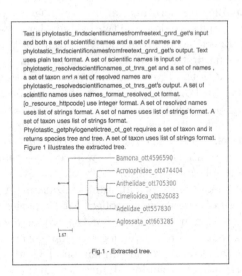

Text is phylotastic_findscientificnamesfromfreetext_gnrd_get's input and both a set of scientific names and a set of names are phylotastic_findscientificnamesfromfreetext_gnrd_get's output. Text uses plain text format. A set of scientific names is input of phylotastic_resolvedscientificnames_ot_tnrs_get and a set of names , a set of taxon and a set of resolved names are phylotastic_resolvedscientificnames_ot_tnrs_get's output. A set of scientific names uses names_format_resolved_ot format. [o_resource_httpcode] use integer format. A set of resolved names uses list of strings format. A set of names uses list of strings format. A set of taxon uses list of strings format. Phylotastic_getphylogenetictree_ot_get requires a set of taxon and it returns species tree and tree. A set of taxon uses list of strings format. Figure 1 illustrates the extracted tree.

Fig.1 - Extracted tree.

Fig. 1. An automatically generated workflow (Color figure online)

Fig. 2. Description generated for workflow in Fig. 1 by `nlgPhylogeny` (Color figure online)

choose which versions to include in their paper. Moreover, we recognize that our general idea can be a bridge between ontology developers and ontology users or engineers who use the ontology in question-answering system. While ontology developers just need to add a little more annotations on their work, the benefit for ontology users is huge because they will no longer need to develop the answering module from scratch. The answer generated from our idea will mimic the grammar structure of annotations provided by ontology developers, but different in content corresponding to the queried data.

As discussed in detail later, `nlgPhylogeny` exploits the NLG capabilities of the *Grammatical Framework (GF)* [8]. This requires the development of a GF for the entities in the Phylostatic projects (described by the ontology). For small ontologies, the manual development of the GF for the NLG task is feasible, but it is an improbable task for large ontologies. Furthermore, `nlgPhylogeny` will not be applicable for other ontologies. It is, however, feasible to consider a situation where an ontology engineer has the necessary domain knowledge to explicitly add meta-information to the concepts as they are progressively added to the ontology. The `nlgOntology`[A] system demonstrates that, as long as meta-information is added in the ontology following proper guidelines, it is possible to generate the description for the atoms derived from annotated ontologies without the manual creation of a GF.

The project critically relies on logic programming. ASP is employed by the composition system and to manage the connection with the ontology. The Attempto Parsing Engine is available in GitHub[4] and it is written in SWI-Prolog. The program to convert lexicon extracted from annotations in the ontologies to lexicon to generate the GF concrete syntax is also a Prolog-based program.

The rest of the paper is organized as follows. We begin with a brief review of the *Grammatical Framework* and *Attempto Controlled English,* the two frameworks used in this paper. The following two sections describe `nlgPhylogeny` and `nlgOntology`^{A}, respectively. We conclude the paper with a discussion of potential uses of `nlgOntology`^{A} and of the proposed technologies developed in this paper.

2   Background

2.1   Grammatical Framework

The Grammatical Framework (GF) [8] is a system used for working with grammars; it is composed of a programming language used to design grammars along with a theory about grammars and languages. GF also comes with a GF Resource Grammar Library and a GF runtime API for working with GF programs.

A GF program has two main parts. The first part is the *Abstract syntax* which defines what meanings can be expressed by a grammar. The abstract syntax defines categories (i.e., types of meaning) and functions (i.e., meaning-building components). The following is an example of an abstract syntax component:

```
abstract Food = {
        flags    startcat = Phrase ;
        cat
                 Phrase ; Item ; Kind ; Quality ;
        fun
                 Is : Item -> Quality -> Phrase ;
                 This : Kind -> Item ;
                 QKind : Quality -> Kind -> Kind ;
                 Cheese, Fish : Kind ;
                 Very : Quality -> Quality ;
                 Warm, Italian, Delicious : Quality ;
}
```

In this syntax, `Phrase`, `Item`, `Kind` and `Quality` are types of meanings. The `startcat flag` declaration states that `Phrase` is the default start category for parsing and generation. Is is a function accepting two parameters, of type `Item` and `Quality`. This function returns a meaning of `Phrase` category.

---

[4] https://github.com/Attempto/APE.

The second part is composed of *one or more concrete syntax specifications.* Each concrete syntax defines the representation of meanings in each output language. For example, the corresponding concrete syntax that maps functions in the `abstract Food` grammar above to strings in English is:

```
concrete FoodEng of Food = {
  lincat
    Phrase, Item, Kind, Quality = {s : Str} ;
  lin
    Is item quality = {s = item.s ++ "is" ++ quality.s} ;
    This kind = {s = "this" ++ kind.s} ;
    QKind quality kind = {s = quality.s ++ kind.s} ;
    Cheese = {s = "cheese"} ;
    Fish = {s = "fish"} ;
    Very quality = {s = "very" ++ quality.s} ;
    Warm = {s = "warm"} ;
    Italian = {s = "Italian"} ;
    Delicious = {s = "delicious"} ;
}
```

In this concrete syntax, the linearization type definition (`lincat`) states that `Phrase`, `Item`, `Kind` and `Quality` are strings (`s`). Linearization definitions (`lin`) indicate what strings are assigned to each of the meanings defined in the abstract syntax. Various types of linearization type definitions are considered in GF (e.g., string, table). Some functions represent a simple string but some functions (e.g., `Is` or `This`) defines a concatenation of strings.

Intuitively, each function in the abstract syntax represents a rule in a grammar. The combination of rules used to construct a meaning type can be seen as a syntax tree. The visualization of the tree representing the `Phrase` *"this delicious cheese is very Italian"* is illustrated in Fig. 3. GF has been used in a variety of applications, such as query-answering systems, voice communication, language learning,

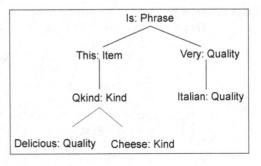

Fig. 3. Example syntax tree

text analysis and translation, and natural language generation [3,9]. GF has been used extensively in automated translation and it is the main vehicle behind the MOLTO project, that aims at developing a set of tools for high-quality and real-time translation of text between multiple languages[5]. To see how it works, let us augment our program with a concrete syntax for Italian as follows:

```
concrete FoodIta of Food = {
  lincat
```

---
[5] http://www.molto-project.eu.

```
      Phrase, Item, Kind, Quality = {s : Str} ;
  lin
      Is item quality = {s = item.s ++ "e'" ++ quality.s} ;
      This kind = {s = "questo" ++ kind.s} ;
      QKind quality kind = {s = kind.s ++ quality.s} ;
      Cheese = {s = "formaggio"} ;
      Fish = {s = "pesce"} ;
      Very quality = {s = "molto" ++ quality.s} ;
      Warm = {s = "caldo"} ;
      Italian = {s = "italiano"} ;
      Delicious = {s = "delizioso"} ;
  }
```

The translation from English to Italian can be performed as follows in the GF API:

```
> parse -lang=FoodEng "this fish is warm" | linearize -lang=FoodIta
  questo pesce e' caldo
```

We use a pipe which includes the **parse** and **linearize** commands to find the syntax tree of the sentence *"this fish is warm"* then turn that tree into a **FoodIta** sentence. The last line is the result of the translation process. The translation process is very similar to currency exchange in the old days, when exchange was done only in gold. Assume we want to exchange US Dollars for Euros; we first exchange US Dollars for gold, then, exchange gold for Euros. Correspondingly, in GF the intermediate result in the translation process is the syntax tree which contains the meaning of the translated sentence.

2.2   Attempto Controlled English

A GF program produces sentences whose syntax is specified by its abstract syntax; this structure also determines the quality of its output. Developing a GF syntax (abstract or concrete) requires understanding functional programming; this is a level of knowledge that might not be suitable for users who are not familiar with programming—as is the case of biologists using Phylotastic to create and execute phylogenetic workflows. As we will see in the next section, our **nlgPhylogeny** system can utilize GF to generate descriptions of Phylotastic workflows. It requires, however, a considerable amount of domain-specific knowledge. To alleviate this problem, we investigate a combination of annotated ontologies and the *Attempto Controlled English (ACE)* [4] for the same task, which results in the system **nlgOntology**[A].

ACE is a controlled natural language, i.e., a subset of standard English with a restricted syntax and restricted semantics, described by a small set of construction and interpretation rules. ACE sentences are normal English sentences and can be read and understood by any English speaker. However, ACE is a formal language that can be used for knowledge representation; ACE texts are computer-processable and can be unambiguously translated into discourse representation structures, a syntactic variant of first-order logic. An ACE grammar consists of construction rules for both simple and composite sentences, interrogative and imperative sentences. ACE can be encoded in GF and used for NLG.

3 Generating Sentences from GF

In this section, we describe the `nlgPhylogeny` system. Figure 4 shows the overall architecture of `nlgPhylogeny`. The main component of the system is the *GF generator* whose inputs are the Phylotastic ontology and the elements necessary for the NLG task (i.e., the set of linearizations, the set of pre-defined conjunctives, the set of vocabularies, and the set of sentence models). The output of the *GF generator* is a GF program, i.e., a pair of GF abstract and concrete syntax. This GF program is used for generating the descriptions of workflows via the GF runtime API. The adapter provides the GF generator with the information from the ontology, such as the classes, instances, and relations. We will describe in more details the elements of `nlgPhylogeny`in Sect. 3.2.

3.1 Web Service Ontology (WSO)

Phylotastic uses web service composition to generate workflows for the extraction/construction of phylogenetic trees. It makes use of two ontologies: WSO and PO. WSO encodes information about the registered web services, classified in a taxonomy of classes of services. In the following discussion, we refer to a simplified version of the ASP encoding of the ontologies used in [6], to facilitate readability.

In WSO, a service has a name and is associated with a list of inputs and outputs. For example, the service named *FindScientificNamesFromWeb_GET* in the ontology is an instance of the class *names_extraction_web*. The outputs and inputs of *FindScientificNamesFromWeb_GET* are encoded by the three atoms:

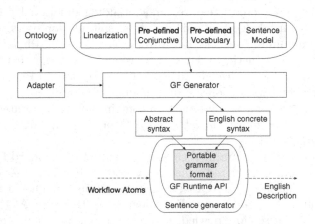

Fig. 4. Overview of `nlgPhylogeny`.

```
has_input(FindScientificNamesFromWeb_GET,resource_WebURL,url_format).
has_output(FindScientificNamesFromWeb_GET,resource_SetOfSciName,
        scientific_names_format).
has_output(FindScientificNamesFromWeb_GET,resource_SetOfNames,
        list_of_strings).
```

In the above atoms, the first argument is the name of the service, the second is the service input or output, and the last argument is the data type of the second argument.

The web service ontology of the Phylotastic project is exported to an ASP program (from its original OWL encoding) and enriched with a collection of ASP rules to draw inferences about classes, inheritance, etc. `nlgPhylogeny` employs these rules to identify information related to the set of atoms whose description is requested by a user—e.g., What are the inputs of a service? What is the data type of an input x of a service y?

3.2   GF Generator

Each Phylotastic workflow is an acyclic directed graph, where the nodes are web services, each consumes some resources (inputs) and produces some resources (outputs). An example of the specification of a workflow is as follows.[6]

```
occur_concrete(GenerateGeneTree_From_Genes,0).
occur_concrete(ExtractSpeciesNames_From_Gene_Tree_GET,1).
occur_concrete(GeneTree_Scaling,2).
occur_concrete(ResolvedScientificNames_OT_TNRS_GET,3).
```

This set of atoms is a partial description of the result of a web service composition process, as described in [6]. Intuitively, this set of atoms represents a plan consisting of 4 steps. At each step, a concrete instance of the service class named by the first argument of the atom `occur_concrete/2` is executed.

To generate the description of a workflow, we adapt the general theoretical framework proposed in [10]. This framework consists of three major processing phases: **(1)** Document planning (content determination), **(2)** Microplanning, and **(3)** Surface realization. The document planning phase is used to determine the structure of the text to be generated. Based on the structure determined in the document planning phase, the microplanner makes lexical/syntatic choices to generate the content of the sentences, and the realization phase generates the actual sentences. In our work, we combine the microplanning and surface realization phase into a single phase due to the nature of the grammar definition and the capability of GF in sentence generation.

In the document planning step, we create, for each occurrence atom, a sentence which specifies the input(s) and output(s) of the service mentioned in the first argument of the atom. Optionally, users can choose to describe the service in more details, one or two more sentences about the data type of the service's

---

[6] For simplicity, we use examples which are linear sequences of services. We also trim the names of services for readability.

inputs or outputs can be included. As we have mentioned in the previous sub-section, the information about the inputs, outputs, and data types of the inputs and outputs of a service can be obtained via the ASP reasoning engine of the Phylotastic system. In general, we identify the document planning structure described in Table 1.

Table 1. Document planning structure

message 1	
argument_1:	instance or class in ontology
argument_2:	list of service inputs
argument_3:	list of service outputs
message 2 (optional)	
argument_1:	name of input or output of service
argument_2:	data type of argument_1
message 3 (optional)	
argument:	actual data involved in the workflow

The document planning phase determines three messages for the sentence generation phase. Each message will be constructed using the arguments as mentioned in Table 1. While the first message is mandatory, the other two messages are optional.

In the microplanning step, we focus on developing a GF generator that can produce a portable grammar format (**pgf**) file [2]. This file is able to encode and generate 3 types of sentences as mentioned above. The GF generator (see Fig. 4) accepts two flows of input data. The first one is the flow of data from the ontology, which is maintained by an adapter. The *adapter* is the glue code that connects the ontology to the GF generator. Its main function is to extract classes and properties from the ontology.

The second flow is the flow of data from predefined resources that cannot be automatically obtained from the ontology—instead they require manual effort from both the ontology experts and the linguistic developers.

– A list of *linearizations:* the translations of ontology entities into linguistic terms. This translation is performed by experts who have knowledge of the ontology domain. An important reason for the existence of this component is that some classes or terms used in the ontology might not be directly understandable by the end user. This may be the result of very special-ized strings used in the encoding of the ontology. For example, the class *phylotastic_ResolvedScientificNames_OT_TNRS_POST* can be meaningfully linearized to *Name Resolution service provided by OpenTree* in Phylotastic ontology.

- Some *sentence models* which are principally Grammatical Framework syntax trees with meta-information. The meta-information denotes which part of syntax tree can be replaced by some *vocabulary* or *linearization*. As indicated above, we decided that each occurrence atom in a workflow will be described by at most three sentences. For example, if we consider the first message in the document planning structure, the generated sentence will have the inputs and the outputs of a service; the second message indicates a sentence about the data type of its first argument (input or output); the third message is about the actual data used during the execution of the workflow. However, the messages do not specify how many inputs and outputs should be included in the generated sentence. This means that sentences have different structures, i.e., the structure of a sentence representing a service that requires one input and one output is different from the structure of a sentence representing a service that does not require any inputs. These variations in sentences are recorded in the *model sentence* component.
- A list of *pre-defined vocabularies* which are domain-specific components for the ontology. A *pre-defined vocabulary* is different from linearizations, in the sense that some lexicon may not be present in the ontology but might be needed in the sentence construction. The predefined vocabulary is also useful to bring variety in word choices when parts of a *model sentence* are replaced by the GF generator. For example, we would not want the system to keep generating a sentence of the form *"The service A has input X"* given an atom of the form occur_concrete(A, T), but sometimes *"The service A requires input X"*, or *"The service A needs input X"*, etc. To achieve this, we keep "have", "require" and "need" in the set of *pre-defined vocabularies* and randomly select a verb to replace the verb in *model sentence*.
- A configuration of *pre-defined conjunctives*, which depend on the document planning result. Basically, this configuration defines which sentences accept a conjunctive adverb in order to provide generated text transition and smoothness.

To encode sentences, the GF generator defines 3 categories: Input, Output and Format in the abstract syntax. The corresponding English concrete syntax is as follows:

```
concrete PhyloEng of Phylo = open SyntaxEng, ParadigmsEng,
ConstructorsEng
     in {
          lincat
               Message = S; Input = NP; Output = NP; Format = NP;
     ... }
```

SyntaxEng, ParadigmsEng, ConstructorsEng are GF Resources Grammar libraries[7] providing constructors for sentence components like Verb, Noun Phrase, etc. in English.

---

[7] http://www.grammaticalframework.org/lib/doc/synopsis.html.

The GF generator obtains information about the services (e.g., how many inputs/outputs has the service? what are the data types of the inputs/outputs? etc.) by querying the ontology (via the adapter). Based on the number of inputs and outputs of a service, the GF generator determines how many parameters will be included in the GF abstraction function corresponding to the service. Furthermore, for each input or output of a service, the GF generator includes an *Input* or *Output* in the GF abstract function. For example, the encoding of $occur\_concrete(FindScientificNamesFromWeb\_GET, 1)$ in the GF abstract syntax is

```
f_FindScientificNamesFromWeb_GET: Input -> Output -> Message;
i_resource_WebURL: Input;
o_resource_SetOfNames: Output;
```

Next, the GF generator looks up in the *sentence models* a model syntax tree whose structure is suitable for the number of inputs and outputs of the service. If such syntax tree exists, the GF generator will replace parts of the syntax tree with the GF service input and output functions, to create a new GF syntax tree which can be appended to the GF concrete function. The functions in the abstract syntax correspond to the following functions in the GF concrete syntax:

```
f_phylotastic_FindScientificNamesFromWeb_GET i_resource_WebURL
  o_resource_SetOfNames = mkS and_Conj
    (mkS (mkCl phylotastic_FindScienticNamesFromWeb_GET_in
             (mkV2 "require") i_resource_WebURL))
    (mkS (mkCl phylotastic_FindScienticNamesFromWeb_GET_out
             (mkV2 "return" ) o_resource_SetOfSciName ));
  i_resource_WebURL = mkNP(mkCN (mkN "webURL"));
  i_resource_SetOfNames = mkNP(mkCN (mkN "asetof names"));
```

The above functions consist of several syntactic construction functions which are implemented in the GF Resources Grammar:

- mkN which creates a noun from a string;
- mkCN which creates a common noun from a noun;
- mkNP which creates a noun phrase from a common noun;
- mkV2 which creates a verb from a string;
- mkCl which creates a clause. A clause can be constructed from sequence of a noun phrase, a verb and another noun phrase (NP V2 NP);
- mkS which creates a sentence. A sentence can be constructed from a clause (Cl) or from 2 other sentences and a conjunction word (and_Conj S S).

From the abstract and concrete syntax specifications built by the GF generator, the atom
    $occur\_concrete(phylotastic\_FindScientificNamesFromWeb\_GET, 1)$
is translated into the sentence

The input of phylotastic_FindScientificNamesFromWeb_GET is a web link, and its outputs are a set of species names and a set of scientific names.

We use the same technique to encode the other types of sentences indicated by the document planning structure. This is how the GF generator has been implemented. Figure 1 is an example output of the current version of `nlgPhylogeny`.

4   Automatic Natural Language Generation from Annotated Ontology: `nlgOntology`[A]

The previous section shows that, with sufficient knowledge about the ontology and pre-defined descriptions about elements in the ontology, we can utilize the current technology in NLG to generate a description of a set of atoms derived from the ontology. It also highlights that the process requires manual labor and domain expertise. Such approach is feasible only in small ontologies related to uncomplicated grammars and elementary lexicons. The application of the same process to medium or large ontologies is likely to be too costly or time consuming. On the other hand, we can observe that ontologies often include meta-data encoding of their elements. Fur-

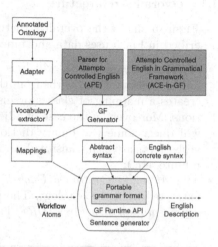

Fig. 5. Overview of `nlgOntology`[A]

thermore, information extracted from the meta-data of an ontology is often sufficient for a basic understanding of the concepts that can be derived from the ontology. Motivated by this observation, we develop an automatic natural language generation method for ontologies whose meta-data can be understood by an ACE parser. We will refer to ontologies satisfying this assumption simply as *annotated ontology*. A simple annotated ontology is as following.

```
%% @n: Company
class(Com)

%% @pn: Apple_Inc
instanceOf(Com, Apple)

%% @pn: Beats
instanceOf(Com, Beats)
```

```
%% @lin: Beats is a company of Apple_Inc
own(Apple, Beats)

%% @pn: Silicon_Grail_Corp_Chalice
instanceOf(Com, Sgcc)

%% @pn: Silicon_Grail
instanceOf(Com, Sg)

%% @lin: Apple_Inc acquires Beats
acquire(Apple, Beats)
```

In the above ontology, `Com` is a class, `Apple`, `Beats`, `Sgcc` and `Sg` are instances of the class `Com`, and `acquire` and `own` are two properties. The tags

- `%% @n` marks a noun
- `%% @pn` denotes a proper noun
- `%% @lin` signals a translation of an atom to an Attempto English sentence

Ontologies annotated in this way can be understood by `nlgOntology`[A]. We now describe the `nlgOntology`[A] system.

4.1   Overall Architecture

Figure 5 shows the overall structure of `nlgOntology`[A]. The GF generator described in Fig. 5 uses data and functions from three main components:

- A *vocabulary extractor*, which is responsible for collecting nouns, proper nouns, adjectives and verbs from the ontology. The *vocabulary extractor* also creates a mapping of classes or instances in the ontology to their linearizations. Moreover, in the case of adjectives and verbs, the *vocabulary extractor* will query some vocabulary dictionaries to collect information like type of verbs (transitive, intransitive) and verbs in different forms (finite singular, infinite, etc.).
- The *Attempto Controlled English Parser (APE)*, which analyzes sentences extracted from the ontology. The parser translates ACE text into *discourse representation structures (DRS)* [5].

Algorithm 1. Generation of portable grammar format

Require: annotated ontology, some annotations are ACE parable sentences
1: $n \leftarrow$ extract nouns and proper nouns from ontology
2: $s \leftarrow$ extract sentences from ontology
3: $a \leftarrow empty, v \leftarrow empty$
4: add n to APE lexicon
5: **for** i in n **do**
6:     $n', a', v' \leftarrow$ parse i using APE
7:     $n := n \cup n', a := a \cup a', v := v \cup v'$
8: **end for**
9: **for** i in n **do**
10:     find singular and plural form of i
11: **end for**
12: **for** i in a **do**
13:     find comparative and supercomparative form of i
14: **end for**
15: **for** i in v **do**
16:     find transitive and intransitive form of i
17: **end for**
18: generate vocabulary, generate mappings
19: convert vocabulary to GF syntax
20: compile grammar in ACE-in-GF and generated syntax

- *Attempto Controlled English in Grammatical Framework (ACE-in-GF)*, which is an implementation of the Attempto Controlled English grammar in the Grammatical Framework syntax.

The outputs of the generator are a portable grammar format (**pgf**) file, a mapping of annotated atoms in the ontology into GF syntax trees, and a mapping of concepts used in the ontology into GF functions. These data will be used in the re-construction sentence progress which is described next.

4.2 Generation of Portable Grammar Format

To generate the **pgf** file, the GF generator performs the procedure shown in Procedure 1. Lines 1–2 extract annotations from the ontology. Lines 3 initialize variables holding adjectives and verbs. Line 4 enriches the APE lexicon with the nouns and proper nouns. This allows the APE to recognize proper nouns that are possibly present in the sentences extract in *s*. Furthermore, it helps increase the accuracy when a sentence is parsed by APE. Next, the for-loop in lines 5–8 iterates through all sentences to collect new lexicon. Lines 9–17 find all possible forms of words. Line 18 creates the vocabulary file and mapping file from information obtained from previous steps. The vocabulary file is written in Prolog. For example, a portion of the vocabulary file extracted from the annotations from the ontology in the beginning of this section looks as follows:

```
noun_pl('companies', company, neutr).
noun_sg('company', company, neutr).
pn_sg('Apple_Inc', 'Apple_Inc', neutr).
pn_sg('Beats', 'Beats', neutr).
pn_sg('Silicon_Grail_Corp_Chalice', 'Silicon_Grail_Corp_Chalice',
neutr).
pn_sg('Silicon_Grail', 'Silicon_Grail', neutr).
tv_finsg(acquires, acquire).
iv_finsg(is, be).
```

Line 19 converts the vocabulary file to GF syntax. As an example, the conversion produces the GF concrete syntax file:

```
lin
    company_N = aceN "company" ;
    Apple_Inc_PN = acePN "Apple_Inc" ;
    Beats_PN = acePN "Beats" ;
    Silicon_Grail_Corp_Chalice_PN = acePN "Silicon_Grail_Corp_Chalice"
;
    Silicon_Grail_PN = acePN "Silicon_Grail" ;
    acquire_V2 = aceV2 "acquire" "acquires" "acquire";
```

Finally, line 20 uses ACE-in-GF to compile the Attempto grammar and the vocabulary extracted from the ontology into a portable grammar format.

4.3   Sentence Construction

Given an input *atom*, the generated **pgf** file and a mapping file, the sentence generator implements the algorithm presented in Procedure 2. Lines 1–3 initialize variables as well as load the information in the **pgf** and mapping files. Line 4 finds the atom in the mapping file that has the same name as the input *atom*. We call it *model_atom*. Line 5 finds the *syntax_tree* of the *model_atom*. The for-loop in lines 6–12 replaces parts of the syntax tree with the mapping of arguments of *atom*. This process creates a new syntax tree which keeps the same structure as the *model_atom*'s syntax tree. Finally, line 13 converts the new syntax tree back to a sentence.

Algorithm 2. Sentence re-construction

Require: an atom
Require: portable grammar format file, mapping file
1: $a \leftarrow$ atom
2: $pgf \leftarrow$ load pgf
3: $map \leftarrow$ mapping
4: $model\_atom \leftarrow map.keys.find(name(a))$
5: $syntax\_tree \leftarrow map(model\_atom)$
6: **for** *part* is a part of *syntax_tree* **do**
7:     **for** arg, arg_index in $arguments(model\_atom)$ **do**
8:         **if** $part == map(arg)$ **then**
9:             $syntax\_tree[part] = map(arguments(a)[arg\_index])$
10:        **end if**
11:    **end for**
12: **end for**
13: $sentence = pgf(syntax\_tree)$

As an example, given an annotated ontology describing Apple Inc. and its acquired companies as mentioned in Sect. 4, from the set of atoms:

```
acquire(Apple,Sg).    own(Sg,Sgcc).    acquire(Apple,Sgcc).
```

we are able to generate the following sentences:

```
Apple_Inc acquires Silicon_Grail .
Silicon_Grail_Corp_Chalice is a company of Silicon_Grail .
Apple_Inc acquires Silicon_Grail_Corp_Chalice .
```

The above example illustrates the feature of nlgOntology[A]; it emulates the annotations in the ontology to generate sentences. From the annotations provided for the specific case *"Apple acquires Beats"*, nlgOntology[A] can generate sentences for other cases that have similar meaning but with different objects. The repetition of narration can be seen in many question-answering systems. In particular, nlgOntology[A] uses the annotation of acquire(Apple, Beats) to generate the sentences for acquire(Apple, Sg) and acquire(Apple, Sgcc). The sentence generation for own(Sg,Sgcc) provides the annotation for own(Apple, Beats).

5   Related Work and Analysis

The closest effort to what proposed here is the work in [3], which reports on generating natural language text from class diagrams. In [3], the author developed a system to generate specifications for UML class design while the present work focuses on natural language text generation for a given ontology and a Grammatical Framework, which is manually encoded or automatically generated from the annotations of the ontology.

The work in [11] targets generating an ASP program from controlled natural language, and vice versa. The author uses a bi-directional grammar as the intermediate conversion in combination with reordering atoms for aggregation. There is a correlation between our work and the work in [11] in terms of processing the controlled input format and generating the natural language text. The key difference between our work and that work in [11] is that our system only relies on the structure of the annotated sentences (for nlgOntology^A) in the text generation and thus could potentially be more flexible.

In order to assess the feasibility of our approach to automatically generate text based on an ontology, we performed an experiment using the *Software ontology*,[8] which is apart of The Open Biological and Biomedical Ontology (OBO) Foundry.[9] We annotated some concepts in the ontology using the tag oboInOwl:comment as in the following example:

```
<!-- http://edamontology.org/operation_0244 -->
<owl:Class rdf:about="http://edamontology.org/operation_0244">
  <rdfs:subClassOf rdf:resource="http://edamontology.org/operation_0243
     "/>
  ...
  <rdfs:label>
    Protein flexibility and motion analysis
  </rdfs:label>
  <oboInOwl:comment rdf:datatype="http://www.w3.org/2001/XMLSchemastring
     ">
    %% @n: protein_flexibility_and_motion_analysis
  </oboInOwl:comment>
  <oboInOwl:comment rdf:datatype="http://www.w3.org/2001/XMLSchemastring
     ">
    %% @lin: a protein_flexibility_and_motion_analysis is a
        molecular_dynamics_simulation .
  </oboInOwl:comment>
</owl:Class>
```

We implicitly bind the annotations with the relation subclassOf due to the simplicity of the Software ontology. Given the annotated Software ontology, nlgOntology^A is able to generate some sentences like

---

[8] http://theswo.sourceforge.net.
[9] http://www.obofoundry.org.

```
A DNA_substitution_modelling is a Modelling_and_simulation_operation .
A Molecular_dynamics_simulation is a Modelling_and_simulation_operation .
A Protein_flexibility_and_motion_analysis is a Modelling_and_simulation .
```

6 Conclusions, Discussions, and Future Work

In this paper, we presented two NLG systems, nlgPhylogeny and nlgOntology^A, for automatic generation of English descriptions for a set of atoms derived from ontologies. Both achieve the goal by creating a GF program and relying on the ability to generate sentences of the Grammatical Framework. nlgPhylogeny uses pre-defined resources (e.g., linearizations, vocabularies, etc.) to build the sentence generator (GF program), while nlgOntology^A extracts and manipulates information directly from an annotated ontology. Observe that the structure of the generated text in nlgPhylogeny is richer than that in the current nlgOntology^A due to the fact that the pre-defined resources are hand-crafted and nlgOntology^A employs a very simple grammar for its sentence structure. For this reason, nlgPhylogeny can generate sentences that are more complex than the sentences generated by nlgOntology^A. On the other hand, nlgOntology^A relies on meta-information in the ontologies and can be used in any ontology that is annotated and can be parsed by an Attempto Controlled English parser. As such, nlgOntology^A can save significant efforts before it can be deployed in an application.

We conclude the paper with a short discussion about the applications and possible extensions of nlgOntology^A. It is easy to see that the current system can be very useful in applications that require shallow explanations. We envision the possibility of using nlgOntology^A for query-answering or information retrieval systems that, at the end of their complex computations, need to present the result—a set of atoms—to their users and do not need to explain the computation process. In such systems, the answers are often crafted manually or using some templates. This is certainly achievable with nlgOntology^A as such templates can be provided as annotations for instances in the ontologies. nlgOntology^A can add some flexibility to such system if multiple linearizations for an instance are provided in the ontologies, since they are translated to potentially different syntax trees. This will result in different sentences during the generation phase. The current system is, on the other hand, not as good, compared to nlgPhylogeny, in dealing with ordered sets of atoms, i.e., the explanation needs to be presented in a certain order. For example, nlgPhylogeny needs to present a plan which is a set of atoms with an ordering in the second parameter of the atoms $occur\_concrete/2$ to the users. The implementation of this feature in nlgOntology^A will be our main immediate future work. This will allow nlgOntology^A to provide natural language explanation detailing the steps involved in the computation of a result (e.g., the steps of a procedure or workflow).

To improve the usability of nlgOntology^A, we intend to extend the system to consider the problem when the ontology comes with annotations in natural language, i.e., to remove the restrictions that the ontology is annotated using controlled natural language. Interestingly, this idea is closely related to the idea proposed in a Blue Sky Ideas of the 17th International Semantic Web Conference [12].

Acknowledgement. We thank the reviewers for the comments and the references, especially [12]. We would like to acknowledge the partial support of the NSF grants 1458595, 1401639, and 1345232.

References

1. Stoltzfus, A., et al.: Phylotastic! making tree-of-life knowledge accessible, reusable and convenient. BMC Bioinform. **14**, 158 (2013)
2. Angelov, K., Bringert, B., Ranta, A.: PGF: a portable run-time format for type-theoretical grammars. J. Logic Lang. Inf. **19**, 201–228 (2010)
3. Burden, H., Heldal, R.: Natural language generation from class diagrams. In: Proceedings of the 8th International Workshop on Model-Driven Engineering, Verification and Validation (MoDeVVa 2011), Wellington, New Zealand. ACM (2011)
4. Fuchs, N.E., Schwitter, R.: Attempto controlled English (ACE). CoRR cmp-lg/9603003 (1996)
5. Kamp, H., Reyle, U.: From Discourse to Logic. Springer, Dordrecht (1993). https://doi.org/10.1007/978-94-017-1616-1
6. Nguyen, T.H., Son, T.C., Pontelli, E.: Automatic web services composition for phylotastic. In: Calimeri, F., Hamlen, K., Leone, N. (eds.) PADL 2018. LNCS, vol. 10702, pp. 186–202. Springer, Cham (2018). https://doi.org/10.1007/978-3-319-73305-0_13
7. Prosdocimi, F., Chisham, B., Thompson, J., Pontelli, E., Stoltzfus, A.: Initial implementation of a comparative data analysis ontology. Evol. Bioinform. **5**, 47–66 (2009)
8. Ranta, A.: Grammatical framework. J. Funct. Program. **14**(2), 145–189 (2004)
9. Ranta, A.: Grammatical framework: Programming with multilingual grammars. CSLI Publications, Center for the Study of Language and Information (2011)
10. Reiter, E., Dale, R.: Building Natural Language Generation Systems. Cambridge University Press, Cambridge (2000)
11. Schwitter, R.: Specifying and verbalising answer set programs in controlled natural language (2018). arXiv preprint: arXiv:1804.10765
12. Vrandei, D.: Capturing meaning: Toward an abstract wikipedia. http://ceur-ws.org/Vol-2180/

Improving Residuation
in Declarative Programs

Michael Hanus$^{(\boxtimes)}$ (iD)

Institut für Informatik, CAU Kiel, 24098 Kiel, Germany
mh@informatik.uni-kiel.de

Abstract. Residuation is an operational principle to evaluate functions
in logic-oriented languages. Residuation delays function calls until the
arguments are sufficiently instantiated in order to evaluate the function deterministically. It has been proposed as an alternative to the
non-deterministic narrowing principle and is useful to connect externally defined operations. Residuation can be implemented in Prolog systems supporting corouting, but this comes with a price: the coroutining mechanism causes a considerable overhead even if it is not used.
To overcome this dilemma, we propose a compile-time analysis which
approximates the run-time residuation behavior. Based on the results of
this analysis, we improve an existing implementation of residuation and
evaluate the potential efficiency gains by a number of benchmarks.

1 Introduction

Declarative programming is an attempt to build reliable software systems in
a high-level manner on sound theoretical principles. Functional languages support functions as programming entities and use reduction for evaluation. Logic
languages support relations as main entities and use unification-based resolution for evaluation. When combining both kinds of languages in order to provide a single declarative language, there are two principle choices for evaluation. *Narrowing* extends reduction by unification so that functions can also be
invoked with partially known arguments. Thus, functions might be evaluated
non-deterministically like relations in logic programming. *Residuation* restricts
non-deterministic evaluation to predicates only so that functions are suspended
if their arguments are not sufficiently instantiated for deterministic reduction.
Both operational mechanisms are applied in functional logic languages that combine the most important features of functional and logic programming in a single
language (see [6,12] for recent surveys).

Both narrowing and residuation have their justifications. Optimal evaluation
strategies are known for narrowing [4] whereas residuation supports concurrent
computations and allows to connect externally defined operations in a declarative manner [7]. This motivated the development of the functional logic language

The research described in this paper has been partially supported by the German
Federal Ministry of Education and Research (BMBF) under Grant No. 01IH15006B.

© Springer Nature Switzerland AG 2019
J. J. Alferes and M. Johansson (Eds.): PADL 2019, LNCS 11372, pp. 82–97, 2019.
https://doi.org/10.1007/978-3-030-05998-9_6

Curry [16] as a unified language for functional logic programming which combines narrowing and residuation in a single evaluation principle [11]. A functional logic language can be implemented with limited efforts by compiling it into Prolog (e.g., [5,9,18]). To implement residuation, one can exploit coroutining facilities supported by many Prolog systems: if some argument of a residuating operation is not sufficiently instantiated, the evaluation of the corresponding Prolog predicate is suspended so that another predicate can be activated [5]. Although this implementation is quite simple, it causes additional costs if residuation is not used, i.e., all function calls are sufficiently instantiated, since one has to check each function call before activating them. To avoid these costs, we develop in this paper a compile-time analysis which approximates operations w.r.t. their runtime residuation behavior. Based on this analysis, we improve a Curry compiler and evaluate the efficiency gains for some benchmarks.

This paper is structured as follows. After a short introduction to functional logic programming and Curry, we sketch in Sect. 3 an existing implementation of residuation in Prolog. Our compile-time analysis of residuation is described in Sect. 4. The improved implementation of residuation w.r.t. analysis information is sketched in Sect. 5 and evaluated in Sect. 6. Section 7 discusses related work before we conclude in Sect. 8.

2   Declarative Programming with Curry

The declarative programming language Curry [16] amalgamates the most important features of functional and logic programming as well as operational principles of combined functional logic languages [6,12], such as narrowing and residuation, in a single language. Conceptually, Curry extends Haskell [21] with nondeterminism, free variables, and constraint solving. Thus, the syntax of Curry is close to Haskell but Curry applies rules with overlapping left-hand sides in a (don't know) non-deterministic manner and allows *free* (*logic*) *variables* in conditions and right-hand sides of rules. These variables must be explicitly declared unless they are anonymous. Similarly to Haskell, functions are evaluated lazily to support modular programming, infinite data structures, and optimal evaluation [4]. Unlike Haskell, function calls might contain free (unbound) variables, i.e., without a value at call time. If the value of such an argument is demanded, the function call is either suspended (which corresponds to residuation) or the variable is non-deterministically instantiated (which corresponds to narrowing [4]).

Example 1. Consider the following definition of natural numbers in Peano representation, the addition on natural numbers, and a predicate which is true on natural numbers:

```
data Nat = Z | S Nat

add :: Nat  → Nat  → Nat          nat :: Nat  → Bool
add Z     y = y                   nat Z     = True
add (S x) y = S (add x y)         nat (S x) = nat x
```

If `add` is evaluated by narrowing (such functions are also called *flexible*), the equation

```
let x free in add x (S Z) == S (S Z)
```

is solved by instantiating the free variable x to (S Z). However, if `add` is evaluated by residuation (in this case `add` is called *rigid*), the equation solving suspends. To proceed with suspended computations, Curry has a *concurrent conjunction* operator "&" which evaluates both arguments concurrently, i.e., if the evaluation of one argument suspends, the other is evaluated. Thus, if the function `add` is rigid and the predicate `nat` is flexible (as in languages like Le Fun [2] or Oz [23]), the conjunction

```
let x free in add x (S Z) == S (S Z) & nat x
```

is successfully evaluated by interleaving the evaluation of `add` and `nat` (which instantiates x to (S Z)). This kind of concurrent computation is also called *declarative concurrency* [24].

In the first version of Curry, functions were rigid and predicates flexible by default, similarly to residuation-based languages [1,2,20,23]. Later, narrowing became the default for all defined operations so that only externally defined operations and conditionals, like "if-then-else" or "case-of", are evaluated by residuation. There is also an explicit "suspension" combinator for concurrent programming: `ensureNotFree` returns its argument evaluated to head normal form but suspends as long as the result is a free variable.

3   Implementing Residuation in Prolog

A scheme to compile functional logic languages with residuation, such as Curry, into Prolog is proposed in [5] and used in the Curry implementation PAKCS [14] which is part of recent Debian und Ubuntu Linux distributions. Coroutining features of contemporary Prolog systems can be exploited to implement residuating operations. SICStus-Prolog[1] offers `block` declarations to enforce the suspension of predicate calls under particular conditions. For instance, the declaration ":- block p(?,-,?)." specifies that a call to p is delayed if the second argument is a free variable. Thus, the following code defines the multiplication function on integers as a predicate which suspends if one of the arguments is a free variable:

```
:- block mult(-,?,?), mult(?,-,?).
mult(X,Y,R) :- R is X*Y.
```

An alternative to block declarations is the predicate `freeze(X,G)` which suspends the evaluation of the goal G if the first argument X is a free variable. Since `freeze` is less efficient than `block` [5], PAKCS uses `block` declarations when it compiles to SICStus-Prolog and `freeze` declarations when it compiles to SWI-Prolog (since SWI-Prolog does not offer `block` declarations).

Unfortunately, such simple `block` declarations are not sufficient when compiling functional logic programs into Prolog due to nested function calls. Since functions are compiled into Prolog predicates by adding a result argument and

---

[1] http://sicstus.sics.se/.

evaluating demanded inner arguments before outer function calls [5,9], it must be ensured that all predicates involved in a function call are suspended when some argument suspends. For instance, consider the Curry program

```
g x = ensureNotFree x
h []      = []
h (y:ys) = h ys
main x = h (g x)
```

If we evaluate main x where x is a free variable, the evaluation of (g x) suspends due to the call of ensureNotFree. Hence, the calls to h and, thus, main also suspend. The Prolog code obtained by translating functions into predicates is[2]

```
:- block g(-,?).
g(X,R)  :- R=X.
h(A,R)  :- hnf(A,B), h_1(B,R).
h_1([],R)  :- R=[].
h_1([Y|Ys],R)  :- h(Ys,R).
main(A,R)  :- h(g(A),R).
```

The evaluation of main(A,R) leads to the evaluation of hnf(g(A),B) and g(A,B), which suspends. However, the subsequent literal h_1(B,R) can still be evaluated which results in an infinite search space by applying the second rule of h_1 forever.

In order to avoid such problems, more control is needed so that the call to h_1 is activated only if the evaluation of the call to g is not suspended. For this purpose, [5] proposes to add specific input and output arguments to each predicate. These arguments are either uninstantiated or bound to the constant eval (the actual value is irrelevant). A computation of a predicate (implementing some Curry function) is activated only if the input control argument is instantiated. If this computation is complete, i.e., without suspension, the output control argument is bound to eval. Thus, one can implement the required control by chaining these control arguments through the program. As a concrete example, our program above is implemented as follows:

```
:- block g(-,?,?,?), g(?,?,-,?).
g(X,R,E0,E1)  :- R=X, E1=E0.
:- block h(?,?,-,?).
h(A,R,E0,E2)  :- hnf(A,B,E0,E1), h_1(B,R,E1,E2).
:- block h_1(?,?,-,?).
h_1([],R,E0,E1)  :- R=[], E1=E0.
h_1([Y|Ys],R,E0,E1)  :- h(Ys,R,E0,E1).
:- block main(?,?,-,?).
main(A,R,E0,E1)  :- h(g(A),R,E0,E1).
```

---

[2] The predicate hnf computes the head normal form of its first argument. It can be defined by a case distinction on all function and constructor symbols in the program. The use of hnf instead of simply flattening nested function calls is essential to implement lazy evaluation.

Now, the evaluation of the goal `main(A,R,eval,E)` suspends where the call to `h_1` is also suspended.

This scheme together with a sophisticated implementation of sharing (see [5] for details) is the basis of the Curry implementation PAKCS [14]. However, this implementation has some cost since *every* predicate is annotated with a `block` declaration. The costs are even higher when `block` declarations are replaced by `freeze` declarations (as shown later by our benchmarks). On the other hand, residuation is not a dominating principle in actual programs. Originally, residuation has been proposed as an alternative to narrowing in order to avoid evaluating functions in a non-deterministic manner, see, for instance, the languages Escher [17], Le Fun [2], Life [1], NUE-Prolog [20], or Oz [23]. Since the language Curry is an attempt to unify the different approaches to combine functional and logic programming, it supports residuation and narrowing in a unified way [11]. As time has passed, residuation became less important so that functions are now non-residuating by default [12]. Nevertheless, residuation is still interesting to support concurrent computations and to connect externally defined operations in a declarative way [7]. This demands for an implementation where the overhead of residuation is accepted only if it is actually used in the program. For this purpose, we develop in the next section a program analysis to approximate the actual usage of residuation during run time in a Curry program.

4   Approximating Residuation Behavior

In order to improve the implementation of potentially residuating programs sketched above, it is important to characterize programs or part of programs where residuation is not used. This is the case if residuating functions are not invoked at run time or they are invoked with sufficiently instantiated arguments. Since such properties are obviously undecidable, we develop a compile-time technique to approximate them.

4.1   CASS: An Analysis Framework for Curry

CASS [15] is an incremental and modular analysis system for Curry programs. Since CASS provides a good infrastructure to implement new program analyses, we will use it for our purpose. A new program analysis can be added to CASS if it is defined in a bottom-up manner, i.e., the analysis computes some abstract information about a given operation from the definition of this operation together with abstract information about the operations used in this definition. Then CASS performs the necessary fixpoint computations, incremental analysis of imported modules, etc., to analyze a given module.

To be more precise, an analysis added to CASS must be defined on an intermediate language, called FlatCurry, which is used in compilers, optimization, and verification tools, and to specify the operational semantics of Curry programs [3]. In FlatCurry, the syntactic sugar of the source language is eliminated and the pattern matching strategy is explicit. The abstract syntax of FlatCurry

$$
\begin{array}{lll}
P ::= D_1 \ldots D_m & & \text{(program)} \\
D ::= f(x_1, \ldots, x_n) = e & & \text{(function definition)} \\
e ::= x & & \text{(variable)} \\
\quad | \quad c(e_1, \ldots, e_n) & & \text{(constructor call)} \\
\quad | \quad f(e_1, \ldots, e_n) & & \text{(function call)} \\
\quad | \quad case\ e\ of\ \{p_1 \to e_1; \ldots; p_n \to e_n\} & & \text{(rigid case)} \\
\quad | \quad fcase\ e\ of\ \{p_1 \to e_1; \ldots; p_n \to e_n\} & & \text{(flexible case)} \\
\quad | \quad e_1\ or\ e_2 & & \text{(disjunction)} \\
\quad | \quad let\ x\ free\ in\ e & & \text{(free variable)} \\
\quad | \quad let\ x = e\ in\ e' & & \text{(let binding)} \\
p ::= c(x_1, \ldots, x_n) & & \text{(pattern)}
\end{array}
$$

Fig. 1. Syntax of the intermediate language FlatCurry [12]

is summarized in Fig. 1. A FlatCurry program consists of a sequence of function definitions, where each function is defined by a single rule. We assume that all variables introduced in the left-hand side, patterns, and let expressions are disjoint. Patterns in source programs are compiled into flexible case expressions and overlapping rules are joined by explicit disjunctions. The difference between *case* and *fcase* corresponds to residuation and narrowing: when the argument e evaluates to a free variable, *case* suspends whereas *fcase* nondeterministically binds this variable to a pattern in a branch of the case expression.

Any Curry program can be translated into a FlatCurry program by making the pattern matching strategy explicit. For instance, the operation h defined in Sect. 3 has the following FlatCurry representation:

$$
\text{h(xs)} \quad = \quad fcase\ \text{xs}\ of\ \{\ [] \ \to\ []; \ \text{y:ys} \ \to\ \text{h(ys)}\ \}
$$

In principle, let bindings as shown in Fig. 1 are not required to translate standard Curry programs. However, they can be used to translate circular data structures and are convenient to express sharing without the use of complex graph structures. Operationally, let bindings introduce new structures in memory that are updated after evaluation, which is essential for lazy computations [3].

4.2 A Domain for Residuation Analysis

We use FlatCurry to specify our analysis of the residuation behavior of Curry programs. Since residuation, i.e., the suspension of function calls, might occur if variables are unbound during run time, we have to approximate which arguments are ground at run time and under which conditions functions do not residuate. For instance, the addition operation (+) does not residuate if both arguments are ground. However, the constant function

```
const :: a  →  _  → a
const x y = x
```

does not residuate if the first argument is ground and the second argument is arbitrary, since the latter is not evaluated by const due to lazy evaluation. Therefore, our analysis associates to each n-ary operation f a set $f^\alpha \subseteq \{1, \ldots, n\}$ with the following interpretation: if $e = f\ t_1 \ldots t_n$ and t_i is a ground constructor term for each $i \in f^\alpha$, then the evaluation of e does not suspend and each value of e is ground. For instance, $+^\alpha = \{1, 2\}$ and $\mathtt{const}^\alpha = \{1\}$. Since there are also operations without such a strong property or where our analysis is not precise enough, we also add a top element $\top$. $f^\alpha = \top$ means that a call to f might residuate or does not yield a ground term.[3] Finally, there is also an abstract bottom element $\bot$, representing no information, which is used to start the fixpoint analysis. Thus, our analysis associates to an n-ary operation f an element of the abstract domain

$$\{\bot, \top\} \cup \{s \mid s \subseteq \{1, \ldots, n\}\}$$

Note that $\bot$ has a different meaning than $\varnothing$. $\bot$ means "unknown" or "no analysis result" (e.g., $\mathtt{loop}^\alpha = \bot$ for the definition $\mathtt{loop} = \mathtt{loop}$), whereas $\varnothing$ means "no suspension." For instance, if $\mathtt{main}^\alpha = \varnothing$, then the evaluation of $\mathtt{main}$ will never residuate. Similarly, if f is n-ary, the abstract value $\{1, \ldots, n\}$ is different from $\top$. If $f^\alpha = \{1, \ldots, n\}$, then $f\ t_1 \ldots t_n$ does not suspend and has a ground result value if each $t_1, \ldots, t_n$ are ground constructor terms, whereas $f^\alpha = \top$ means that any call to f might residuate or does not yield a ground term.

Abstract elements are ordered as usual, i.e., $\bot \sqsubseteq x$, $x \sqsubseteq \top$, and, for $\bot \neq s_i \neq \top$ $(i = 1, 2)$, $s_1 \sqsubseteq s_2$ iff $s_1 \subseteq s_2$. Consequently, the least upper bound $s_1 \sqcup s_2$ of two abstract elements s_1, s_2 is defined as follows:

$$s_1 \sqcup s_2 = \begin{cases} s_1 & \text{if } s_2 = \bot \\ s_2 & \text{if } s_1 = \bot \\ \top & \text{if } s_1 = \top \text{ or } s_2 = \top \\ s_1 \cup s_2 & \text{otherwise} \end{cases}$$

4.3   Residuation Analysis

The analysis of a single operation f uses an assumption $\mathcal{A}$ which maps operations and variables into abstract elements. $\mathcal{A}[x \mapsto \alpha]$ denotes the extended assumption $\mathcal{A}'$ which is defined by

$$\mathcal{A}'(y) = \begin{cases} \alpha & \text{if } y = x \\ \mathcal{A}(y) & \text{if } y \neq x \end{cases}$$

To analyze a function f w.r.t. an assumption $\mathcal{A}$ about operations defined in the program, we apply the inference rules shown in Fig. 2. Rule $FDecl$ is the main rule to analyze a function defined by $f(x_1, \ldots, x_n) = e$. For this purpose, the right-hand side e is analyzed with the assumption extended by information about the position of the argument variables. Rule Var simply returns the abstract element associated to the variable so that we obtain the information of arguments passed as results. For instance, rules $FDecl$ and Var are sufficient to derive the judgement $\mathcal{A} \vdash \mathtt{const}(x, y) = x : \{1\}$. Rule $Cons$ combines the information of all

---

[3] One could also refine the abstract domain in order to distinguish between residuation and non-ground results, but this does not seem to provide better results in practice.

$FDecl$
$$\frac{\mathcal{A}[x_1 \mapsto \{1\}, \ldots, x_n \mapsto \{n\}] \vdash e : \alpha}{\mathcal{A} \vdash f(x_1, \ldots, x_n) = e : \alpha}$$

Var $\mathcal{A} \vdash x : \mathcal{A}(x)$

$Cons$
$$\frac{\mathcal{A} \vdash e_1 : \alpha_1 \ \ldots \ \mathcal{A} \vdash e_n : \alpha_n}{\mathcal{A} \vdash c(e_1, \ldots, e_n) : \alpha_1 \sqcup \ldots \sqcup \alpha_n}$$

Fun
$$\frac{\mathcal{A} \vdash e_1 : \alpha_1 \ \ldots \ \mathcal{A} \vdash e_n : \alpha_n}{\mathcal{A} \vdash f(e_1, \ldots, e_n) : \alpha}$$

where $\alpha = \alpha_{i_1} \sqcup \ldots \sqcup \alpha_{i_k}$ if $\mathcal{A}(f) = \{i_1, \ldots, i_k\}$, otherwise $\alpha = \mathcal{A}(f)$

$Case$
$$\frac{\mathcal{A} \vdash e : \alpha \quad \mathcal{A}_1 \vdash e_1 : \alpha_1 \ \ldots \ \mathcal{A}_n \vdash e_n : \alpha_n}{\mathcal{A} \vdash case \ e \ of \ \{p_1 \to e_1; \ldots; p_n \to e_n\} : \alpha \sqcup \alpha_1 \sqcup \ldots \sqcup \alpha_n}$$

where $\mathcal{A}_i = \mathcal{A}[x_{i_1} \mapsto \alpha, \ldots, x_{i_{k_i}} \mapsto \alpha]$ if $p_i = c_i(x_{i_1}, \ldots, x_{i_{k_i}})$

$FCase$
$$\frac{\mathcal{A} \vdash e : \alpha \quad \mathcal{A}_1 \vdash e_1 : \alpha_1 \ \ldots \ \mathcal{A}_n \vdash e_n : \alpha_n}{\mathcal{A} \vdash fcase \ e \ of \ \{p_1 \to e_1; \ldots; p_n \to e_n\} : \alpha \sqcup \alpha_1 \sqcup \ldots \sqcup \alpha_n}$$

where $\mathcal{A}_i = \mathcal{A}[x_{i_1} \mapsto \alpha, \ldots, x_{i_{k_i}} \mapsto \alpha]$ if $p_i = c_i(x_{i_1}, \ldots, x_{i_{k_i}})$

Or
$$\frac{\mathcal{A} \vdash e_1 : \alpha_1 \ \ldots \ \mathcal{A} \vdash e_2 : \alpha_2}{\mathcal{A} \vdash e_1 \ or \ e_2 : \alpha_1 \sqcup \alpha_2}$$

$Free$
$$\frac{\mathcal{A}[x \mapsto \top] \vdash e : \alpha}{\mathcal{A} \vdash let \ x \ free \ in \ e : \alpha}$$

Let
$$\frac{\mathcal{A}[x \mapsto \bot] \vdash e : \alpha \quad \mathcal{A}[x \mapsto \alpha] \vdash e' : \alpha'}{\mathcal{A} \vdash let \ x = e \ in \ e' : \alpha'}$$

Fig. 2. Abstract semantics for residuation analysis

arguments by returning their least upper bound. Hence, one can derive the judgement $\mathcal{A} \vdash \mathtt{pair}(x, y) = (x, y) : \{1, 2\}$ showing that $\mathtt{pair}$ does not residuate and returns a ground value if both arguments are ground. In case of function applications (rule Fun), the computation of the least upper bound can be restricted to the arguments required by the assumption about the function. Rules $Case$ and $FCase$ simply combine the information of the discriminating expression and all branches since all of these expressions might contribute to the overall result. Note that the operational difference between $case$ and $fcase$ is not considered here since our abstract domain does not distinguish between non-ground and possibly residuating expressions. Such a distinction could be introduced in principle, but practical evaluations showed that such a refined domain does not yield more useful results for our intended application. Rule Or combines both branches since both will be executed at run time. Rule $Free$ assigns the top element to the introduced variable so that the overall result will be "possibly non-ground/suspending" if this variable is used. Finally, rule Let analyzes the bound expression with no information about the bound variable and, then, analyzes the main expression with the information computed for the bound variable.

External operations, like "+", are not explicitly mentioned in the analysis rules. They can be simply covered by defining $\mathcal{A}(f) = \{1, \ldots, n\}$ for each external operation f of arity n. This is a correct approximation for all currently supported external operations, since they do not residuate and yield a ground value if all arguments are ground values.

One might wonder why higher-order functions are not explicitly mentioned in the analysis rules. This is because they can be transformed into first-order ones by providing an "apply" operation between two expressions (this technique is known as "defunctionalization" [22] and also used to extend logic programs with higher-order features [25]). In this implementation, partially applied function calls are considered as constructor applications where the operation `apply` adds an argument and, if all arguments are provided, calls the actual function. Thus, partial applications are analyzed by *Cons* and `apply` is considered as a predefined operation with $\mathcal{A}(\texttt{apply}) = \{1, 2\}$. The only disadvantage of this simple approach is a possible over-approximation since *all* arguments of a partial application are assumed to be evaluated. For instance, consider the definitions

```
f x y = y+1
main = map (f x) [1,2,3]  where x free
```

Then the analysis yields the result that `main` might residuate although `main` evaluates to a ground value. This over-approximation can be avoided by the following specialized rule for partial applications which takes into account the abstract information about functions even for partial applications:

$$PFun \quad \frac{\mathcal{A} \vdash e_1 : \alpha_1 \ \ldots \ \mathcal{A} \vdash e_m : \alpha_m}{\mathcal{A} \vdash f(e_1, \ldots, e_m) : \alpha} \qquad f \ n\text{-ary function and } m < n$$

where $\alpha = \bigsqcup\{\alpha_i \mid i \in \mathcal{A}(f) \text{ and } i \leq m\}$, otherwise $\alpha = \mathcal{A}(f)$

An assumption $\mathcal{A}$ is correct if, for all operations f defined by $f(x_1, \ldots, x_n) = e$, $\mathcal{A}(f) = \alpha$ and $\mathcal{A} \vdash f(x_1, \ldots, x_n) = e : \alpha$ is derivable. Since all abstract operations used in Fig. 2 are monotone and the abstract domain is finite, we can compute a correct assumption as a least fixpoint by starting with the initial assumption $\mathcal{A}_0(f) = \bot$ for all operations f. Since such fixpoint computations are supported by CASS, the residuation analysis can be implemented by encoding the rules of Fig. 2 in a straightforward way and adding this code to CASS. The analysis is available in the current implementation of CASS (install package `cass` with the Curry package manager [13]) or via the online version of CASS.[4]

The soundness of the residuation analysis can be proved by induction on the evaluation steps of the concrete semantics. For this purpose, one has to extend the operational semantics of Curry programs presented in [3] to cover suspended computations by returning a specific SUSPEND result when the discriminating expression of a *case* expression is a free variable. Then one can show that an expression e will not be evaluated to SUSPEND if all variables required to be ground by the analysis of e are actually bound to ground expressions,

---

[4] https://www-ps.informatik.uni-kiel.de/~mh/webcass/.

where the latter means that these expressions evaluate to ground values (and not to SUSPEND). Thus, if $\mathcal{A} \vdash main : \varnothing$ is a correct judgement, then the evaluation of *main* never suspends. Due to lack of space, we omit the detailed definitions and proofs which can be found in a long version of this paper.

In order to evaluate the precision of the presented analysis, we analyzed the system libraries distributed with PAKCS. For instance, the library `Prelude`, which is the largest one and contains the predefined standard operations of Curry, contains 867 operations (including auxiliary operations that are not exported) but only one operation has the analysis result $\top$: the operation `unknown` which yields a fresh variable:

```
unknown = let x free in x
```

For all other operations, our analysis yields an argument index set, i.e., these operations do not residuate if they are called with ground values. When analyzing all system libraries, only 25 of 2616 operations might residuate or yield non-ground values. These are mainly operations in logic-oriented libraries for combinatorial programming or encapsulated search.

5 Implementing Residuation with Analysis Information

In this section we sketch how one can use the results of the residuation analysis to improve the implementation of residuation shown in Sect. 3.

As discussed in Sect. 3, suspension declarations, like `block` or `freeze`, are necessary to suspend the evaluation of an expression if some of its demanded subexpressions are suspended. However, if it is ensured that these subexpressions do not suspend, the run-time checking of suspension declarations become superfluous since the conditions under which they fire (i.e., suspend a goal) are never satisfied. Unfortunately, these conditions might not be the same in all calls to an operation. For instance, the factorial function can be evaluated without residuation if its argument is a number, but it is suspended when it is called with an unbound variable until this variable is instantiated by some other thread. Thus, if we want to keep the overall functionality of a program but improve it on calls with sufficiently instantiated arguments, we have to duplicate the code: in addition to the original Prolog code, we add code without suspension declarations which is activated only on sufficiently instantiated arguments. If the compiler uses the information of the residuation analysis, calls to the appropriate version of the code can be generated.

For instance, consider the translation of a function `f(x) = g(x,h(0))`. We add the suffix `_NR` to Prolog predicates implementing non-residuating code. If $f^\alpha \neq \top$, there are sufficient conditions to evaluate `f` without residuation so that we generate the non-residuating version of the code:[5]

```
f_NR(X,R,E0,E1) :- g_NR(X,h_NR(0),R,E0,E1).
```

---

[5] Although the control arguments E0 and E1 are superfluous in non-residuating computations, we leave them in the code in order to simplify the interaction of residuating and non-residuating code. Improving this scheme is a topic for future work.

Thus, non-residuating code always calls other non-residuating code. If $f^\alpha = \{1\}$, the predicate f_NR is invoked when f is called with an expression that evaluates to a ground value and does not suspend.

However, f might also be called with non-ground arguments or expressions which residuate. For this purpose, we also need the standard code for f but we can improve the translation of some subexpressions if they are non-residuating. For instance, if $h^\alpha = \{1\}$, the following code is generated:

```
:- block f(?,?,-,?).
f(X,R,E0,E1) :- g(X,h_NR(0),R,E0,E1).
```

If $g^\alpha = \{2\}$, i.e., g does not use its first argument, the code can be improved even more:

```
:- block f(?,?,-,?).
f(X,R,E0,E1) :- g_NR(X,h_NR(0),R,E0,E1).
```

Thus, standard code can call non-residuating code but not vice versa.

Although the code duplication is a slight a drawback of our approach, it is acceptable in practice since Prolog compilers often generate compact executables, e.g., by using virtual machine (WAM) instructions. This is shown in the next section where we evaluate our approach in a concrete compiler.

6   Benchmarks

In order to evaluate our approach, we added to PAKCS [14], which compiles Curry programs into Prolog programs based on the scheme sketched in Sect. 3 and described in detail in [5], a compilation flag to select one of the following three *residuation compilation modes*:

Full residuation: This is the existing compilation scheme sketched in Sect. 3 where block declarations (if SICStus-Prolog is used as the back end) or freeze goals (if SWI-Prolog is used as the back end) are used in the translation of all Curry operations.

No residuation: In this compilation mode, block and freeze are completely omitted. Instead, run-time errors are emitted in cases where residuation should occur according to the definition of Curry. Although this mode changes the semantics of Curry, it shows the best efficiency gain which can be obtained by removing coroutining annotations.

Optimized residuation: This is the compilation mode described in the previous section, i.e., the code generated for each operation is duplicated and the non-residuating code is invoked depending on the results of the program analysis described in Sect. 4.

All benchmarks were executed on a Linux machine (Debian 9.4) with an Intel Core i7-7700K (4.20 GHz) processor and 32 GiB of memory. The Curry implementation PAKCS (Version 2.0.2) uses SICStus-Prolog (Version 4.3.5) or SWI-Prolog (Version 7.6.4) as back ends. Timings were performed with the Unix **time** command measuring the execution time to compute all solutions (in seconds) of a compiled executable for each benchmark as a mean of three runs.

Program	Full Res. Time	No Residuation Time	No Residuation Speedup	Optimized Resid. Time	Optimized Resid. Speedup
ReverseUser	14.72	9.07	1.62	9.10	1.62
Reverse	13.06	7.75	1.69	7.77	1.68
TakPeano	6.09	2.89	2.11	4.00	1.52
Tak	4.68	3.34	1.40	4.00	1.17
ReverseHO	3.55	3.03	1.17	3.32	1.07
Primes	11.42	7.90	1.45	9.82	1.16
PrimesPeano	7.89	3.82	2.07	4.14	1.91
Queens	9.74	6.36	1.53	7.84	1.24
QueensUser	10.61	6.63	1.60	8.13	1.31
PermSort	9.57	6.50	1.47	7.81	1.23
PermSortPeano	6.20	3.18	1.95	4.84	1.28
RegExp	5.18	4.06	1.28	4.39	1.18

Fig. 3. Run times (in seconds) and speedups with SICStus-Prolog

The concrete benchmarks are Curry programs that were already used to compare different Curry implementations [8]. "ReverseUser" is the naive list reverse program applied to a list of 16384 elements, where all data (lists, numbers) are user-defined. "Reverse" is the same but with built-in lists. "Tak" is a highly recursive function on naturals applied to arguments (24,16,8) and "TakPeano" is the same but with user-defined natural numbers in Peano representation (see Example 1) so that no built-in arithmetic operations are used. "ReverseHO" reverses a list with one million elements in linear time using higher-order functions like `foldl` and `flip`. "Primes" computes the 2000th prime number via the sieve of Eratosthenes using higher-order functions, and "PrimesPeano" computes the 256th prime number but with Peano numbers and user-defined lists. "Queens" (and "QueensUser" with user-defined lists) computes the number of safe positions of 10 queens on a 10 × 10 chess board. Finally, "PermSort" sorts a list containing 15 elements by enumerating all permutations and selecting the sorted ones ("PermSortPeano" does the same for Peano numbers and 14 elements), and "RegExp" matches a regular expression in a string of length 400,000 following the non-deterministic specification of `grep` shown in [6]. In all these examples, residuation is not used so that, in principle, our optimization is applicable.

Figures 3 and 4 show the execution times and speedups for these programs with the SICStus-Prolog and SWI-Prolog back end, respectively. The speedups are computed relative to the "full residuation" compilation mode. The timings and speedups show that our proposed improvement is effective, in particular, if `freeze` is used for coroutining, as in SWI-Prolog. This is of practical relevance, since the SWI-Prolog implementation of PAKCS is used in the Debian package "`pakcs`" which is part of recent distributions of the Ubuntu Linux system. Our analysis can detect, for all benchmark programs, that the main expression is non-residuating. The difference in the timings between "no residuation" and "optimized residuation" can be explained by the fact that the run-time system

Program	Full Res. Time	No Residuation Time	Speedup	Optimized Resid. Time	Speedup
ReverseUser	136.47	29.65	4.60	29.85	4.57
Reverse	133.62	29.01	4.61	28.29	4.72
TakPeano	53.76	16.91	3.18	23.00	2.34
Tak	42.97	24.90	1.73	32.52	1.32
ReverseHO	17.97	8.16	2.20	9.83	1.83
Primes	140.56	75.46	1.86	97.70	1.44
PrimesPeano	91.34	22.38	4.08	22.50	4.06
Queens	124.75	63.78	1.96	87.15	1.43
QueensUser	190.68	90.94	2.10	122.73	1.55
PermSort	82.61	52.74	1.57	64.20	1.29
PermSortPeano	49.09	20.80	2.36	30.52	1.61
RegExp	34.36	15.93	2.16	21.82	1.57

Fig. 4. Run times (in seconds) and speedups with SWI-Prolog

of PAKCS (i.e., the implementation of predefined operations) is not optimized in the optimized residuation mode, since it might also be used by operations requiring residuation.

Program	Full Residuation	No Residuation	Optimized Res.
ReverseUser	612,257	612,126	857,588
Reverse	612,227	612,085	856,735
TakPeano	611,661	611,030	855,907
Tak	608,459	608,586	851,502
ReverseHO	612,979	611,896	859,200
Primes	610,701	610,482	855,398
PrimesPeano	614,630	614,056	864,129
Queens	610,413	609,681	852,238
QueensUser	612,797	612,715	858,428
PermSort	610,339	609,244	853,135
PermSortPeano	613,505	613,778	862,806
RegExp	614,466	613,096	859,765

Fig. 5. Program sizes (in bytes) with SICStus-Prolog

Another interesting question is the increase of the program size due to the code duplication in the optimized residuation mode. Figures 5 and 6 show the sizes (in bytes) of the executables ("saved state") of all benchmark programs with the SICStus-Prolog and SWI-Prolog back end, respectively. Note that also all standard operations defined in the prelude are duplicated in the optimized residuation mode. Since the run-time system is the largest part of the executable, the difference in program size is not really relevant for such small programs. In order to get some idea of the different sizes for realistic applications, we compiled

Program	Full Residuation	No Residuation	Optimized Res.
ReverseUser	1,433,607	1,179,270	1,800,747
Reverse	1,432,692	1,178,537	1,799,469
TakPeano	1,431,921	1,178,003	1,798,219
Tak	1,427,842	1,175,038	1,791,529
ReverseHO	1,434,424	1,179,887	1,802,239
Primes	1,431,504	1,177,585	1,797,703
PrimesPeano	1,438,153	1,182,305	1,808,340
Queens	1,429,760	1,176,368	1,794,638
QueensUser	1,434,593	1,179,992	1,802,729
PermSort	1,429,425	1,176,095	1,794,054
PermSortPeano	1,436,714	1,181,373	1,805,870
RegExp	1,437,173	1,181,854	1,806,103

Fig. 6. Program sizes (in bytes) with SWI-Prolog

the Curry package manager [13], a non-trivial Curry application consisting of 116 modules, with different residuation modes. The following table contains the sizes of the executables (in bytes):

Back end	Full Residuation	No Residuation	Optimized Res.
SICStus-Prolog	3,230,549	3,153,585	5,644,240
SWI-Prolog	7,720,682	5,490,839	11,641,481

Although the increase in the program size is considerable, it is not relevant for the practical execution if we take into account the memory sizes of contemporary computer hardware.

7   Related Work

The integration of functions into logic-oriented languages by suspending function calls with free variables has been proposed for various languages, e.g., Escher [17], Le Fun [2], Life [1], NUE-Prolog [20], or Oz [23]. The main motivation for this alternative to narrowing is to evaluate functions in a deterministic manner and to delegate all non-determinism to relations, as in logic programming. Although this principle sounds reasonable at a first glance, there are no strong results about completeness and optimality, as for narrowing [4]. Actually, there are examples where residuation has an infinite derivation space whereas the search space of narrowing is finite [10]. Abandoning residuation completely is also not desirable, since it is a good principle to connect external operations [7] and to support concurrent computations [24].

The potential incompleteness of residuation is investigated in [10] where a program analysis to approximate the groundness of variables for residuating logic program is proposed. Although this has some similarities with our approach, the analysis is different due to the different underlying languages (e.g., functions in [10] are always strict).

Coroutining is also used in logic programming to delay insufficiently instantiated negated subgoals to avoid logically incorrect answers. This delay might cause "floundering" if only delayed negated subgoals remain. A program analysis to analyze such situations is presented in [19]. Although the overall objective of this work is similar to our work, the underlying operational semantics is quite different to the work presented in this paper.

There are many approaches to implement functional features in logic languages (see [9] and the survey in [12]). Some of them support residuation and use block/freeze [5] or when [20] declarations. As shown by our benchmarks, such declarations have considerable costs which can be reduced by the techniques developed in this paper.

8   Conclusions

We have presented a method to improve the implementation of declarative programs with residuation. Since residuation is implemented in Prolog by coroutining annotations and these annotations have run-time costs even if they are not activated, we developed a compile-time analysis to approximate classes of programs or parts of programs where residuation is not used. For these parts, specific code without residuation annotations is generated. Our benchmarks show that the code optimized in this way can be more than four times faster than the original code if freeze is used to implement residuation. This also shows that freeze is a costly operation for coroutining (in SWI-Prolog). The use of block declarations (in SICStus-Prolog) is less expensive but, even in this case, we could measure a significant speedup by our optimization.

References

1. Aït-Kaci, H.: An overview of life. In: Schmidt, J.W., Stogny, A.A. (eds.) EWDW 1990. LNCS, vol. 504, pp. 42–58. Springer, Heidelberg (1991). https://doi.org/10.1007/3-540-54141-1_4
2. Aït-Kaci, H., Lincoln, P., Nasr, R.: Le fun: logic, equations, and functions. In: Proceedings of the 4th IEEE International Symposium on Logic Programming, San Francisco, pp. 17–23 (1987)
3. Albert, E., Hanus, M., Huch, F., Oliver, J., Vidal, G.: Operational semantics for declarative multi-paradigm languages. J. Symb. Comput. **40**(1), 795–829 (2005)
4. Antoy, S., Echahed, R., Hanus, M.: A needed narrowing strategy. J. ACM **47**(4), 776–822 (2000)
5. Antoy, S., Hanus, M.: Compiling multi-paradigm declarative programs into Prolog. In: Kirchner, H., Ringeissen, C. (eds.) FroCoS 2000. LNCS (LNAI), vol. 1794, pp. 171–185. Springer, Heidelberg (2000). https://doi.org/10.1007/10720084_12
6. Antoy, S., Hanus, M.: Functional logic programming. Commun. ACM **53**(4), 74–85 (2010)
7. Bonnier, S., Maluszynski, J.: Towards a clean amalgamation of logic programs with external procedures. In: Proceedings of the 5th Conference on Logic Programming and 5th Symposium on Logic Programming, Seattle, pp. 311–326. MIT Press, Cambridge (1988)

8. Braßel, B., Hanus, M., Peemöller, B., Reck, F.: KiCS2: a new compiler from Curry to Haskell. In: Kuchen, H. (ed.) WFLP 2011. LNCS, vol. 6816, pp. 1–18. Springer, Heidelberg (2011). https://doi.org/10.1007/978-3-642-22531-4_1

9. Casas, A., Cabeza, D., Hermenegildo, M.V.: A syntactic approach to combining functional notation, lazy evaluation, and higher-order in LP systems. In: Hagiya, M., Wadler, P. (eds.) FLOPS 2006. LNCS, vol. 3945, pp. 146–162. Springer, Heidelberg (2006). https://doi.org/10.1007/11737414_11

10. Hanus, M.: On the completeness of residuation. In: Proceedings of the 1992 Joint International Conference and Symposium on Logic Programming, pp. 192–206. MIT Press, Cambridge (1992)

11. Hanus, M.: A unified computation model for functional and logic programming. In: Proceedings of the 24th ACM Symposium on Principles of Programming Languages, pp. 80–93 (1997)

12. Hanus, M.: Functional logic programming: from theory to Curry. In: Voronkov, A., Weidenbach, C. (eds.) Programming Logics. LNCS, vol. 7797, pp. 123–168. Springer, Heidelberg (2013). https://doi.org/10.1007/978-3-642-37651-1_6

13. Hanus, M.: Semantic versioning checking in a declarative package manager. In: Technical Communications of the 33rd International Conference on Logic Programming (ICLP 2017), Open Access Series in Informatics (OASIcs), pp. 6:1–6:16. Schloss Dagstuhl - Leibniz-Zentrum fuer Informatik (2017)

14. Hanus, M., et al.: PAKCS: The Portland Aachen Kiel Curry System (2017). http://www.informatik.uni-kiel.de/~pakcs/

15. Hanus, M., Skrlac, F.: A modular and generic analysis server system for functional logic programs. In: Proceedings of the ACM SIGPLAN 2014 Workshop on Partial Evaluation and Program Manipulation (PEPM 2014), pp. 181–188. ACM Press (2014)

16. Hanus, M. (ed.): Curry: An integrated functional logic language (vers. 0.9.0) (2016). http://www.curry-language.org

17. Lloyd, J.W.: Combining functional and logic programming languages. In: Proceedings of the International Logic Programming Symposium, pp. 43–57 (1994)

18. Loogen, R., Fraguas, F.L., Artalejo, M.R.: A demand driven computation strategy for lazy narrowing. In: Bruynooghe, M., Penjam, J. (eds.) PLILP 1993. LNCS, vol. 714, pp. 184–200. Springer, Heidelberg (1993). https://doi.org/10.1007/3-540-57186-8_79

19. Marriott, K., Søndergaard, H., Dart, P.: A characterization of non-floundering logic programs. In: Proceedings of the 1990 North American Conference on Logic Programming, pp. 661–680. MIT Press, Cambridge (1990)

20. Naish, L.: Adding equations to NU-Prolog. In: Maluszyński, J., Wirsing, M. (eds.) PLILP 1991. LNCS, vol. 528, pp. 15–26. Springer, Heidelberg (1991). https://doi.org/10.1007/3-540-54444-5_84

21. Peyton Jones, S. (ed.): Haskell 98 Language and Libraries—The Revised Report. Cambridge University Press, Cambridge (2003)

22. Reynolds, J.C.: Definitional interpreters for higher-order programming languages. In: Proceedings of the ACM Annual Conference, pp. 717–740. ACM Press (1972)

23. Smolka, G.: The Oz programming model. In: van Leeuwen, J. (ed.) Computer Science Today: Recent Trends and Developments. LNCS, vol. 1000, pp. 324–343. Springer, Heidelberg (1995). https://doi.org/10.1007/BFb0015252

24. Van Roy, P., Haridi, S.: Concepts, Techniques, and Models of Computer Programming. MIT Press, Cambridge (2004)

25. Warren, D.H.D.: Higher-order extensions to Prolog: are they needed? Mach. Intell. **10**, 441–454 (1982)

Incremental Evaluation of Lattice-Based Aggregates in Logic Programming Using Modular TCLP

Joaquín Arias[✉] and Manuel Carro

IMDEA Software Institute and Universidad Politécnica de Madrid, Madrid, Spain
{joaquin.arias,manuel.carro}@imdea.org, joaquin.arias@alumnos.upm.es,
manuel.carro@upm.es

Abstract. Aggregates are used to compute single pieces of information from separate data items, such as records in a database or answers to a query to a logic program. The maximum and minimum are well-known examples of aggregates. The computation of aggregates in Prolog or variant-based tabling can loop even if the aggregate at hand can be finitely determined. When answer subsumption or mode-directed tabling is used, termination improves, but the behavior observed in existing proposals is not consistent. We present a framework to incrementally compute aggregates for elements in a lattice. We use the entailment and join relations of the lattice to define (and compute) aggregates and decide whether some atom is compatible with (entails) the aggregate. The semantics of the aggregates defined in this way is consistent with the LFP semantics of tabling with constraints. Our implementation is based on the TCLP framework available in Ciao Prolog, and improves its termination properties w.r.t. similar approaches. Defining aggregates that do not fit into the lattice structure is possible, but some properties guaranteed by the lattice may not hold. However, the flexibility provided by this possibility justifies its inclusion. We validate our design with several examples and we evaluate their performance.

1 Introduction

Aggregates, in general and informally, are operations which take all the records in a database table or all the answers to a logic programming query and synthesize a result using these data items. Common aggregates include maximum, minimum, and the set of all answers, counting the number of solutions, or computing an average. A straightforward way to compute aggregates is to compute all solutions and then calculate the aggregate. However, this has several drawbacks. In some cases, computing an aggregate can be done without computing all possible answers: for example, if the operational semantics of the underlying language include mechanisms to avoid repeating useless computations [1,2]. Also, the computation of the aggregate may involve (recursively)

© Springer Nature Switzerland AG 2019
J. J. Alferes and M. Johansson (Eds.): PADL 2019, LNCS 11372, pp. 98–114, 2019.
https://doi.org/10.1007/978-3-030-05998-9_7

using the aggregate itself (see Example 1), so computing a full aggregate-less model with a fixpoint procedure may simply be not correct, and several iterations of fixpoint procedures may be necessary.

Several tabling systems [11,14,16] include the so-called *modes*, which make it possible to implement some specific aggregates incrementally. However, while being very helpful in some situations, a careful examination of their behavior reveals inconsistencies with the LFP semantics which makes reasoning about simple programs unsound.

In this paper we present a semantics for a class of common aggregates, derived from an interpretation of their meaning in a lattice. This interpretation makes it possible to give them a consistent least fixed point semantics. We observe that it is possible to take advantage of existing implementation techniques for tabled logic programming and extend them in order to implement the additional machinery necessary for aggregates: tabling, in all of its variants, needs to store the answers returned by the different branches of the computation, which is a first step towards computing aggregates. We further develop this initial implementation by adding the necessary support (in the form of syntax and underlying infrastructure) to incrementally compute aggregates based on the answers that are added to the table.

In particular, we base our proposal in the Modular TCLP [1,2] framework, which already has infrastructure to perform tabling with constraints. This infrastructure includes the possibility of storing answers and using entailment between stored answers to increase expressiveness, termination properties, and speed of tabling.

In Sect. 2 we briefly describe the Modular TCLP interface. In Sect. 3 we present a semantics for aggregates based on entailment and/or join operation over a lattice which is consistent with the LFP semantics. In Sect. 4 we present the generic framework for lattice-based aggregates with an improvement in Modular TCLP which allows the combination of answers. In Sect. 5 we evaluate the expressiveness and performance of ATCLP versus Prolog and tabling. Finally, in Sect. 6, we offer some conclusions.

2 Background: Tabling and Constraints

Tabled Logic Programming with Constraints (TCLP) [2,5,12] improves program expressiveness and, in many cases, efficiency and termination properties. Let us consider a program to compute distances between nodes in a graph written using tabling and using TCLP (Fig. 1, left and right, resp.).

Tabling records the first occurrence of each call to a tabled predicate (the *generator*) and its answers. In variant tabling (the most usual form of tabling), when a call is found to be equal, modulo variable renaming, to a previous generator, the execution of the call is suspended and it is flagged as a *consumer* of the generator. For example dist(a,Y,D) is a variant of dist(a,Z,D) if Y and Z are free variables. Upon suspension, execution switches to evaluating another, untried branch. A branch which does not suspend due to the existence of a repeated call can generate an answer for an initial goal. When a generator finitely finishes exploring all the clauses and all answers are collected, its consumers are resumed and are fed the answers of the generator. This may make consumers produce new answers which can in turn resume more consumers. This process finishes when no new answers can be generated — i.e., a fixpoint has been reached. Tabling is sound and, for programs with a finite Herbrand model, is complete.

```
1  :- table dist/3.
2
3  dist(X, Y, D) :-
4      dist(X, Z, D1),
5      edge(Z, Y, D2),
6      D is D1 + D2.
7  dist(X, Y, D) :-
8      edge(X, Y, D).
```

```
1  :- table dist/3.
2
3  dist(X, Y, D) :-
4      D1 #> 0, D2 #> 0,
5      D #= D1 + D2,
6      dist(X, Z, D1),
7      edge(Z, Y, D2).
8  dist(X, Y, D) :-
9      edge(X, Y, D).
```

Fig. 1. Left-recursive distance traversal in a graph: Tabling (left)/TCLP (right). Note: The symbols #> and #= are (in)equalities in CLP.

The program in Fig. 1 would always loop under SLD due to the left-recursive rule. Under tabling, a query such as ?- dist(a,Y,D),D < K would terminate for acyclic graphs. In a cyclic graph, however, dist/3 has an infinite Herbrand model: every cycle can be traversed repeatedly and create paths of increasing length. Therefore, that query will not terminate under variant tabling.

However, the integration of tabling and CLP makes it possible to execute the dist/3, right, using *constraint entailment* [4] to suspend calls which are more particular than previous calls, and to keep only the most general answers. The query ?- D #< K, dist(a,Y,D) terminates under TCLP because by placing the constraint D #< K before dist(a,Y,D), the search is pruned when the values in D are larger than or equal to K.

This illustrates the main idea underlying the use of entailment in TCLP: more particular calls (consumers) can suspend and later reuse the answers collected by more general calls (generators). In order to make this entailment relationship explicit, we will represent a TCLP goal as $\langle g, c_g \rangle$ where g is the call (a literal) and c_g is the projection of the current constraint store onto the variables of the call. For example, $\langle \text{dist(a,Y,D)}, D > 0 \wedge D < 75 \rangle$ entails the goal $\langle \text{dist(a,Y,D)}, D < 150 \rangle$ because $(D > 0 \wedge D < 75) \sqsubseteq D < 150$. We also say that the latter (the generator) is more general than the former (the consumer). All the solutions of a consumer are solutions for its generator, since the space of solutions of the consumer is a subset of that of the generator. However, not all answers from a generator are valid for its consumers. For example $Y = b \wedge D > 125 \wedge D < 135$ is a solution for our generator, but not for our consumer, since the consumer call was made under a constraint store more restrictive than the generator. Therefore, the tabling engine has to filter, via the constraint solver, the answers from the generator that are consistent w.r.t. the constraint store of the consumer.

Some tabling systems offer facilities that improve termination in this situation. Tabling engines that implement *mode-directed tabling* [6,17] and/or *answer subsumption* [13] can use policies other than being a variant to decide whether a call is a consumer and should be suspended. These are expressed by specifying the *modes* of some arguments. For example, the directive :- table dist(_,_,min) specifies the (aggregate) mode min for the third argument. The call will in this case terminate because only the shortest distance will be returned. However, note that the standard least fixpoint semantics (calculated by tabling) is not well-suited to programs with aggregates [8,9,15]. For example, let us consider the following program:

1 p(1).   2 p(0) :- p(1).

and let us assume that we want to minimize the (single) argument to p/1, i.e., we want to evaluate this program under the constraint that the argument of p/1 has to be as small as possible. On the one hand, this means that only one literal (the p(X) having the smallest value for X) should be in the model. On the other hand, it turns out that neither {p(0)} nor {p(1)} are consistent with this intended semantics. For p(0) to be the literal with the minimum value, p(1) needs to be true. But then p(1) would be in the model and therefore it should be the minimum. This paradox points to the need of an ASP semantics for the general case (and clarifies why there is not an accepted, consistent semantics for aggregates in Prolog-based logic programming — see at the end of Sect. 3.1). We will present here an alternative, defensible meaning for a class of aggregates that can stay within the least fixpoint semantics.

3   Aggregates in Lattices

We consider first the case of aggregates that can be embedded into a lattice: the elements on which we operate can be viewed as points in a lattice whose structure depends on the particular aggregate we are computing, and where the aggregation operation can be expressed based on the partial order of the lattice. As an intuitive example, the minimum of a set of elements is the element x for which there is no other element y s.t. $y \sqsubseteq x$. This view gives rise to a view of aggregates returning designated representatives of a class.

3.1   Aggregates Based on Entailment

The simplest type of aggregation operations can be defined using only the $\sqsubseteq$ operation of the lattice. Since $\sqsubseteq$ is related to constraint entailment, we have used this name.

Definition 1 (Entailment-Based Aggregates). *Given a partial order relation $\sqsubseteq$ over a multiset S,[1] the aggregate of S over $\sqsubseteq$, denoted as $Agg_{\sqsubseteq}$, is the set of more general values of S w.r.t. $\sqsubseteq$:*

$$Agg_{\sqsubseteq}(S) = \{x \in S \mid \not\exists y \in S, y \neq x \cdot x \sqsubseteq y\}$$

minimum and maximum are two widely used entailment-based aggregates. But it is interesting to note that other policies that select a subset of answers to a query, such as variant or subsumption, can also be expressed as aggregates in a lattice.

---

[1] This definition would usually be based on a set instead of a multiset. The reason to choose explicitly a multiset will be clear in Sect. 4.5, when we apply our implementation to operations that cannot be embedded in a lattice.

Example 1 (min). The minimum of a set of values is the least upper bound of the lattice ordered by ' > '. The aggregate of S over min is defined as:

$$Agg_{min}(S) = \{x \in S \mid \nexists y \in S, y \neq x \cdot x > y\}$$

The minimum of a set of values is unique and, as aggregate, is a set: $Agg_{min}(\{2,3,4\}) = \{2\}$. Note that $Agg_{min}(\{2,3,4,5,6\}) = \{2\}$, as well. Therefore, one can view the aggregation of a set of values as another (potentially different) set that in some sense summarizes or represents the initial set of values. As such, several sets can have the same aggregate, or, conversely, a single aggregate can represent many initial sets. As we will see, we define $Agg_{min}(\{2,3,4\}) = \{x \mid x \geq 2\}$ as this brings interesting properties to aggregates that are compatible with the intuitive idea of what an aggregate is.

We will see how this definition of aggregates can be applied to the previous min case to generate a model that is compatible with the least fixpoint of a logic program. Let us consider the following variant of an example taken from [15].[2]

Example 2 (p(min)). In the program below, `:- table p(min)` is intended to mean that we want to restrict the model of the program to the atoms that minimize the value of the single argument of p/1.

```
1   :- table p(min).           4   p(1) :- p(2).
2   p(3).                       5   p(0) :- p(3).
3   p(2).
```

In absence of the `table` aggregate declaration, the set of answers would be {p(0), p(1), p(2), p(3)} and, therefore, the expected aggregated answer using the minimum should be p(0). This is the model that ATCLP returns as the aggregated answer for the previous program and query. It also behaves consistently with an LFP semantics if p(k) is intended to mean p(x) s.t. $x \geq k$. In that case, using the clause p(0):-p(3) does not fall into a contradiction: if p(x) s.t. $x \geq 0$ is the model of the program, the atom p(3) is true under that model (because $3 \geq 0$). Therefore, p(3) can be used to support p(0).

We want to note that the current state of affairs in other systems is far from being satisfactory. Following [15], none of the current *answer subsumption* implementations seems to behave correctly: XSB and B-Prolog return p(1), and Yap, which uses batch scheduling[3] returns, on backtracking, p(3), p(2), and p(1) the *first time* the query is issued, and only p(1) in subsequent calls.

3.2 Aggregates Based on Join

Some interesting aggregates need to be based on an operation richer than the entailment, because they have to generate a new element based on previous elements. For these cases, we posit an aggregate similar to the one in Definition 1, but using the join operation instead of the entailment.

---

[2] The original example used max. For coherence with the rest of the cases in this paper, we have converted it to use min.

[3] Batch scheduling returns answers as soon as they are found.

Definition 2 (Join-Based Aggregates). *Given a join-semilattice domain D with a join operation $\sqcup$ (that is commutative, associative and idempotent), the aggregated value of any multiset $S \in D$ over $\sqcup$, denoted as $Agg_\sqcup$, is the least upper bound of S w.r.t. $\sqcup$:*

$$Agg_\sqcup(S) = LUB_\sqcup(S)$$

The main difference w.r.t. entailment-based aggregates is that when using the join operator, the resulting aggregate could be a value that is not in S. In our case, it may not be a logical consequence of the program.

*Example 3 (*min of pairs*).* Let us build on Example 1 and define the minimum of a set of pairs as element-wise minima. We define the join operation $(a_1, b_1) \sqcup (a_2, b_2) = (\min(a_1, a_2), \min(b_1, b_2))$. The aggregate value of $S = \{(a_i, b_i)\}, i = 1 \ldots n$ over this join operator is:

$$Agg_{min}(S) = LUB_{min}(\{(a_i, b_i) \in S\}) = (min(a_i), min(b_i)) \text{ for } i = 1 \ldots n$$

Note that the minimum of a set of pairs using an entailment-based aggregate and an element-wise order (i.e., $(a_1, b_1) > (a_2, b_2) \leftrightarrow a_1 > a_2 \wedge b_1 > b_2$) can return a non-singleton set $Agg_{min}(\{(4,4), (4,2), (3,3)\}) = \{(4,2), (3,3)\}$ that defines a Pareto frontier. The join-based definition, however, returns a unique value which was not an element of the initial set: $Agg_{min}(\{(4,4), (4,2), (3,3)\}) = \{(3,2)\}$. Similarly to Definition 1, the model derived from a join-based aggregate is assumed to capture the constraint used to generate the aggregate – i.e., $Agg_{min}(\{(4,4), (4,2), (3,3)\}) \sqsubseteq (5,7)$.

4 The ATCLP Framework

We present here the ATCLP framework: how aggregated predicates are declared, how the aggregates are defined, and how the implementation works. This implementation is based on a program transformation that uses the underlying infrastructure of Modular TCLP. Finally, we present an extension to the Modular TCLP framework that makes it possible to combine answers and write aggregation operations that do not follow a lattice structure.

4.1 From Lattices to Constraints

We built our system upon the infrastructure used in Modular TCLP [2] to handle constraints. Indeed, many of the operations are similar: entailment in a lattice can be handled similarly (from an implementation point of view) to entailment in a constraint system and the implementation of the join operation can also be executed in the same places where previous, less general answer constraints are discarded in a TCLP system. We are looking at the aggregate operations in a lattice as a counterpart of similar operations among constraints, including the removal of answers that, from the point of view of the aggregates, are entailed by other answers.

4.2 Design of the ATCLP Interface

ATCLP provides a directive to declare the aggregated predicates and a generic interface designed to facilitate the use of different user-defined aggregates.

For homogeneity, aggregated predicates are declared with the same directive used by mode-directed tabling: `:- table p(agg1,...,aggn)`, where agg_i denotes the aggregate used for the ith argument. For the arguments that should be evaluated under variant tabling, we use the mode `'_'`.

```
1   :- use_package(tclp_aggregates).
2   :- table dist(_,_,min).
3
4   dist(X,Y,D) :-
5       edge(X,Y,D).
6   dist(X,Y,D) :-
7       edge(X,Z,D1),
8       dist(Z,Y,D2),
9       D is D1 + D2.
10
11  entails(min,A,B) :- A >= B.
12
13  edge(a,b,10).
14  ...
```

```
1   :- include(aggregate_rt).
2   :- table '$dist'/3.
3
4   dist(X,Y,A1) :-
5       put(V1,(min,F1)),
6       '$dist'(X,Y,V1),
7       ( var(A1) -> A1=F1
8       ; entails(min,A1,F1) ).
9   '$dist'(X,Y,V1) :-
10      get(V1,(min,A1)), A1 = D,
11      edge(X,Y,D).
12  '$dist'(X,Y,V1) :-
13      get(V1,(min,A1)), A1 = D,
14      edge(X,Z,D1),
15      dist(Z,Y,D2),
16      D is D1 + D2.
17  ...
```

Fig. 2. Left: minimum distance traversal program using aggregates. Right: transformation of the program.

Figure 2, left, shows the minimum distance traversal program using aggregates. The directive `:- use_package(tclp_aggregate)` initializes the TCLP engine, and the directive `:- table path(_,_,min)` states that the answers of `path/3` should be aggregated using the `min` of its third argument. The aggregation operation is defined as an entailment, by specifying with the predicate `entails/3` when two values are entailed from the point of view of `min` (the first argument to `entails/3`). Note that the rest of the program remains as in Fig. 1. The entailment and join operations for a given aggregate are provided by the user with predicates that implement these operations. The two predicates that a user can define are:

- `entails(Agg,A,B)` defines an entailment-based aggregate. It succeeds when the answer A entails the answer B w.r.t. the aggregate Agg, e.g., when $A \sqsubseteq_{Agg} B$.
- `join(Agg,A,B,New)` defines a join-based aggregate. It returns in New the combination of the answers A and B w.r.t. the aggregate Agg, e.g. $New = A \sqcup_{Agg} B$.

Examples of Entailment-Based Aggregates

Example 4 (Implementation of min*).* The implementation of Example 1 would be complete by providing the `entails/3` predicate as:

```
1   entails(min, A, B) :- A >= B.
```

In order to further clarify the relationship between the aggregates and the model of the program where they appear, we show now a program that captures the semantics of the program in Example 2.

Example 5 (interpretation of p(min)*).* The code below exemplifies how Example 2 is expected to behave under ATCLP, according to Definition 1 and the entailment definition in Example 4:

```
1   p(X) :- entails(min,X,3).
2   p(X) :- entails(min,X,2).
3   p(X) :- entails(min,X,1), p(Y), entails(min,2,Y).
4   p(X) :- entails(min,X,0), p(Y), entails(min,3,Y).
```

With this interpretation, p(2), inferred by the second clause, is more general than p(3), inferred from the first clause, since $\{x \geq 3\} \sqsubseteq \{x \geq 2\}$. p(3) is therefore discarded when the second clause is executed and only p(2) remains in the model (which, in our implementation, lives in the answer table of the tabling engine). After this, the first entailment goal of the third clause succeeds, p(Y) then succeeds with Y=2 followed by `entails(min,2,2)`, which also succeeds because $2 \leq 2$, and p(1) is inferred. At this point, p(2) is discarded because p(1) is more general: $\{x \geq 2\} \sqsubseteq \{x \geq 1\}$. Finally, the first entailment goal in the last clause succeeds and the rest of the clause succeeds as well because we had p(1) and $3 \geq 1$. p(0) is then inferred and p(1) is discarded because it entails p(0), i.e., p(1) $\sqsubseteq_{p(min)}$ p(0).

The interpretation of a query is similar to that of a body goal: ?- p(2) is to be understood as ?- p(X), entails(min,2,X) which in our example succeeds because p(X) returns X=0 and `entails(min,2,0)` succeeds because $2 \geq 0$.

As noted before, this interpretation extends the range of atoms which are true to include some that were not in the program without the aggregate declaration. The model for the latter was {p(0), p(1), p(2), p(3)}, but the intended meaning of ?- p(X) under the new semantics is {p(X) | entails(min,X,0)}, and therefore the query ?- p(5) also succeeds. While this may seem strange, we also want to note that by seeing aggregates as constraints defining a domain for a variable plus a value to *anchor* these constraints, this interpretation is similar to an answer in a CLP system or to the behavior of subsumption tabling in the Herbrand domain, as the following example highlights:

*Example 6 (*p(sub)*).* In the program below, `:- table p(sub)` means that we want to keep the more general answers.

```
1  :- table p(sub).                    4  :- use_module(terms_check).
2  p(f(X,Y)).                          5  entails(sub,A,B) :-
3  p(f(g(Z),a)).                       6       instance(A,B).
```

Without the aggregate declaration, the set of answers for the query ?- p(X) is {p(f(X,Y)),p(f(g(Z),a))}. In the Herbrand domain with subsumption tabling, the answer A = f(X,Y) covers the answer A = f(g(Z),a). Therefore, the expected aggregated answer using subsumption is p(f(X,Y)). Note that the query ?-p(f(1,g(-1))) succeeds under ATCLP, but also in Prolog under the standard LFP semantics, even if the literal was not present in the set of answers obtained without the aggregate declaration. Therefore, our interpretation of the meaning of a model for a program with aggregates can be viewed as an extension of the Herbrand model with subsumption for constraint domains.

An Example of Join-Based Aggregates

Example 7 (path(set)). Let us consider a program to compute the set of nodes that are reachable from a given node in a graph. Figure 3 shows, on the left, a simple Prolog program and, on the right, an ATCLP program using the set aggregate (see below). While both seem to have the same expressiveness, the Prolog program would loop for graphs with cycles and cannot to answer some queries that the ATCLP program can (see at the end of this example). Adding tabling to the Prolog program helps in this case, but note that mixing all-solution predicates and tabling does not always work, as the suspension and resumption mechanism of tabling interacts with the usual failure- and assert-driven implementations of setof/3 and similar predicates.

```
1  path(X,Set) :-                        1  :- table path(_,set).
2     setof(Y, path_(X,Y), Set).         2  path(X,[Y]) :- edge(X,Y).
3  path_(X,Y) :- edge(X,Y).              3  path(X,Ys) :- edge(X,Z),
4  path_(X,Y) :- edge(X,Z), path_(Z,Y).  4                path(Z,Ys).
```

```
1  edge(a,b).  edge(b,c).  edge(b,a).  edge(c,d).
```

Fig. 3. Set of reachable nodes from a given node.

The set aggregate generates sets from the union of subsets. It can therefore generate values that are not logical consequences of the program without aggregates. Assuming that we have a library implementing basic operations on sets (e.g., Richard O'Keefe's well-known ordset.pl), we can define the set aggregate as:

```
1  :- use_module(library(sets)).
2  entails(set, SetA, SetB) :- ord_subset(SetA, SetB).
3  join(set, SetA, SetB, NewSet) :- ord_union(SetA, SetB, NewSet).
```

Note that in this case we define both the entailment and the join (although the former can be defined in terms of the latter).

This example returns the set (as an ordered list without repetitions) L=[a,b,c,d] for the query ?- path(a,L). Moreover, if we want to know which nodes can reach a set of nodes, the query ?- path(X,[a,d]) returns X=a and X=b under ATCLP, which neither Prolog nor tabling can if setof/3 is used.

In general, for lattice-based aggregates, entails/3 can be defined in terms of join/4 or vice versa. However, join-based aggregates allows us to aggregate the answers in a unique value, and in some cases its gain in efficiency, in space, and time comes with a loss of precision. Nevertheless, there are applications where this trade-off can remain feasible, e.g., abstract interpretation and stream data analysis.

4.3 Implementation Sketch

In this section we present the program transformation used to execute programs with aggregates and we describe how ATCLP is implemented using Modular TCLP as underlying infrastructure.

Modular TCLP: Modular TCLP is a tabling engine that handles constraints natively. It can use constraint entailment to perform suspension and to save and return only the most general answers to a query. Its modularity comes from the existence of a generic interface with constraint solvers that defines what operations a constraint solver needs to provide to the tabling engine [2]. By extending the code (written in Prolog) that calls these external solver operations, we can *hack* the existing TCLP engine to execute aggregates as described before.

Program Transformation: Figure 2, right, shows the transformation applied to the predicate dist/3. The original entry point is rewritten to call an auxiliary predicate where the aggregated arguments are substituted by attributed variables [7]. These are later on caught by the tabling engine [5] and their execution is derived to the TCLP code written in Prolog. The auxiliary predicate corresponds to the original one, but the original arguments are retrieved from the attributed variables with get/2. The attributes are tuples of the form (Agg_i, F_i), where Agg_i is the aggregate mode declared for that argument and F_i is a fresh variable where the aggregated value will be collected. Once the auxiliary predicate collects the aggregated answer, it is either returned (if called with an unbound variable) or checked for entailment against the value in the corresponding argument.

ATCLP Internals: The TCLP tabling engine calls interface predicates from constraint solvers whose implementation depends on that solver. When this interface is used to implement aggregates, its implementation is always the same and ultimately calls the user-provided entails/3 and join/4 predicates. Figure 4 shows the implementation of this interface, under the simplifying assumption that we are aggregating over a single variable. This implementation merely recovers information related to which aggregate is being used and which variables are affected, and passes it to and from the join and entailment operations.

ATCLP uses two objects: the aggregated argument (V) and the aggregate mode and the value for the argument (Agg,A). There are three main phases in the execution of ATCLP:

```
1  store_projection(V, (Agg,A))                :- get(V, (Agg,A)).
2  call_entail((_ ,_), (_ ,B))                 :- var(B),!.
3  call_entail((Agg,A), (Agg,B))               :- entails(Agg,A,B).
4  answer_compare((Agg,A), (Agg,B),'=<')        :- entails(Agg,A,B),!.
5  answer_compare((Agg,A), (Agg,B), '>')        :- entails(Agg,B,A),!.
6  answer_compare((Agg,A), (Agg,B),'$new'((Agg,New))) :- join(Agg,A,B,New).
7  apply_answer(V, (Agg,B))      :- get(V,(Agg,A)), \+ ground(A), A = B, !.
8  apply_answer(V, (Agg,B))      :- get(V,(Agg,A)), entails(Agg,A,B).
```

Fig. 4. Simplified ATCLP interface with the constraint tabling engine.

Call Entailment: the TCLP engine invokes store_projection(+V,-(Agg,A)) to retrieve the representation of the aggregated arguments of a new call. Then call_entail(+(Agg,A),+(Agg,B)) is called to check whether the new call A entails a previous generator B. It succeeds if B is a variable or if A $\sqsubseteq_{Agg}$ B. If so, the new call suspends and consumes answers from the generator; otherwise, the new call is marked as a new generator.

Answer entailment: the TCLP engine invokes store_projection(+V,-(Agg,A)) to retrieve the representation of aggregated arguments of a new answer. Then it invokes answer_compare(+(Agg,A),+(Agg,B),-Res) to compare the new answer A against a previous answer B. If A $\sqsubseteq_{Agg}$ B, the predicate succeeds with Res='=<'; conversely, if B $\sqsubseteq_{Agg}$ A, the predicate returns Res='>'. This entailment check discards/removes more particular answers from the answer table. When the entailment check fails, and if the join operator of the aggregate mode Agg is implemented, the predicate returns Res = '$new'(New), where New = A $\sqcup_{Agg}$ B. Otherwise, answer_compare/3 fails and the new answer is stored in the answer table of the generator.

Answer consistency: In constraint tabling, answers from a generator may not be directly applicable to a consumer: if the environment of the consumer is more restrictive than that of the generator, the generator's answers have to be filtered by applying the constraints in the consumer environment to generate compatible answers. The TCLP engine invokes apply_answer(+V,+(Agg,B)). When A (the aggregate value of V) is a variable, B is returned as the aggregated answer. Otherwise, entailment is checked: if A entails B, appl_answer/2 succeeds, and it fails otherwise.

4.4 Adapting the Answer Management of TCLP

The Modular TCLP framework further rewrites the program in Fig. 2, right, to add at the end of each clause a call to the predicate new_answer/0 (Fig. 6), which saves answers in the answer table.

This rewritten predicate is called through a meta-predicate tabled_call/1 (Fig. 5), that executes the call entailment phase. store_projection/2 retrieves the current value of the aggregate, and call_entail/2 detects if the current call entails a previous generator by comparing their projections, i.e., their aggregates. If that is the case, the call is suspended by suspend_consumer/1; otherwise, the new call is made a generator and executed (with save_generator/3 and execute_generator/2 resp.)

When the generators terminate and/or the consumers are resumed, answer consistency is checked and apply_answer/2 applies all the answers collected during the execution of the generator.

new_answer/0 (Fig. 6) collects the answers executing the answer entailment phase. Lines 7 to 10 perform the entailment check while lines 11 to 13 can join an incoming answer with previous answers into a new answer, and remove the previous answers [12]. This is used to *combine* two points A1 and A2 of a lattice into A1 ⊔ A2 and, for example, store abstractions of answers. Such abstraction may lose some precision, but this can be acceptable for some applications (e.g., in abstract interpretation).

```
1   tabled_call(Call) :-
2       call_lookup_table(Call, Vars, Gen),
3       'store_projection'(Vars, ProjStore),
4       (   projstore_Gs(Gen, List_GenProjStore),
5           member(ProjStore_G, List_GenProjStore),
6           'call_entail'(ProjStore, ProjStore_G) ->
7           suspend_consumer(Call)
8       ;   save_generator(Gen, ProjStore_G, ProjStore),
9           execute_generator(Gen, ProjStore_G),
10      ),
11      answers(Gen, ProjStore_G, List_Ans),
12      member(Ans, List_Ans),
13      projstore_As(Ans, List_AnsProjStore),
14      member(ProjStore_A, List_AnsProjStore),
15      'apply_answer'(Vars, ProjStore_A).
```

Fig. 5. Tabled_call

```
1   new_answer :-
2       answer_lookup_table(Vars, Ans),
3       'store_projection'(Vars, ProjStore),
4       (   projstore_As(Ans, List_AnsProjStore),
5           member(ProjStore_A, List_AnsProjStore),
6           'answer_compare'(ProjStore, ProjStore_A, Res),
7           (   Res == '=<'                         % Discard ProjStore
8           ;   Res == '>',                         % Remove ProjStore_A
9               remove_answer(ProjStore_A),
10              fail
11          ;   Res == '$new'(NewProjStore),        % Save NewProjStore
12              remove_answer(ProjStore_A),
13              save_answer(Ans, NewProjStore)
14          ), !
15      ;   save_answer(Ans, ProjStore)             % Save ProjStore
16      ), !, fail.
```

Fig. 6. Extended implementation of new_answer/0.

4.5 Non-lattice Aggregates

We presented aggregates that are defined over lattices where the join operation is commutative, associative, and idempotent. However, there are many common aggregates that can be implemented using ATCLP but that do not satisfy some of the properties listed above. As a consequence, their execution may not completely align with LFP semantics. This is the case of sum, which can be defined using the join operator, but which does not have a sound definition for entailment.

Example 8 (probability of paths in a graph). Let us consider a (cyclic) graph where each edge has a transition probability. We want the probability P of reaching a node N from another node a. P is the sum of the transition probabilities of all possible paths from a to N. Then, on one hand we have to multiply the probability of every traversed edge to calculate the probability of a path and, on the other hand, we have to add probabilities for every path. We define an aggregate (resp., sum and thr(Epsilon)) for each of these.

Incrementally adding path probabilities (in general, numbers) is easy by adding every new answer to the previous value. This behaves as expected when we have a finite set of answers to add. For non-cyclic graphs, the model is finite and computing all the paths and their sum is possible. However, in case of cycles, edges within loops may have to be traversed an unbounded number of times, and their contribution to the final solution decreases with every loop.

A possible strategy is to *discard* edges when their contribution goes below a certain user-defined threshold. With a somewhat ad-hoc reading of this condition, we can say that new solutions with a difference small enough w.r.t. existing solutions entail these previous solutions and therefore they ought not to be taken into account. This can be expressed in our framework by defining another aggregate that decides, via entailment, when further advancing in a path does not contribute enough.

```
1  :- table reach(_,sum).            9  reach(N,P) :- path(a,N,P).
2  :- table path(_,_,thr(0.001)).   10
3                                    11  path(X,Y,P) :-
4  entails(sum,_,_) :- fails.       12      edge(X,Y,P).
5  join(sum, A, B, C) :-            13  path(X,Y,P) :-
6      C  is A + B.                 14      edge(X,Z,P1),
7  entails(thr(Epsilon), A, B):-    15      path(Z,Y,P2),
8      A < Epsilon * B.             16      P is P1 * P2.
```

In this example, for each node N, the predicate reach(_,sum) aggregates in its second argument the sum of the transition probabilities of the paths from a to N. Note we want to add all distances; therefore we define the entailment of sum to be always false. Since cyclic graphs have infinitely many paths, we have implemented the threshold aggregate, denoted by thr(Epsilon) to discard paths between X and Y whose relative contribution to the final results w.r.t. the contribution of another path falls below Epsilon.

5   Experimental Evaluation

We will now evaluate the expressiveness and performance of ATCLP w.r.t. pure Prolog and tabling. The ATCLP framework presented in this paper is based on TCLP, that is in turn implemented in Ciao Prolog. The examples, benchmarks, and a Ciao Prolog distribution including the libraries and frameworks presented in this paper are available at http://www.cliplab.org/papers/padl2019-atclp/.[4] All the experiments were performed on a Mac OS X 10.13.6 laptop with a 2 GHz Intel Core i5. Times are given in milliseconds.

We will first evaluate some implementations of the well-known minimax algorithm applied to (an extended version of) TicTacToe. Our starting point is the Prolog version from [3, 10] that uses `bagof/3` to collect the possible movements from a TicTacToe position and selects the best one. Thanks to the expressiveness of ATCLP, our code for the core minimax procedure (below) is considerably more compact (i.e., less number of predicates and arguments per predicate) than the equivalent Prolog or tabling code.

```
1   :- table minimax(_, first, best).
2
3   minimax(Pos, NextPos, (Pos,Val)) :-
4       move(Pos, NextPos),                    % Chose a move
5       minimax(NextPos, _, (NextPos, Val)).
6   minimax(Pos, Pos, (Pos,Val)) :-
7       \+ move(Pos, _),                       % Final position
8       utility(Pos,Val).                      % Calculate score
9
10  entails(best,(Pos,ValA),(Pos,ValB)) :-
11      min_to_move(Pos), ValA >= ValB.        % Minimizing
12  entails(best,(Pos,ValA),(Pos,ValB)) :-
13      max_to_move(Pos), ValA =< ValB.        % Maximizing
14  entails(first,_,_) :- true.                % Choose first best option
```

The ATCLP code chooses the best movement by applying the best aggregate which discards movements with worst (resp., best, depending on the current player) value. The infrastructure for aggregates transparently keeps track of gathering solutions and retains only the most relevant one at each moment. Note that we are using two different aggregates functions in the same predicate: best takes care of minimization/maximization and first retains only the first solution found among those with the same score.

We compared execution time and memory usage in two scenarios: determining the best initial movement for a 3×3 TicTacToe board and determining the best movement for a 4×4 TicTacToe starting at two different positions. In all three cases the remaining game tree was completely explored. The results (Table 1) show that the Prolog version is the slowest, with the tabling version being faster than the ATCLP version. However, the ATCLP version behaves considerably better than tabling in terms of table memory consumption (between parentheses, in Mb). This is because viewing aggregates as constraints automatically stops the search as soon as the value of an aggregate is worse than a previously found one. That makes the ATCLP version to terminate for cases where regular tabling runs out of memory.

---

[4] Stable versions of Ciao Prolog are available at http://www.ciao-lang.org. However, ATCLP is still in development and not fully available yet in the stable versions.

Table 1. Run time (ms), between parentheses the memory usage (in Mb) for Minimax with different initial boards.

	Prolog	tabling	ATCLP
3 × 3	1051	**167** (2)	359 **(1)**
4 × 4'	>5 min	**10166** (130)	15194 **(30)**
4 × 4"	>5 min	out of mem.	**134918 (252)**

The second benchmark is the *Game* problem presented in the LP/CP contest of ICLP 2015 (http://picat-lang.org/lp_cp_pc/Games.html). The problem can be seen as a graph traversal where the movements represent a decision regarding whether to repeat the same game or play a new one. There are two parameters to optimize: T, the remaining money, and F, the fun we have had (which can be negative). The final goal have as much fun as possible, for which one has to keep as much money as possible. The core of the algorithm, where we again want to stress its compactness, follows:

```
1   :- table total_fun(max).
2   total_fun(F) :-
3       reach(initial,end,_,F).
4
5   :- table reach(_,_,max,max).
6   reach(GameA,GameB,T,F) :-
7       edge(GameA,GameB,T,F).
8   reach(GameA,GameB,Tf,Ff) :-
9       reach(GameA,GameZ,T1,F1),
10      edge(GameZ,GameB,T2,F2),
11      Ff is F1 + F2,
12      Tm is T1 + T2, Tm >= 0,
13      ( cap(Cap), Tm > Cap ->
14      Tf is Cap ; Tf is Tm ).
```

We developed three versions of a program to solve this problem using Prolog, tabling, and ATCLP. Table 2 shows that the ATCLP on-the-fly aggregate computation performs better than either Prolog or tabling, since ATCLP does not try to evaluate states where T and F are worse than in states already evaluated.

Table 2. Run time (ms) comparison for *Games* with different scenarios.

	Prolog	Tabling	ATCLP
game_data_01	8062.49	14.66	**2.89**
game_data_02	>5 min.	37.59	**4.87**
game_data_03	>5 min.	1071.26	**19.61**
game_data_04	>5 min.	4883.00	**23.21**

6   Conclusion and Future Work

We have presented a framework to implement a type of aggregates, defined over a lattice structure, whose behavior is consistent with the least fixpoint semantics. We provide an interface so that final users can define the basic operations on which the aggregates are built. We validated the flexibility and expressiveness of our framework through several examples; we also evaluated their performance in a couple of benchmarks, which showed a positive balance between memory consumption and execution speed.

Among the immediate future plans, we want to work on increasing the performance of the system and improve the user interface. In many cases, the entails/3 and join/4 predicates can directly be generated from a mode definition by providing a predicate name. While this will not enhance performance or give more flexibility, it will make using the ATCLP interface more user-friendly. We also plan to include with ATCLP a library of commonly-used aggregate functions.

References

1. Arias, J., Carro, M.: Description and evaluation of a generic design to integrate CLP and tabled execution. In: International Symposium on Principles and Practice of Declarative Programming, pp. 10–23. ACM, September 2016
2. Arias, J., Carro, M.: Description, implementation, and evaluation of a generic design for tabled CLP. Theory and Practice of Logic Programming (2018) (to appear)
3. Bratko, I.: Prolog Programming for Artificial Intelligence. Pearson Education, London (2001)
4. Chico de Guzmán, P., Carro, M., Hermenegildo, M.V., Stuckey, P.: A general implementation framework for tabled CLP. In: Schrijvers, T., Thiemann, P. (eds.) FLOPS 2012. LNCS, vol. 7294, pp. 104–119. Springer, Heidelberg (2012). https://doi.org/10.1007/978-3-642-29822-6_11
5. Cui, B., Warren, D.S.: A system for tabled constraint logic programming. In: Lloyd, J., Dahl, V., Furbach, U., Kerber, M., Lau, K.-K., Palamidessi, C., Pereira, L.M., Sagiv, Y., Stuckey, P.J. (eds.) CL 2000. LNCS (LNAI), vol. 1861, pp. 478–492. Springer, Heidelberg (2000). https://doi.org/10.1007/3-540-44957-4_32
6. Guo, H.F., Gupta, G.: Simplifying dynamic programming via mode-directed tabling. Softw. Pract. Exp. 1, 75–94 (2008)
7. Holzbaur, C.: Metastructures vs. attributed variables in the context of extensible unification. In: Bruynooghe, M., Wirsing, M. (eds.) PLILP 1992. LNCS, vol. 631, pp. 260–268. Springer, Heidelberg (1992). https://doi.org/10.1007/3-540-55844-6_141
8. Kemp, D.B., Stuckey, P.J.: Semantics of logic programs with aggregates. In: Saraswat, V.A., Ueda, K. (eds.) International Symposium on Logic Programming, pp. 387–401. October 1991
9. Pelov, N., Denecker, M., Bruynooghe, M.: Well-founded and stable semantics of logic programs with aggregates. Theory Pract. Log. Program. 3, 301–353 (2007)
10. Picard, G.: Artificial intelligence - implementing minimax with prolog. https://www.emse.fr/~picard/cours/ai/minimax/
11. Santos Costa, V., Rocha, R., Damas, L.: The YAP prolog system. Theory Pract. Log. Program. 1–2, 5–34 (2012)
12. Schrijvers, T., Demoen, B., Warren, D.S.: TCHR: a Framework for tabled CLP. Theory Pract. Log. Program. 4, 491–526 (2008)
13. Swift, T., Warren, D.S.: Tabling with answer subsumption: implementation, applications and performance. In: Janhunen, T., Niemelä, I. (eds.) JELIA 2010. LNCS (LNAI), vol. 6341, pp. 300–312. Springer, Heidelberg (2010). https://doi.org/10.1007/978-3-642-15675-5_26
14. Swift, T., Warren, D.S.: XSB: extending prolog with tabled logic programming. Theory Pract. Log. Program. 1–2, 157–187 (2012)

15. Vandenbroucke, A., Pirog, M., Desouter, B., Schrijvers, T.: Tabling with sound answer sub-sumption. Theory Pract. Log. Program. **16**(5–6), 933–949 (2016). 32nd International Conference on Logic Programming
16. Zhou, N.F.: The language features and architecture of B-Prolog. Theory Pract. Log. Program. **1–2**, 189–218 (2012)
17. Zhou, N.F., Kameya, Y., Sato, T.: Mode-directed tabling for dynamic programming, machine learning, and constraint solving. In: International Conference on Tools with Artificial Intelligence, No. 2, pp. 213–218. IEEE, October 2010

A Combinatorial Testing Framework for Intuitionistic Propositional Theorem Provers

Paul Tarau[✉]

Department of Computer Science and Engineering,
University of North Texas, Denton, USA
paul.tarau@unt.edu

Abstract. Proving a theorem in intuitionistic propositional logic, with *implication* as its single connective, is known as one of the simplest to state PSPACE-complete problem. At the same time, via the Curry-Howard isomorphism, it is instrumental to find lambda terms that may inhabit a given type.

However, as hundreds of papers witness it, all starting with Gentzen's **LJ** calculus, conceptual simplicity has not come in this case with comparable computational counterparts. Implementing such theorem provers faces challenges related not only to soundness and completeness but also too termination and scalability problems.

In search for an efficient but minimalist theorem prover, on the two sides of the Curry-Howard isomorphism, we design a combinatorial testing framework using types inferred for lambda terms as well as all-term and random term generators.

We choose Prolog as our meta-language. Being derived from essentially the same formalisms as those we are covering, it reduces the semantic gap and results in surprisingly concise and efficient declarative implementations. Our implementation is available at: https://github.com/ptarau/TypesAndProofs.

Keywords: Curry-Howard isomorphism
Propositional implicational intuitionistic logic
Type inference and type inhabitation
Simply typed lambda terms
Logic programming · Propositional theorem provers
Combinatorial testing algorithms

1 Introduction

The implicational fragment of propositional intuitionistic logic can be defined by two axiom schemes:

$$K : \quad A \to (B \to A)$$
$$S : \quad (A \to (B \to C)) \to ((A \to B) \to (A \to C))$$

© Springer Nature Switzerland AG 2019
J. J. Alferes and M. Johansson (Eds.): PADL 2019, LNCS 11372, pp. 115–132, 2019.
https://doi.org/10.1007/978-3-030-05998-9_8

and the modus ponens inference rule:

$$MP: \quad A,\ A \to B \vdash B.$$

Our interest in theorem provers for this minimalist logic fragment has been triggered by its relation, via the Curry-Howard isomorphism, to the inverse problem, corresponding to inferring types for lambda terms, *type inhabitation*. In its simplest form, the Curry-Howard isomorphism [1,2] connects the implicational fragment of propositional intuitionistic logic and types in the *simply typed lambda calculus*. A low polynomial type inference algorithm associates a type (when it exists) to a lambda term. Harder (PSPACE-complete, see [3]) algorithms associate inhabitants to a given type expression with the resulting lambda term (typically in normal form) serving as a witness for the existence of a proof for the corresponding tautology in implicational propositional intuitionistic logic. As a consequence, a theorem prover for implicational propositional intuitionistic logic can also be seen as a tool for program synthesis, as implemented by code extraction algorithms in proof assistants like Coq [4].

This provides a simple and effective testing mechanism: by using as input the type of a lambda term known to have as an inhabitant the term itself. While only providing "positive examples" - formulas known to be tautologies, this is becoming increasingly difficult with size, as the asymptotic density of typable terms in the set of closed lambda terms has been shown to converge to 0 [5]. As a consequence, even our best generators [6], based on Boltzmann samplers, are limited to lambda terms in normal form of about size 60–70, given the very large number of retries needed to filter out untypable terms.

Thus, besides generating large simply typed lambda terms, we will need to devise testing methods also ensuring correct rejection of non-theorems and termination on arbitrary formulas.

This will lead us to a stepwise refinement from simpler to more efficient equivalent provers. We will start from a known, proven to be sound and complete prover as a first step, and use a *test-driven* approach to improve its performance and scalability while having soundness and completeness as invariants. As even small, apparently obvious changes in sound and complete provers can often break these properties, one must chose between writing a formal proof for each variant or setting up an extensive combinatorial and random testing framework, able to ensure correctness, with astronomically low chance of error, "at the push of a button".

We chose the second approach. Besides the ability to also evaluate scalability and performance of our provers, our combinatorial generation library, released as open source software, has good chances to be reused as a testing harness for other propositional solvers, (e.g., SAT, ASP or SMT solvers) with structurally similar formulas.

Our combinatorial testing framework comprises generators for

- simply typed lambda terms (in normal form) and their types
- formulas of the implicational subset of propositional calculus, requiring
  - generation of binary trees with internal nodes labeled with '->'
  - generation of set partitions helping to label variables in leaf position.

For quick correctness tests we build *all-formula* generators. Total counts for formulas of a given size for tautologies and non-tautologies provide an instant indicator for high-probability correctness. It also provides small false positives or negatives, helpful to explain and debug unexpected behavior.

For performance, scalability and termination tests, in the tradition of QuickCheck [7,8] we build *random formula generators*, with focus on ability to generate very large simply typed lambda terms and implicational formulas.

While our code at (https://github.com/ptarau/TypesAndProofs), covers a few dozen variants of implicational as well as full propositional provers, we will describe here a few that win on simplicity and/or scalable performance.

Notations and Assumptions. As we will use **Prolog** as our meta-language, our notations will be derived as much as possible from its syntax (including token types and operator definitions). Thus, variables will be denoted with upper-case letters and, as programmer's conventions final s letters indicate a plurality of items (e.g., when referring to the content of Γ contexts). We assume that the reader is familiar with basic Prolog programming, including, besides the pure Horn clause subset, well-known builtin predicates like `memberchk/2` and `select/3`, elements of higher order programming (e.g., `call/N`), and occasional use of CUT and `if-then-else` constructs.

Lambda terms are built using the function symbols $a/2$ = application, $l/2$ = lambda binder, with a logic variable as first argument and expression as second, as well as *logic variables* representing the variables of the terms.

Type expressions (also seen as implicational formulas) are built as binary trees with the function symbol `->/2` and *logic variables at their leaves*.

The Paper Is Organized as Follows. Section 2 overviews the **LJT** sequent calculus for implicational propositional intuitionistic logic. Section 3 describes, starting with a direct encoding of the **LJT** calculus as a Prolog program, derivation steps leading to simpler and faster provers. Section 4 describes our testing framework. Section 5 overviews related work and Sect. 6 concludes the paper.

2   Proof Systems for Implicational Propositional Intuitionistic Logic

Initially, like for other fields of mathematics and logic, Hilbert-style axioms were considered for intuitionistic logic. While simple and directly mapped to SKI-combinators via the Curry-Howard isomorphism, their usability for automation is very limited. In fact, their inadequacy for formalizing even "hand-written" mathematics was the main trigger of Gentzen's work on natural deduction and sequent calculus, inspired by the need for formal reasoning in the foundation of mathematics [9].

Thus, we start with Gentzen's own calculus for intuitionistic logic, simplified here to only cover the purely implicational fragment, given that our focus is on theorem provers working on formulas that correspond to types of simply-typed lambda terms.

2.1 Gentzen's LJ Calculus, Restricted to the Implicational Fragment of Propositional Intuitionistic Logic

We assume familiarity with basic sequent calculus notation. Gentzen's original LJ calculus [9] (with the equivalent notation of [10]) uses the following rules.

$$LJ_1 : \quad \frac{}{A, \Gamma \vdash A}$$

$$LJ_2 : \quad \frac{A, \Gamma \vdash B}{\Gamma \vdash A \to B}$$

$$LJ_3 : \quad \frac{A \to B, \Gamma \vdash A \quad B, \Gamma \vdash G}{A \to B, \Gamma \vdash G}$$

As one can easily see, when trying a goal-driven implementation that uses the rules in upward direction, the unchanged premises on left side of rule LJ_3 would not ensure termination as nothing prevents A and G from repeatedly trading places during the inference process.

2.2 Roy Dyckhoff's LJT Calculus, Restricted to the Implicational Fragment of Propositional Intuitionistic Logic

Motivated by problems related to loop avoidance in implementing Gentzen's **LJ** calculus, Roy Dyckhoff [10] splits rule LJ_3 into LJT_3 and LJT_4.

$$LJT_1 : \quad \frac{}{A, \Gamma \vdash A}$$

$$LJT_2 : \quad \frac{A, \Gamma \vdash B}{\Gamma \vdash A \to B}$$

$$LJT_3 : \quad \frac{B, A, \Gamma \vdash G}{A \to B, A, \Gamma \vdash G}$$

$$LJT_4 : \quad \frac{D \to B, \Gamma \vdash C \to D \quad B, \Gamma \vdash G}{(C \to D) \to B, \Gamma \vdash G}$$

This avoids the need for loop checking to ensure termination as one can identify a multiset ordering-based size definition that decreases after each step [10]. The rules work with the context Γ being a multiset, but it has been shown later [11] that Γ can be a set, with duplication in contexts eliminated.

As it is not unusual with logic formalisms, the same calculus had been discovered independently in the 50's by Vorob'ev and in the 80's–90's by Hudelmaier [12,13].

3   The Test-Driven Prover Derivation Process

Starting from this calculus, we will describe our "test-driven" derivation process for simpler and/or more efficient provers that will be validated at each step by our testing framework described in the next section.

3.1   An Executable Specification: Dyckhoff's LJT Calculus, Literally

Roy Dyckhoff has implemented the **LJT** calculus as a Prolog program.

We have ported it to SWI-Prolog as a reference implementation (see https://github.com/ptarau/TypesAndProofs/blob/master/third_party/dyckhoff_orig.pro). However, it is a fairly large (420 lines) program, partly because it covers the full set of intuitionistic connectives and partly because of the complex heuristics that it implements.

This brings up the question if, in the tradition of "lean theorem provers", we can build one directly from the LJT calculus, in a goal oriented style, by reading the rules from conclusions to premises.

Thus, we start with a simple, almost literal translation of rules $LJT_1 \ldots LJT_4$ to Prolog with values in the environment Γ denoted by the variable Vs.

```
lprove(T):-ljt(T,[]),!.

ljt(A,Vs):-memberchk(A,Vs),!.           % LJT_1
ljt((A->B),Vs):-!,ljt(B,[A|Vs]).        % LJT_2
ljt(G,Vs1):- %atomic(G),                % LJT_3
  select((A->B),Vs1,Vs2),
  memberchk(A,Vs2),
  !,
  ljt(G,[B|Vs2]).
ljt(G,Vs1):-                            % LJT_4
  select( ((C->D)->B),Vs1,Vs2),
  ljt((C->D), [(D->B)|Vs2]),
  !,
  ljt(G,[B|Vs2]).
```

Note the use of `select/3` to extract a term from the environment (a nondeterministic step) and termination, via a multiset ordering based measure [10]. An example of use is:

```
?- lprove(a->b->a).
true.
?- lprove((a->b)->a).
false.
```

Note also that integers can be used instead of atoms, flexibility that we will use as needed.

Besides the correctness of the **LJT** rule set (as proved in [10]), given that the prover has passed our tests, it looks like being already quite close to our interest in a "lean" prover for the implicational fragment of propositional intuitionistic logic.

However, given the extensive test set (see Sect. 4) that we have developed, it is not hard to get tempted in getting it simpler and faster, knowing that the smallest error will be instantly caught.

3.2 Concentrating Nondeterminism into One Place

We start with a transformation that keeps the underlying implicational formula unchanged. It merges the work of the two `select/3` calls into a single call, observing that their respective clauses do similar things after the call to `select/3`. That avoids redoing the same iteration over candidates for reduction.

```
bprove(T):-ljb(T,[]),!.

ljb(A,Vs):-memberchk(A,Vs),!.
ljb((A->B),Vs):-!,ljb(B,[A|Vs]).
ljb(G,Vs1):-
   select((A->B),Vs1,Vs2),
   ljb_imp(A,B,Vs2),
   !,
   ljb(G,[B|Vs2]).

ljb_imp((C->D),B,Vs):-!,ljb((C->D),[(D->B)|Vs]).
ljb_imp(A,_,Vs):-atomic(A),memberchk(A,Vs).
```

This results on our tests (see Sect. 4 for details) in an improvement on a mix of tautologies and non-tautologies, in exchange for a slowdown on formulas known to be tautologies.

3.3 Implicational Formulas as Nested Horn Clauses

Given the equivalence between: $B_1 \to B_2 \ldots B_n \to H$ and (in Prolog notation) $H :- B_1, B_2, \ldots, B_n$, (where we choose H as the *atomic* formula ending a chain of implications), we can, recursively, transform an implicational formula into one built form nested clauses, as follows.

```
toHorn((A->B),(H:-Bs)):-!,toHorns((A->B),Bs,H).
toHorn(H,H).

toHorns((A->B),[HA|Bs],H):-!,toHorn(A,HA),toHorns(B,Bs,H).
toHorns(H,[],H).
```

Note also that the transformation is reversible and that lists (instead of Prolog's conjunction chains) are used to collect the elements of the body of a clause.

```
?- toHorn(((0->1->2->3->4)->(0->1->2)->0->2->3),R).
R =  (3:-[(4:-[0, 1, 2, 3]),  (2:-[0, 1]), 0, 2]).
```

This suggests transforming provers for implicational formulas into equivalent provers working on nested Horn clauses.

```
hprove(T0):-toHorn(T0,T),ljh(T,[]),!.

ljh(A,Vs):-memberchk(A,Vs),!.
ljh((B:-As),Vs1):-!,append(As,Vs1,Vs2),ljh(B,Vs2).
ljh(G,Vs1):-                % atomic(G), G not in Vs1
  memberchk((G:-_),Vs1),    % if not, we just fail!
  select((B:-As),Vs1,Vs2),  % outer select loop
  select(A,As,Bs),          % inner select loop
  ljh_imp(A,B,Vs2),         % A is an element of the body of B
  !,
  trimmed((B:-Bs),NewB),    % trim off empty bodies
  ljh(G,[NewB|Vs2]).

ljh_imp((D:-Cs),B,Vs):-!,ljh((D:-Cs),[(B:-[D])|Vs]).
ljh_imp(A,_B,Vs):-memberchk(A,Vs).

trimmed((B:-[]),R):-!,R=B.
trimmed(BBs,BBs).
```

A first improvement, ensuring quicker rejection of non-theorems is the call to memberchk in the 3-rd clause to ensure that our goal G is the head of at least one of the assumptions. Once that test is passed, the 3-rd clause works as a reducer of the assumed hypotheses. It removes from the context a clause B:-As and it removes from its body a formula A, to be passed to ljh_imp, with the remaining context. Should A be atomic, we succeed if and only if it is already in the context. Otherwise, we closely mimic rule LJT_4 by trying to prove A = (D:-Cs), after extending the context with the assumption B:-[D]. Note that in both cases the context gets smaller, as As does not contain the A anymore. Moreover, should the body Bs end up empty, the clause is downgraded to its atomic head by the predicate trimmed/2. Also, by having a second select/3 call in the third clause of ljh, will give ljh_imp more chances to succeed and commit.

Thus, besides quickly filtering out failing search branches, the nested Horn clause form of implicational logic helps bypass some intermediate steps, by focusing on the head of the Horn clause, which corresponds to the last atom in a chain of implications.

The transformation brings to hprove/1 an extra 66% performance gain over bprove/1 on terms of size 15, which scales up to run as much as 29 times faster on terms of size 16.

3.4 Propagating Back the Elimination of Non-matching Heads

We can propagate back to the implicational forms used in bprover the observation made on the Horn-clause form that heads (as computed below) should match at least one assumption.

```
head_of(_->B,G):-!,head_of(B,G).
head_of(G,G).
```

We can apply this to bprove/1 as shown in the 3-rd clause of lje, where we can also prioritize the assumption found to have the head G, by placing it first in the context.

```
eprove(T):-lje(T,[]),!.

lje(A,Vs):-memberchk(A,Vs),!.
lje((A->B),Vs):-!,lje(B,[A|Vs]).
lje(G,Vs0):-
  select(T,Vs0,Vs1),head_of(T,G),!,
  select((A->B),[T|Vs1],Vs2),lje_imp(A,B,Vs2),!,
  lje(G,[B|Vs2]).

lje_imp((C->D),B,Vs):-!,lje((C->D),[(D->B)|Vs]).
lje_imp(A,_,Vs):-atomic(A),memberchk(A,Vs).
```

This brings the performance of eprove within a few percents of hprove.

3.5 Extracting the Proof Terms

Extracting the *proof terms* (lambda terms having the formulas we prove as types) is achieved by decorating in the code with application nodes a/2, lambda nodes l/2 (with first argument a logic variable) and leaf nodes (with logic variables, same as the identically named ones in the first argument of the corresponding l/2 nodes).

The simplicity of the predicate eprove/1 and the fact that this is essentially the inverse of a type inference algorithm (e.g., the one in [14]) help with figuring out how the decoration mechanism works.

```
sprove(T):-ljs(X,T,[]),!.

ljs(X,A,Vs):-memberchk(X:A,Vs),!. % leaf variable
ljs(l(X,E),(A->B),Vs):-!,ljs(E,B,[X:A|Vs]). % lambda term
ljs(E,G,Vs1):-
  select(S:(A->B),Vs1,Vs2),    % source of application
  ljs_imp(T,A,B,Vs2),          % target of application
  !,
  ljs(E,G,[a(S,T):B|Vs2]).     % application

ljs_imp(X,A,_,Vs):-atomic(A),!,memberchk(X:A,Vs).
ljs_imp(E,(C->D),B,Vs):-ljs(E,(C->D),[_:(D->B)|Vs]).
```

Thus, lambda nodes decorate *implication introductions* and application nodes decorate *modus ponens* reductions in the corresponding calculus. Note that the two clauses of ljs_imp provide the target node T. When seen from the type inference side, T is the type resulting from cancelling the source type S and the application type $S \rightarrow T$.

Calling `sprove/2` on the formulas corresponding to the types of the S, K and I combinators, we obtain:

```
?- sprove(((0->1->2)->(0->1)->0->2),X).
X = l(A, l(B, l(C, a(a(A, C), a(B, C))))).          % S
?- sprove((0->1->0),X).
X = l(A, l(B, A)).                                  % K
?- sprove((0->0),X).
X = l(A, A).                                        % I
```

4   The Testing Framework

Correctness can be checked by identifying false positives or false negatives. A false positive is a non-tautology that the prover proves, breaking the *soundness* property. A false negative is a tautology that the prover fails to prove, breaking the *completeness* property. While classical tautologies are easily tested (at small scale against truth tables, at medium scale with classical propositional provers and at larger scale with a SAT solver), intuitionistic provers require a more creative approach, given the absence of a finite truth-value table model.

As a first bootstrapping step, assuming that no "gold standard" prover is available, one can look at the other side of the Curry-Howard isomorphism, and rely on generators of (typable) lambda terms and generators implicational logic formulas, with results being checked against a trusted type inference algorithm.

As a next step, a trusted prover can be used as a "gold standard" to test both for false positives and negatives.

4.1   Finding False Negatives by Generating the Set of Simply Typed Normal Forms of a Given Size

A false negative is identified if our prover fails on a type expression known to have an inhabitant. Via the Curry-Howard isomorphism, such terms are the types inferred for lambda terms, generated by increasing sizes. In fact, this means that all implicational formulas having proofs shorter than a given number are all covered, but possibly small formulas having long proofs might not be reachable with this method that explores the search by the size of the proof rather than the size of the formula to be proven. We refer to [14] for a detailed description of efficient algorithms generating pairs of simply typed lambda terms in normal form together with their principal types. The code we use here is at: https://github.com/ptarau/TypesAndProofs/blob/master/allTypedNFs.pro

4.2   Finding False Positives by Generating All Implicational Formulas/Type Expressions of a Given Size

A false positive is identified if the prover succeeds finding an inhabitant for a type expression that does not have one.

We obtain type expressions by generating all binary trees of a given size, extracting their leaf variables and then iterating over the set of their set partitions, while unifying variables belonging to the same partition. We refer to [14] for a detailed description of the algorithms.

The code describing the all-tree and set partition generation as well as their integration as a type expression generator is at:

https://github.com/ptarau/TypesAndProofs/blob/master/allPartitions.pro.

We have tested the predicate lprove/1 as well as all other provers derived from it for false negatives against simple types of terms up to size 15 (with size defined as 2 for applications, 1 for lambdas and 0 for variables) and for false positives against all type expressions up to size 7 (with size defined as the number of internal nodes).

An advantage of exhaustive testing with all formulas of a given size is that it implicitly ensures coverage: no path is missed simply because there are no paths left unexplored.

4.3   Testing Against a Trusted Reference Implementation

Assuming we trust an existing reference implementation (e.g., after it passes our generator-based tests), it makes sense to use it as a "gold standard". In this case, we can identify both false positives and negatives directly, as follows:

```
gold_test(N,Generator,Gold,Silver, Term, Res):-call(Generator,N,Term),
  gold_test_one(Gold,Silver,Term, Res),
  Res\=agreement.

gold_test_one(Gold,Silver,T, Res):-
  ( call(Silver,T) -> \+ call(Gold,T),
    Res = wrong_success
  ; call(Gold,T) -> % \+ Silver
    Res = wrong_failure
  ; Res = agreement
  ).
```

When specializing to a generator for all well-formed implication expressions, and using Dyckhoff's dprove/1 predicate as a gold standard, we have:

```
gold_test(N, Silver, Culprit, Unexp):-
  gold_test(N,allImpFormulas,dprove,Silver,Culprit,Unexp).
```

To test the tester, we design a prover that randomly succeeds or fails.

```
badProve(_) :- 0 =:= random(2).
```

We can now test lprove/1 and badprove/1 as follows:

```
?- gold_test(6,lprove,T,R).
false. % indicates that no false positive or negative is found

?- gold_test(6,badProve,T,R).
```

```
T =  (0->1->0->0->0->0->0),
R = wrong_failure ;
...
?- gold_test(6,badProve,T,wrong_success).
T =  (0->1->0->0->0->0->2) ;
...
```

A more interesting case is when a prover is only guilty of false positives. For instance, let's naively implement the intuition that a goal is provable w.r.t. an environment Vs if all its premises are provable, with implication introduction assuming premises and success achieved when the environment is reduced to empty.

```
badSolve(A):-badSolve(A,[]).

badSolve(A,Vs):-atomic(A),!,memberchk(A,Vs).
badSolve((A->B),Vs):-badSolve(B,[A|Vs]).
badSolve(_,Vs):-badReduce(Vs).

badReduce([]):-!.
badReduce(Vs):-select(V,Vs,NewVs),badSolve(V,NewVs),badReduce(NewVs).
```

As the following test shows, while no tautology is missed, the false positives are properly caught.

```
?- gold_test(6,badSolve,T,wrong_failure).
false.

?- gold_test(6,badSolve,T,wrong_success).
T =  (0->0->0->0->0->0->1) ;
...
```

4.4   Random Simply-Typed Terms, with Boltzmann Samplers

Once passing correctness tests, our provers need to be tested against large random terms. The mechanism is similar to the use of all-term generators.

We generate random simply-typed normal forms, using a Boltzmann sampler along the lines of that described in [6]. The code variant, adapted to our different term-size definition is at: https://github.com/ptarau/TypesAndProofs/blob/master/ranNormalForms.pro.   It works as follows:

```
?- ranTNF(60,XT,TypeSize).
XT = l(l(a(a(0, l(a(a(0, a(0, l(...))), s(s(0)))),
             l(l(a(a(0, a(l(...), a(..., ...))), l(0))))))))
      :
        (A->((((A->A)- ...)->D)->D)->M)->M),
TypeSize = 34.
```

Interestingly, partly due to the fact that there's some variation in the size of the terms that Boltzmann samplers generate, and more to the fact that the distribution of types favors (as seen in the second example) the simple tautologies where an atom identical to the last one is contained in the implication chain leading to it [5,15], if we want to use these for scalability tests, additional filtering mechanisms need to be used to statically reject type expressions that are large but easy to prove as intuitionistic tautologies.

4.5 Random Implicational Formulas

The generation of random implicational formulas is more intricate.

Our code combines an implementation of Rémy's algorithm [16], along the lines of Knuth's algorithm **R** in [17] for the *generation of random binary* trees at https://github.com/ptarau/TypesAndProofs/blob/master/RemyR.pro with code to generate *random set partitions* at:
https://github.com/ptarau/TypesAndProofs/blob/master/ranPartition.pro.

We refer to [18] for a declarative implementation of Rémy's algorithm in Prolog with code adapted for this paper at:
https://github.com/ptarau/TypesAndProofs/blob/master/RemyP.pro.

As automatic Boltzmann sampler generation of set partitions is limited to fixed numbers of equivalence classes from which a CF- grammar can be given, we build our random set partition generator that groups variables in leaf position into equivalence classes by using an urn-algorithm [19]. Once a random binary tree of size N is generated with the ->/2 constructor labeling internal nodes, the $N + 1$ leaves of the tree are decorated with variables denoted by successive integers starting from 0. As variables sharing a name define equivalence classes on the set of variables, each choice of them corresponds to a set partition of the $N+1$ nodes. Thus, a set partition of the leaves $\{0,1,2,3\}$ like $\{\{0\},\{1,2\},\{3\}\}$ will correspond to the variable leaf decorations

$$0, 1, 1, 2$$

The partition generator works as follows:

```
?- ranSetPart(7,Vars).
Vars = [0, 1, 2, 1, 1, 2, 3] .
```

Note that the list of labels it generates can be directly used to decorate the random binary tree generated by Rémy's algorithm, by unifying the list of variables Vs with it.

```
?- remy(6,T,Vs).
T =   ((((A->B)->C->D)->E->F)->G),
Vs = [A, B, C, D, E, F, G] .
```

The combined generator, that produces in a few seconds terms of size 1000, works as follows:

```
?- time(ranImpFormula(1000,_)).
% includes tabling large Stirling numbers
% 37,245,709 inferences,7.501 CPU in
7.975 seconds (94% CPU, 4965628 Lips)

?- time(ranImpFormula(1000,_)). % fast, thanks to tabling
% 107,163 inferences,0.040 CPU in
0.044 seconds (92% CPU, 2659329 Lips)
```

Note that we use Prolog's *tabling* (a form of automated dynamic programming) to avoid costly recomputation of the (very large) Stirling numbers in the code at: https://github.com/ptarau/TypesAndProofs/blob/master/ranPartition.pro.

4.6 Testing with Large Random Terms

Testing for false positives and false negatives for random terms proceeds in a similar manner to exhaustive testing with terms of a given size.

Assuming Roy Dyckhoff's prover as a gold standard, we can find out that our bprove/1 program can handle 20 terms of size 50 as well as the gold standard.

```
?- gold_ran_imp_test(20,100,bprove, Culprit, Unexpected).
false. % indicates no differences with the gold standard
```

In fact, the size of the random terms handled by bprove/1 makes using provers an appealing alternative to random lambda term generators in search for very large (lambda term, simple type) pairs. Interestingly, on the side of random simply typed terms, limitations come from their vanishing density, while on the other side they come from the known PSPACE-complete complexity of the proof procedures.

4.7 Scalability Tests

Besides the correctness and completeness test sets described so far, one might want also ensure that the performance of the derived provers scales up to larger terms. Given space constraints, we only show here a few such performance tests and refer the reader to our benchmarks at: https://github.com/ptarau/TypesAndProofs/blob/master/bm.pro.

Time is measured in seconds. The tables in Fig. 1 compare several provers on exhaustive "all-terms" benchmarks, derived from our correctness test.

First, we run them on the types inferred on all simply typed lambda terms of a given size. Note that some of the resulting types in this case can be larger and some smaller than the sizes of their inhabitants. We place them in the column *Positive* - as they are known to be all provable.

Prover	Size	Positive	Mix	Total Time
lprove	13	0.979	0.261	1.24
lprove	14	4.551	5.564	10.116
lprove	15	30.014	5.568	35.583
lprove	16	3053.202	168.074	3221.277
bprove	13	0.943	0.203	1.147
bprove	14	4.461	4.294	8.755
bprove	15	32.206	4.306	36.513
bprove	16	3484.203	129.91	3614.114
dprove	13	5.299	0.798	6.098
dprove	14	23.161	13.514	36.675
dprove	15	107.264	13.645	120.909
dprove	16	1270.586	240.301	1510.887

Prover	Size	Positive	Mix	Total Time
hprove	13	1.007	0.111	1.119
hprove	14	4.413	1.818	6.231
hprove	15	20.09	1.836	21.927
hprove	**16**	**90.595**	**30.713**	**121.308**
eprove	13	1.07	0.132	1.203
eprove	14	4.746	2.27	7.017
eprove	15	21.562	2.248	23.81
eprove	16	97.811	43.18	140.991
sprove	13	1.757	0.173	1.931
sprove	14	8.037	2.966	11.003
sprove	15	38.266	2.941	41.208
sprove	16	188.317	54.802	243.12

Fig. 1. Performance of provers on exhaustive tests (faster ones in the right table)

Next, we run them on all implicational formulas of a given size, set to be about half of the former (integer part of size divided by 2), as the number of these grows much faster. We place them in the column *Mix* as they are a mix of provable and unprovable formulas.

The predicate hprove/1 turns out to be an overall winner, followed closely by eprove/1 that applies to implicational forms a technique borrowed from hprove/1 to quickly filter out failing search branches.

Testing exhaustively on small formulas, while an accurate indicator for average speed, might not favor provers using more complex heuristics or extensive preprocessing, as it is the case of Dyckhoff's original dprove/1.

We conclude that early rejection via the test we have discovered in the nested Horn clause form is a clear separator between the slow provers in the left table and the fast ones in the right table, a simple and useful "mutation" worth propagating to full propositional and first order provers.

As the focus of this paper was to develop a testing methodology for propositional theorem provers, we have not applied more intricate heuristics to further improve performance or to perform better on "human-made" benchmarks or compare them on such tests with other provers, as there are no purely implicational tests among at the ILTP library [20] at http://www.iltp.de/. On the other hand, for our full intuitionistic propositional provers at https://github.com/ptarau/TypesAndProofs, as well as our Python-based ones at https://github.com/ptarau/PythonProvers, we have adapted the ILTP benchmarks on which we plan to report in a future paper.

5   Related Work

The related work derived from Gentzen's **LJ** calculus is in the hundreds if not in the thousands of papers and books. Space constraints limit our discussion to the most closely related papers, directly focusing on algorithms for implicational intuitionistic propositional logic, which, as decision procedures, ensure termination without a loop-checking mechanism.

Among them the closest are [10,11], that we have used as starting points for deriving our provers. We have chosen to implement the **LJT** calculus directly rather than deriving our programs from Roy Dyckhoff's Prolog code. At the same time, as in Roy Dyckhoff's original prover, we have benefitted from the elegant, loop-avoiding rewriting step also present in Hudelmaier's work [12,13]. Similar calculi, key ideas of which made it into the Coq proof assistant's code, are described in [21].

On the other side of the Curry-Howard isomorphism, the thesis [22], described in full detail in [23], finds and/or counts inhabitants of simple types in long normal form. But interestingly, these algorithms have not crossed, at our best knowledge, to the other side of the Curry-Howard isomorphism, in the form of theorem provers.

Using hypothetical implications in Prolog, although all with a different semantics than Gentzen's **LJ** calculus or its **LJT** variant, go back as early as [24,25], followed by a series of λProlog-related publications, e.g., [26]. The similarity to the propositional subsets of N-Prolog [25] and λ-Prolog [26] comes from their close connection to intuitionistic logic. The hereditary Harrop formulas of [26], when restricted to their implicational subset, are much easily computable with a direct mapping to Prolog, without the need of theorem prover. While closer to an **LJ**-based calculus, the execution algorithm of [25] uses restarts on loop detection instead of ensuring termination along the lines the **LJT** calculus. In [27] backtrackable linear and intuitionistic assumptions that mimic the implication introduction rule are used, but they do not involve arbitrarily deep nested implicational formulas.

Overviews of closely related calculi, using the implicational subset of propositional intuitionistic logic are [11,28].

For generators of random lambda terms and related functional programming constructs we refer to [7,8]. We have shared with them the goal of achieving high-probability correctness via automated combinatorial testing. Given our specific focus on propositional provers, we have been able to use all-term and all-formula generators as well as comparison mechanisms with "gold-standard" provers. We have also taken advantage of the Curry-Howard isomorphism between types and formulas to provide an initial set of known tautologies, usable as "bootstrapping mechanism" allowing to test our provers independently from using a "gold-standard".

6   Conclusions and Future Work

Our code base at https://github.com/ptarau/TypesAndProofs provides an extensive test-driven development framework built on several cross-testing opportunities between type inference algorithms for lambda terms and theorem provers for propositional intuitionistic logic.

It also contains the code of the provers presented in the paper together with several other provers and "human-made" test sets.

Our lightweight implementations of these theoretically hard (PSPACE-complete) combinatorial search problems, are also more likely than provers using complex heuristics, to be turned into parallel implementations using multi-core and GPU algorithms.

Among them, provers working on nested Horn clauses outperformed those working directly on implicational formulas. The fact that conjunctions in their body are associative and commutative also opens opportunities for AND-parallel execution.

Given that they share their main data structures with Prolog, it also seems interesting to attempt their partial evaluation or even compilation to Prolog via a source-to-source transformation. At the same time, the nested Horn clause provers might be worth formalizing as a calculus and subject to deeper theoretical analysis. We plan future work in formally describing the nested Horn-clause prover in sequent-calculus as well as exploring compilation techniques and new parallel algorithms for it. A generalization to nested Horn clauses with conjunctions and universally quantified variables seems also promising to explore, especially with grounding techniques as used by SAT and ASP solvers, or via compilation to Prolog.

Acknowledgement. This research has been supported by NSF grant 1423324. We thank the reviewers of PADL'19 for their constructive comments and suggestions for improvement.

References

1. Howard, W.: The formulae-as-types notion of construction. In: Seldin, J., Hindley, J. (eds.) To H.B. Curry: Essays on Combinatory Logic, Lambda Calculus and Formalism, pp. 479–490. Academic Press, London (1980)
2. Wadler, P.: Propositions as types. Commun. ACM **58**, 75–84 (2015)
3. Statman, R.: Intuitionistic propositional logic is polynomial-space complete. Theor. Comput. Sci. **9**, 67–72 (1979)
4. The Coq development team: The Coq proof assistant reference manual (2018) Version 8.8.0
5. Kostrzycka, Z., Zaionc, M.: Asymptotic densities in logic and type theory. Studia Logica **88**(3), 385–403 (2008)

6. Bendkowski, M., Grygiel, K., Tarau, P.: Random generation of closed simply typed λ-terms: a synergy between logic programming and Boltzmann samplers. TPLP **18**(1), 97–119 (2018)
7. Claessen, K., Hughes, J.: QuickCheck: a lightweight tool for random testing of haskell programs. SIGPLAN Not. **46**(4), 53–64 (2011)
8. Palka, M.H., Claessen, K., Russo, A., Hughes, J.: Testing an optimising compiler by generating random lambda terms. In: Proceedings of the 6th International Workshop on Automation of Software Test, AST 2011, pp. 91–97. ACM, New York (2011)
9. Szabo, M.E.: The collected papers of Gerhard Gentzen. Philos. Sci. **39**(1), 91 (1972)
10. Dyckhoff, R.: Contraction-free sequent calculi for intuitionistic logic. J. Symbolic Logic **57**(3), 795–807 (1992)
11. Dyckhoff, R.: Intuitionistic decision procedures since Gentzen. In: Kahle, R., Strahm, T., Studer, T. (eds.) Advances in Proof Theory. PCSAL, vol. 28, pp. 245–267. Springer, Cham (2016). https://doi.org/10.1007/978-3-319-29198-7_6
12. Hudelmaier, J.: A PROLOG Program for Intuitionistic Logic. SNS-Bericht-. Universität Tübingen (1988)
13. Hudelmaier, J.: An O(n log n)-space decision procedure for intuitionistic propositional logic. J. Logic Comput. **3**(1), 63–75 (1993)
14. Tarau, P.: A hiking trip through the orders of magnitude: deriving efficient generators for closed simply-typed lambda terms and normal forms. In: Hermenegildo, M.V., Lopez-Garcia, P. (eds.) LOPSTR 2016. LNCS, vol. 10184, pp. 240–255. Springer, Cham (2017). https://doi.org/10.1007/978-3-319-63139-4_14
15. Genitrini, A., Kozik, J., Zaionc, M.: Intuitionistic vs. classical tautologies, quantitative comparison. In: Miculan, M., Scagnetto, I., Honsell, F. (eds.) TYPES 2007. LNCS, vol. 4941, pp. 100–109. Springer, Heidelberg (2008). https://doi.org/10.1007/978-3-540-68103-8_7
16. Rémy, J.L.: Un procédé itératif de dénombrement d'arbres binaires et son application à leur génération aléatoire. RAIRO - Theoretical Informatics and Applications - Informatique Théorique et Applications **19**(2), 179–195 (1985)
17. Knuth, D.E.: The Art of Computer Programming, Volume 4, Fascicle 4: Generating All Trees-History of Combinatorial Generation (Art of Computer Programming). Addison-Wesley Professional, Upper Saddle River (2006)
18. Tarau, P.: Declarative algorithms for generation, counting and random sampling of term algebras. In: Proceedings of SAC 2018, ACM Symposium on Applied Computing, PL track. ACM, Pau, April 2018
19. Stam, A.: Generation of a random partition of a finite set by an urn model. J. Comb. Theory Ser. A **35**(2), 231–240 (1983)
20. Raths, T., Otten, J., Kreitz, C.: The ILTP problem library for intuitionistic logic: release v1.1. J. Autom. Reasoning **38**, 261–271 (2007)
21. Herbelin, H.: A λ-calculus structure isomorphic to Gentzen-style sequent calculus structure. In: Pacholski, L., Tiuryn, J. (eds.) CSL 1994. LNCS, vol. 933, pp. 61–75. Springer, Heidelberg (1995). https://doi.org/10.1007/BFb0022247
22. Ben-Yelles, C.B.: Type assignment in the lambda-calculus: syntax and semantics. PhD thesis, University College of Swansea (1979)
23. Hindley, J.R.: Basic Simple Type Theory. Cambridge University Press, New York (1997)

24. Gabbay, D.M., Reyle, U.: N-Prolog: an extension of prolog with hypothetical implications I. J. Logic Program. **1**(4), 319–355 (1984)
25. Gabbay, D.M.: N-Prolog: an extension of prolog with hypothetical implication II. Logical foundations, and negation as failure. J. Logic Program. **2**(4), 251–283 (1985)
26. Miller, D., Nadathur, G.: Programming with Higher-Order Logic. Cambridge University Press, New York (2012)
27. Tarau, P., Dahl, V., Fall, A.: Backtrackable state with linear affine implication and assumption grammars. In: Jaffar, J., Yap, R.H.C. (eds.) ASIAN 1996. LNCS, vol. 1179, pp. 53–63. Springer, Heidelberg (1996). https://doi.org/10.1007/BFb0027779
28. Gabbay, D., Olivetti, N.: Goal-oriented deductions. In: Gabbay, D.M., Guenthner, F. (eds.) Handbook of Philosophical Logic. Handbook of Philosophical Logic, vol. 9, pp. 199–285. Springer, Dordrecht (2002). https://doi.org/10.1007/978-94-017-0464-9_4

Faster Coroutine Pipelines:
A Reconstruction

Ruben P. Pieters$^{(\boxtimes)}$ⓘ and Tom Schrijversⓘ

KU Leuven, 3001 Leuven, Belgium
{ruben.pieters,tom.schrijvers}@cs.kuleuven.be

Abstract. Spivey has recently presented a novel functional representation that supports the efficient composition, or *merging*, of coroutine pipelines for processing streams of data. This representation was inspired by Shivers and Might's three-continuation approach and is shown to be equivalent to a simple yet inefficient executable specification. Unfortunately, neither Shivers and Might's original work nor the equivalence proof sheds much light on the underlying principles allowing the derivation of this efficient representation from its specification.

This paper gives the missing insight by reconstructing a systematic derivation in terms of known transformation steps from the simple specification to the efficient representation. This derivation sheds light on the limitations of the representation and on its applicability to other settings. In particular, it has enabled us to obtain a similar representation for pipes featuring two-way communication, similar to the Haskell **pipes** library. Our benchmarks confirm that this two-way representation retains the same improved performance characteristics.

Keywords: Stream processing · Structured recursion · Algebra

1 Introduction

Coroutine pipelines provide a compositional approach to processing streams of data that is both efficient in time and space, thanks to a targeted form of lazy evaluation interacting well with side-effects like I/O. Two prominent Haskell libraries for coroutine pipelines are **pipes** [5] and **conduit** [11]. Common to both libraries is their representation of pipelines by an algebraic data type (ADT).

Spivey [12] has recently presented a novel Haskell representation that is entirely function-based. His representation is an adaptation of Shivers and Might's earlier three-continuation representation [10] and exhibits a very efficient *merge* operation for connecting pipes.

Spivey proves that his representation is equivalent to a simple ADT-based specification. Yet, neither his proof nor Shivers and Might's explanation sheds much light on the underlying principles used to come up with the efficient representation. This makes it difficult to adapt the representation to other settings.

© Springer Nature Switzerland AG 2019
J. J. Alferes and M. Johansson (Eds.): PADL 2019, LNCS 11372, pp. 133–149, 2019.
https://doi.org/10.1007/978-3-030-05998-9_9

This paper remedies the situation by systematically deriving the efficient function-based representation from the simple, but inefficient ADT-based representation. Our derivation consists of known transformations and constructions that are centered around folds with appropriate algebras. Our derivation clarifies the limitations of the efficient representation, and enables us to derive a similarly efficient representation for the two-way pipes featured in the pipes library.

The specific contributions of this paper are:

- We present a systematic derivation of Spivey's efficient representation starting from a simple executable specification. Our derivation only consists of known transformations, most of which concern structural recursion with folds and algebras. It also explains why the efficient representation only supports the merging of "never-returning" pipes.
- We apply our derivation to a more general definition of pipes used by the pipes library, where the communication between adjacent pipes is bidirectional rather than unidirectional.
- Our benchmarks demonstrate that the merge operator for the bidirectional three-continuation approach improves upon the pipes library's performance.

The rest of this paper is organized as follows. Section 2 briefly introduces both the ADT pipes encoding and the three-continuation approach. Section 3 derives the fast merging operation for a simplified setting. Section 4 derives the fast merging operation for the original pipe setting. Section 5 extends Spivey's approach with the bidirectional pipes operations. Section 6 presents the results of the primes benchmark by Spivey, on the approaches discussed in this paper. Section 7 discusses related work and Sect. 8 concludes this paper. The appendix is included in the extended version[1].

2   Motivation

This section introduces the ADT pipes encoding and then contrasts it with the three-continuation encoding. This serves as both a background introduction and a motivation for a better understanding of the relation between both encodings.

2.1   Pipes

We start with a unidirectional version of the pipes library. A unidirectional *pipe* can receive i values, output o values and return a values. On the other hand, a bidirectional pipe additionally carries an output value when receiving values and an input value when outputting values. We represent a unidirectional pipe as an abstract syntax tree where each node is an input, output or return operation. This is expressed in Haskell with the following ADT.

$$\textbf{data } Pipe\ i\ o\ a = Input\ (i \rightarrow Pipe\ i\ o\ a)$$
$$\mid Output\ o\ (Pipe\ i\ o\ a)$$
$$\mid Return\ a$$

This datatype exhibits a monadic structure where the bind operation ($\ggeq$) grafts one syntax tree onto another.

> **instance** *Monad* (*Pipe i o*) **where**
> *return* = *Return*
> (*Input h*) $\ggeq f = Input\ (\lambda i \rightarrow (h\ i) \ggeq f)$
> (*Output o r*) $\ggeq f = Output\ o\ (r \ggeq f)$
> (*Return a*) $\ggeq f = f\ a$

We define the basic components: *input$_P$*: a pipe returning its received input, *output$_P$*: a pipe outputting a set value and *return$_P$*: a pipe returning a set value.

> *input$_P$* :: *Pipe i o i*
> *input$_P$* = *Input* ($\lambda i \rightarrow$ *Return i*)
>
> *output$_P$* :: $o \rightarrow$ *Pipe i o* ()
> *output$_P$ o* = *Output o* (*Return* ())
>
> *return$_P$* :: $a \rightarrow$ *Pipe i o a*
> *return$_P$ a* = *Return a*

The bind operation assembles these components into larger pipes. For example *doubler$_P$*, a pipe which repeatedly takes its input, multiplies it by two and continually outputs this new value.

> *doubler$_P$* :: *Pipe Int Int a*
> *doubler$_P$* = **do** $i \leftarrow$ *input$_P$*; *output$_P$* ($i * 2$); *doubler$_P$*

Another essential way of combining pipes is *merging* them. This connects the outputs of the upstream to the inputs of the downstream. In the implementation, *merge$_{PL}$* performs a case analysis on the downstream q: if it is trying to output then that is kept and we keep searching, if it finds an input then we call *merge$_{PR}$* on the wrapped continuation and the upstream. Then, in *merge$_{PR}$* we similarly scan the upstream for an output operation, keeping any input operations. If an output operation is found, the output value is passed to the continuation and the merging process starts again. If at any point we see a return, then the merge finishes with this resulting return value. The implementation is given below.

> *merge$_P$* :: *Pipe i m a* $\rightarrow$ *Pipe m o a* $\rightarrow$ *Pipe i o a*
> *merge$_P$ p q* = *merge$_{PL}$ q p* **where**
>   *merge$_{PL}$* :: *Pipe m o a* $\rightarrow$ *Pipe i m a* $\rightarrow$ *Pipe i o a*
>   *merge$_{PL}$* (*Input h*)   *p* = *merge$_{PR}$ p h*
>   *merge$_{PL}$* (*Output o r*) *p* = *Output o* (*merge$_{PL}$ r p*)
>   *merge$_{PL}$* (*Return a*)   *p* = *Return a*
>
>   *merge$_{PR}$* :: *Pipe i m a* $\rightarrow$ ($m \rightarrow$ *Pipe m o a*) $\rightarrow$ *Pipe i o a*
>   *merge$_{PR}$* (*Input f*)   *h* = *Input* ($\lambda v \rightarrow$ *merge$_{PR}$* (*f v*) *h*)
>   *merge$_{PR}$* (*Output o r*) *h* = *merge$_{PL}$* (*h o*) *r*
>   *merge$_{PR}$* (*Return a*)   *h* = *Return a*

The merge operator enables expressing the merge of $doubler_P$ with itself. In this example the left $doubler_P$ is the upstream and the right $doubler_P$ is the downstream. The result of this merge is a pipe which outputs the quadruple of its incoming values.

$$quadrupler_P :: Pipe\ Int\ Int\ a$$
$$quadrupler_P = doubler_P\ `merge_P`\ doubler_P$$

We can run a pipe by interpreting it to IO.

$$toIO_P :: (Read\ i, Show\ o) \Rightarrow Pipe\ i\ o\ a \rightarrow IO\ a$$
$$toIO_P\ (Input\ f)\quad = \textbf{do}\ i \leftarrow readLn; toIO_P\ (f\ i)$$
$$toIO_P\ (Output\ o\ r) = \textbf{do}\ putStrLn\ (\texttt{"out: "} + show\ o); toIO_P\ r$$
$$toIO_P\ (Return\ a)\quad = return\ a$$

An example where we input 10, receive 40 and then exit, is shown below.

$$\lambda >\ toIO_P\ quadrupler_P$$
$$10\ \langle\textbf{Return}\rangle$$
$$out: 40$$
$$\langle\textbf{Ctrl+C}\rangle$$

2.2   Three-Continuation Approach

The function $merge_P$ is suboptimal because it has to recursively scan a pipe for an operation of interest while copying the other operation. When several merges are piled up this leads to repeated scanning and copying of the same operations.

Spivey has introduced $ContPipe$, a different pipe representation which enables a faster merge implementation [12]. It features three continuations, one for each constructor. The first continuation ($a \rightarrow Result\ i\ o$) represents the return constructor. The next two continuations, $InCont\ i$ and $OutCont\ o$ as part of $Result\ i\ o$, represent the input and output constructor respectively.

```
newtype ContPipe i o a =
    MakePipe { runPipe :: (a → Result i o) → Result i o }
type Result i o = InCont i → OutCont o → IO ()
newtype InCont i =
    MakeInCont { resumeᵢ :: OutCont i → IO () }
newtype OutCont o =
    MakeOutCont { resumeₒ :: o → InCont o → IO () }
instance Monad (ContPipe i o) where
    return a = MakePipe (λk → k a)
    p ≫ f = MakePipe (λk → runPipe p (λx → runPipe (f x) k))
```

In the following definitions for the basic pipe components the continuation k is the return constructor—we give it a value and the input and output constructors and receive a pipe. The continuations k_i and k_o are the input and output constructors, we resume them with the newtype unwrapper and the continuations are refreshed once they have been used.

$return_{CP} :: a \rightarrow ContPipe\ i\ o\ a$
$return_{CP}\ a = MakePipe\ (\lambda k\ k_i\ k_o \rightarrow k\ a\ k_i\ k_o)$
$input_{CP} :: ContPipe\ i\ o\ i$
$input_{CP} = MakePipe\ (\lambda k\ k_i\ k_o \rightarrow$
$\quad resume_I\ k_i\ (MakeOutCont\ (\lambda i\ k_i' \rightarrow k\ i\ k_i'\ k_o)))$
$output_{CP} :: o \rightarrow ContPipe\ i\ o\ ()$
$output_{CP}\ o = MakePipe\ (\lambda k\ k_i\ k_o \rightarrow$
$\quad resume_O\ k_o\ o\ (MakeInCont\ (\lambda k_o' \rightarrow k\ ()\ k_i\ k_o')))$

We can use the *Monad* instance for *ContPipe* to compose pipes with **do**-notation, similar to *Pipe*.

$doubler_{CP} :: ContPipe\ Int\ Int\ a$
$doubler_{CP} = \textbf{do}\ i \leftarrow input_{CP};\ output_{CP}\ (i * 2);\ doubler_{CP}$

We can also interpret *ContPipe* to *IO*.

$toIO_{CP} :: (Read\ i, Show\ o) \Rightarrow ContPipe\ i\ o\ () \rightarrow IO\ ()$
$toIO_{CP}\ p = runPipe\ p\ (\lambda()\ \_\_ \rightarrow return\ ())\ k_i\ k_o\ \textbf{where}$
$\quad k_i = MakeInCont\ (\lambda k_o \rightarrow \textbf{do}\ x \leftarrow readLn;\ resume_O\ k_o\ x\ k_i)$
$\quad k_o = MakeOutCont\ (\lambda o\ k_i \rightarrow$
$\quad\quad \textbf{do}\ putStrLn\ (\texttt{"out: "} +\!\!+ show\ o);\ resume_I\ k_i\ k_o)$

The merge function for *ContPipe* is defined as:

$merge_{CP}\ p\ q = MakePipe\ (\lambda k\ k_i\ k_o \rightarrow$
$\quad runPipe\ q\ err\ (MakeInCont\ (\lambda k_o' \rightarrow runPipe\ p\ err\ k_i\ k_o'))\ k_o)$
$\quad \textbf{where}\ err = error\ \texttt{"terminated"}$

With the merge definition we are able to create the quadrupler pipe as before. Running $toIO_{CP}\ quadrupler_{CP}$ results an identical scenario to the *Pipe* scenario from the previous section.

$quadrupler_{CP} :: ContPipe\ Int\ Int\ a$
$quadrupler_{CP} = doubler_{CP}\ `merge_{CP}`\ doubler_{CP}$

While Spivey has demonstrated the remarkable performance advantage of this merge operator, he sheds little light on the origin or underlying principles of the related encoding. The remainder of this paper provides this missing insight by deriving Spivey's efficient *ContPipe* representation from the ADT-style *Pipe* by means of well-known principles. The aim is to improve understanding of the applicability and limitations of the techniques used.

3   Fast Merging for One-Sided Pipes

To offer a firmer grip on the problem, this section considers a simplified setting where pipes are one-sided, either only producing or only consuming data. For example, the *doubler* component can not be defined in this setting. The simplified setting gives a more straightforward path to the fast merging approach, which we generalize back to regular 'mixed' pipes in Sect. 4.

3.1   One-Sided Pipes

In the simplified setting pipes are either pure *Producer*s or pure *Consumer*s. A *Producer only* outputs values, while a *Consumer only* receives them.

> **data** *Producer o* = *Producer o* (*Producer o*)
> **data** *Consumer i* = *Consumer* (*i* → *Consumer i*)

If we specialize $merge_P$ for a *Consumer* and a *Producer*, we get:

> $merge_A$ :: *Producer b* → *Consumer b* → *a*
> $merge_A$ *p q* = $merge_{AL}$ *q p* **where**
> $merge_{AL}$ :: *Consumer b* → *Producer b* → *a*
> $merge_{AL}$ (*Consumer h*) *p* = $merge_{AR}$ *p h*
>
> $merge_{AR}$ :: *Producer b* → (*b* → *Consumer b*) → *a*
> $merge_{AR}$ (*Producer o r*) *h* = $merge_{AL}$ (*h o*) *r*

3.2   Mutual Recursion Elimination

The two auxiliary functions $merge_{AL}$ and $merge_{AR}$ turn respectively a producer and a consumer into the result of type a by means of an additional parameter, which is respectively of type (*Producer b*) and (*b* → *Consumer b*). To highlight these parameters, we introduce type synonyms for them.

> **type** *ProdPar' b* = *Producer b*
> **type** *ConsPar' b* = *b* → *Consumer b*

Now we refactor $merge_{AL}$ and $merge_{AR}$ with respect to their additional parameter in a way that removes the term-level mutual recursion between them. Consider $merge_{AL}$ which does not use its parameter p directly, but only its interpretation by function $merge_{AR}$. We refactor this code to a form where $merge_{AR}$ has already been applied to p before it is passed to $merge_{AL}$. This adapted $merge_{AL}$ would then have type *Consumer b* → (*ConsPar' b* → *a*) → *a*. At the same time we apply a similar transformation to $merge_{AR}$, moving the application of $merge_{AL}$ to *h* out of it. This yields infinite types for the two new parameters, which Haskell only accepts if we wrap them in newtypes.

> **newtype** *ProdPar b a* = *ProdPar* (*ConsPar b a* → *a*)
> **newtype** *ConsPar b a* = *ConsPar* (*b* → *ProdPar b a* → *a*)

The merge is then defined by appropriately placing newtype (un-)wrappers.

$merge_{Par} :: Producer\ b \rightarrow Consumer\ b \rightarrow a$
$merge_{Par}\ p\ q = ml\ q\ (ProdPar\ (mr\ p))$ **where**
   $ml :: Consumer\ b \rightarrow ProdPar\ b\ a \rightarrow a$
   $ml\ (Consumer\ h)\ (ProdPar\ p) = p\ (ConsPar\ (\lambda i \rightarrow (ml\ (h\ i))))$
   $mr :: Producer\ b \rightarrow ConsPar\ b\ a \rightarrow a$
   $mr\ (Producer\ o\ r)\ (ConsPar\ h) = h\ o\ (ProdPar\ (mr\ r))$

Note that we can recover Spivey's *InCont* i and *OutCont* o by instantiating the type parameter a to *IO* () in *ProdPar* $i\ a$ and *ConsPar* $o\ a$ respectively.

3.3   Structural Recursion with Fold

Due to the removal of the term-level mutual recursion in ml and mr, they are easily adapted to their structurally recursive form. By isolating the work done in each recursive step, we obtain alg_L and alg_R.

type $Carrier_L\ i\ a = ProdPar\ i\ a \rightarrow a$

$alg_L :: (i \rightarrow Carrier_L\ i\ a) \rightarrow Carrier_L\ i\ a$
$alg_L\ f = \lambda(ProdPar\ prod) \rightarrow prod\ (ConsPar\ f)$

type $Carrier_R\ o\ a = ConsPar\ o\ a \rightarrow a$

$alg_R :: o \rightarrow Carrier_R\ o\ a \rightarrow Carrier_R\ o\ a$
$alg_R\ o\ prod = \lambda(ConsPar\ cons) \rightarrow cons\ o\ (ProdPar\ prod)$

The functions alg_L and alg_R are now in a form known as algebras. Algebras are a combination of a *carrier* r, the type of the resulting value, and an *action* of type $f\ r \rightarrow r$. This action denotes the computation performed at each node of the recursive datatype, for which the functor f determines the shape of its nodes. We omit the carrier type if it is clear from the context and simply refer to an algebra by its action.

    The structural recursion schemes, or *folds*, for *Consumer* and *Producer* take algebras of the form $(i \rightarrow r) \rightarrow r$ and $o \rightarrow r \rightarrow r$. Their definitions are:

$fold_P :: (o \rightarrow r \rightarrow r) \rightarrow Producer\ o \rightarrow r$
$fold_P\ alg\ (Producer\ o\ r) = alg\ o\ (fold_P\ alg\ r)$
$fold_C :: ((i \rightarrow r) \rightarrow r) \rightarrow Consumer\ i \rightarrow r$
$fold_C\ alg\ (Consumer\ h) = alg\ (\lambda i \rightarrow fold_C\ alg\ (h\ i))$

An example use of folds is an interpretation to *IO* by supplying the inputs for a consumer or printing the outputs of a producer.

type $CarrierCons_{IO}\ i = IO\ ()$

$consume_{IO} :: Read\ i \Rightarrow Consumer\ i \rightarrow IO\ ()$
$consume_{IO} = fold_C\ alg$ **where**

$$alg :: Read\ i \Rightarrow (i \to CarrierCons_{IO}\ i) \to CarrierCons_{IO}\ i$$
$$alg\ f = \textbf{do}\ x \leftarrow readLn; f\ x$$
$$\textbf{type}\ CarrierProd_{IO}\ o = IO\ ()$$
$$produce_{IO} :: Show\ o \Rightarrow Producer\ o \to IO\ ()$$
$$produce_{IO} = fold_P\ alg\ \textbf{where}$$
$$alg :: Show\ o \Rightarrow o \to CarrierProd_{IO}\ o \to CarrierProd_{IO}\ o$$
$$alg\ o\ p = \textbf{do}\ print\ o; p$$

Another example is expressing $merge_{Par}$ with folds using alg_L and alg_R.

$$merge_{fold} :: Producer\ x \to Consumer\ x \to a$$
$$merge_{fold}\ p\ q = fold_C\ alg_L\ q\ (ProdPar\ (fold_P\ alg_R\ p))$$

3.4   A Short-Cut to a Merge-Friendly Representation

Instead of directly defining a *Consumer* or *Producer* value in terms of the data constructors of the respective types, we can also do it in a more roundabout way by abstracting over the constructor occurrences—this is known as *build* form. The *build* function then instantiates the abstracted constructors with the actual constructors; for *Consumer* and *Producer* they are:

$$build_C :: (\forall r.((i \to r) \to r) \to r) \to Consumer\ i$$
$$build_C\ g = g\ Consumer$$
$$build_P :: (\forall r.(o \to r \to r) \to r) \to Producer\ o$$
$$build_P\ g = g\ Producer$$

For instance,

$$prodFrom :: Integer \to Producer\ Integer$$
$$prodFrom\ n = Producer\ n\ (prodFrom\ (n + 1))$$

can be written as:

$$prodFrom\ n = build_P\ (prodFrom'\ n)\ \textbf{where}$$
$$prodFrom' :: Integer \to (\forall r.(Integer \to r \to r) \to r)$$
$$prodFrom'\ n\ p = go\ n\ \textbf{where}\ go\ n = p\ n\ (go\ (n + 1))$$

The motivation for these build functions is use of the fold/build fusion rule, a special form of short-cut fusion [4]. This rule can be applied when a fold directly follows a build, specifically for *Consumer* and *Producer* these fusion rules are:

$$fold_C\ alg\ (build_C\ cons) = cons\ alg$$
$$fold_P\ alg\ (build_P\ prod) = prod\ alg$$

In other words, instead of first building an ADT representation and then folding it to its result, we can directly create the result of the fold. This readily applies to the two folds in $merge_{fold}$. We can directly represent consumers and producers in terms of the carrier types of those two folds,

$$\textbf{type } Consumer_{Alt} \; i = \forall a. Carrier_L \; i \; a \quad \text{-- } \forall a. ProdPar \; i \; a \to a$$
$$\textbf{type } Producer_{Alt} \; o = \forall a. Carrier_R \; o \; a \quad \text{-- } \forall a. ConsPar \; o \; a \to a$$

using their algebras as constructors:

$$input_{Alt} :: (i \to Consumer_{Alt} \; i) \to Consumer_{Alt} \; i$$
$$input_{Alt} = alg_L$$
$$output_{Alt} :: o \to Producer_{Alt} \; o \to Producer_{Alt} \; o$$
$$output_{Alt} = alg_R$$

For instance, after fold/build fusion *prodFrom* becomes:

$$prodFrom_{Alt} :: Integer \to Producer_{Alt} \; Integer$$
$$prodFrom_{Alt} \; n = output_{Alt} \; n \; (prodFrom_{Alt} \; (n + 1))$$

The merge function for the alternate representations $Producer_{Alt}$ and $Consumer_{Alt}$ then becomes an almost trivial operation.

$$merge_{Alt} :: Producer_{Alt} \; b \to Consumer_{Alt} \; b \to a$$
$$merge_{Alt} \; p \; q = q \; (ProdPar \; p)$$

3.5   A Not So Special Representation

This merge-friendly representations of producers and consumers are not just specializations; they are in fact isomorphic to the originals. The inverses of *ml* and *mr* to complete the isomorphism are given by ml^{-1} and mr^{-1}. The proof is included in the appendix.

$$ml^{-1} :: Consumer_{Alt} \; i \to Consumer \; i$$
$$ml^{-1} \; f = f \; (ProdPar \; h) \; \textbf{where}$$
$$\quad h :: ConsPar \; i \; (Consumer \; i) \to Consumer \; i$$
$$\quad h \; (ConsPar \; f) = Consumer \; (\lambda x \to f \; x \; (ProdPar \; h))$$
$$mr^{-1} :: Producer_{Alt} \; o \to Producer \; o$$
$$mr^{-1} \; f = f \; (ConsPar \; (\lambda x \; p \to Producer \; x \; (h \; p))) \; \textbf{where}$$
$$\quad h :: ProdPar \; o \; (Producer \; o) \to Producer \; o$$
$$\quad h \; (ProdPar \; f) = f \; (ConsPar \; (\lambda x \; p \to Producer \; x \; (h \; p)))$$

Hence, we can also fold with other algebras by transforming the merge-friendly representation back to the ADT, and then folding over that.

$$fold_{P_{Alt}} :: (o \to a \to a) \to Producer_{Alt} \; o \to a$$
$$fold_{P_{Alt}} \; alg \; rep = fold_P \; alg \; (mr^{-1} \; rep)$$

$$fold_{C_{Alt}} :: ((i \to a) \to a) \to Consumer_{Alt} \; i \to a$$
$$fold_{C_{Alt}} \; alg \; rep = fold_C \; alg \; (ml^{-1} \; rep)$$

Of course, these definitions are wasteful because they create intermediate datatypes. However, by performing fold/build fusion we obtain their fused versions:

$$fold_{P_{Alt}} \; alg \; rep = rep \; (ConsPar \; (\lambda x \; p \to alg \; x \; (h \; p))) \; \textbf{where}$$
$$\quad h \; (ProdPar \; f) = f \; (ConsPar \; (\lambda x \; p \to alg \; x \; (h \; p)))$$

$$fold_{C_{Alt}} \; alg \; rep = rep \; (ProdPar \; h) \; \textbf{where}$$
$$\quad h \; (ConsPar \; f) = alg \; (\lambda x \to f \; x \; (ProdPar \; h))$$

4   Return to Two-Sided Pipes

The previous section has derived an efficient approach for simplified *Consumer* and *Producer* pipes. This section extends that approach to proper *Pipes* in two steps, first supporting both input and output operations, and then also a *return*.

4.1   Pipe of No Return

Let us consider pipes with both input and output operations, but no *return*.

$$\textbf{data} \; Pipe_\infty \; i \; o = Input_\infty \; (i \to Pipe_\infty \; i \; o)$$
$$\quad\quad\quad\quad\quad\quad | \; Output_\infty \; o \; (Pipe_\infty \; i \; o)$$

We can fold over these pipes by providing algebras for both the input and output operation, agreeing on the carrier type a.

$$foldPipe_\infty :: Pipe_\infty \; i \; o \to ((i \to a) \to a) \to (o \to a \to a) \to a$$
$$foldPipe_\infty \; p \; inAlg \; outAlg = go \; p \; \textbf{where}$$
$$\quad go \; (Input_\infty \; p) \quad = inAlg \; (\lambda i \to go \; (p \; i))$$
$$\quad go \; (Output_\infty \; o \; p) = outAlg \; o \; (go \; p)$$

To merge these pipes, we use alg_L and alg_R developed in the previous section. There is only one snag: the two algebras do not agree on the carrier type. The carrier types were the alternate representations $Consumer_{Alt}$ and $Producer_{Alt}$.

$$\textbf{type} \; Consumer_{Alt} \; i = \forall a.ProdPar \; i \; a \to a$$
$$\textbf{type} \; Producer_{Alt} \; o = \forall a.ConsPar \; o \; a \to a$$

We reconcile these two carrier types by observing that both are functions with a common result type, but different parameter types. A combination of both is a function taking both parameter types as input.

$$\textbf{type} \; Result_R \; i \; o = \forall a.ConsPar \; o \; a \to ProdPar \; i \; a \to a$$

The algebra actions are easily adapted to the additional parameter. They simply pass it on to the recursive positions without using it themselves.

$$input_{Result_R} :: (i \rightarrow Result_R \; i \; o) \rightarrow Result_R \; i \; o$$
$$input_{Result_R} \; f = \lambda cons \; (ProdPar \; prod) \rightarrow$$
$$\quad prod \; (ConsPar \; (\lambda i \; prod' \rightarrow f \; i \; cons \; prod'))$$

$$output_{Result_R} :: o \rightarrow Result_R \; i \; o \rightarrow Result_R \; i \; o$$
$$output_{Result_R} \; o \; result = \lambda(ConsPar \; cons) \; prod \rightarrow$$
$$\quad cons \; o \; (ProdPar \; (\lambda cons' \rightarrow result \; cons' \; prod))$$

Like before, we can avoid the algebraic datatype $Pipe_\infty$ and directly work with $Result_R$ using the algebras as constructor functions.

Finally, we can use the one-sided merge function from the previous section to merge the output side of a $Result_R \; i \; m$ pipe with the input side of a $Result_R \; m \; o$ pipe. Because we defer the interpretation of the i and o sides of the respective pipes, this one-sided merge does not yield a result of type a, but rather one of type $ConsPar \; o \; a \rightarrow ProdPar \; i \; a \rightarrow a$. In other words, the merge of the two pipes yields a $Result_R \; i \; o$ pipe.

$$merge_{Result_R} :: Result_R \; i \; m \rightarrow Result_R \; m \; o \rightarrow Result_R \; i \; o$$
$$merge_{Result_R} \; p \; q = \lambda cons_o \; prod_i \rightarrow$$
$$\textbf{let } q' = q \; cons_o$$
$$\qquad p' = flip \; p \; prod_i$$
$$\textbf{in } q' \; (ProdPar \; p')$$

4.2   Return to *return*

Finally, we reobtain *return* and the monadic structure of pipes in a slightly unusual way, by means of the *continuation* monad.

$$\textbf{newtype } Cont \; r \; a = Cont \; \{ runCont :: (a \rightarrow r) \rightarrow r \}$$
$$\textbf{instance } Monad \; (Cont \; r) \; \textbf{where}$$
$$\quad return \; x = Cont \; (\lambda k \rightarrow k \; x)$$
$$\quad p \ggg f \; = Cont \; (\lambda k \rightarrow runCont \; p \; (\lambda x \rightarrow runCont \; (f \; x) \; k))$$

If we specialize the result type r to $Result_R \; i \; o$, we get:

$$\textbf{newtype } ContP \; i \; o \; a = ContP \; ((a \rightarrow Result_R \; i \; o) \rightarrow Result_R \; i \; o)$$

The merge function for $ContP$ is implemented in terms of $merge_{Result_R}$.

$$merge_{Cont} :: ContP \; i \; m \; Void \rightarrow ContP \; m \; o \; Void \rightarrow ContP \; i \; o \; a$$
$$merge_{Cont} \; (ContP \; p) \; (ContP \; q) = ContP \; (\lambda k \rightarrow$$
$$\quad merge_{Result_R} \; (p \; absurd) \; (q \; absurd))$$

However, there is an issue: before $merge_{Result_R}$ can merge the two pipes, their continuations (the interpretations of the *return* constructor) must be supplied.

Yet, the resulting pipe's continuation type k does not match that of either the upstream or downstream pipe. Thus we are stuck, unless we assume what we have been all along: that the two pipes are infinite. Indeed, in that case it does not matter that we don't have a continuation for them, as their continuation is never reached anyway. In short, $merge_{Cont}$ only works for never-returning pipes, which we signal with the return type $Void$, only inhabited by $\bot$.

4.3   Specialization for *IO*

To get exactly Spivey's representation, we instantiate the polymorphic type variable a in $Result_R\ i\ o$ to $IO\ ()$, which yields:

> **type** $Result\ i\ o = InCont\ i \rightarrow OutCont\ o \rightarrow IO\ ()$

We can rewrite this type as a monad transformer stack, using two reader monad transformers for the two parameters.

> **newtype** $ReaderT\ r\ m\ a = ReaderT\ \{\, runReaderT :: r \rightarrow m\ a\,\}$
> **type** $Result'\ i\ o = ReaderT\ (InCont\ i)\ (ReaderT\ (OutCont\ o)\ IO)\ ()$

Similarly, $ContPipe\ i\ o\ a$ can be written with a transformer stack by adding a $ContT$ layer, since $Cont\ (m\ r)$ is equal to $ContT\ r\ m$ for any monad m.

> **newtype** $ContT\ r\ m\ a = ContT\ \{\, runContT :: (a \rightarrow m\ r) \rightarrow m\ r\,\}$
> **type** $ContPipe'\ i\ o\ a =$
> $\quad ContT\ ()\ (ReaderT\ (InCont\ i)\ (ReaderT\ (OutCont\ o)\ IO))\ a$

This transformer stack view enables two additional useful operations: aborting the pipe and embedding an IO action. Both are specializations of generic functionality from the continuation monad transformer: $abort$ and $lift_{ContT}$.

> $abort :: m\ r \rightarrow ContT\ r\ m\ a$
> $abort\ r = ContT\ (\lambda k \rightarrow r)$
> $lift_{ContT} :: Monad\ m \Rightarrow m\ a \rightarrow ContT\ r\ m\ a$
> $lift_{ContT}\ p = ContT\ (\lambda k \rightarrow p \ggg k)$
> $exit' :: ContPipe'\ i\ o\ a$
> $exit' = abort\ (lift_{ReaderT}\ (lift_{ReaderT}\ (return\ ())))$
> $effect' :: IO\ a \rightarrow ContPipe'\ i\ o\ a$
> $effect'\ e = lift_{ContT}\ (lift_{ReaderT}\ (lift_{ReaderT}\ e))$

5   Bidirectional Pipes

So far we have covered unidirectional pipes where information flows in one direction through the pipe, from the *output* operations in one pipe to the *input* operations in the next pipe downstream. However, some use cases also require information to flow upstream and pipes that support this are called bidirectional.

The *Proxy* data type at the core of the `pipes` library [5] implements bidirectional pipes. The operations *request* and *respond* are respectively downstream and upstream combinations of *input* and *output*. In addition, *Proxy* is also a monad transformer that embed effects of monad m.

$$\textbf{data}\ Proxy\ a'\ a\ b'\ b\ m\ r = Request\ a'\ (a \rightarrow Proxy\ a'\ a\ b'\ b\ m\ r)$$
$$\mid\ Respond\ b\ (b' \rightarrow Proxy\ a'\ a\ b'\ b\ m\ r)$$
$$\mid\ M\qquad (m\ (Proxy\ a'\ a\ b'\ b\ m\ r))$$
$$\mid\ Pure\ r$$

We refer to the `pipes` source code [5] for the implementation of the corresponding $merge_{PL}$ and $merge_{PR}$ functions, which are called $+\!\!\gg$ and $\gg\!\!\sim$.

We obtain a more efficient function-based representation by adapting the derivation of Sects. 3 and 4. This yields the parameter type *PCPar*.

$$\textbf{newtype}\ PCPar\ i\ o\ a = PCPar\ (o \rightarrow PCPar\ o\ i\ a \rightarrow a)$$

The *Result$_R$* counterpart for *Proxy* takes two such *PCPars* as input. In addition, the result type r is now a monadic type $m\ r$ to be able to lift operations once it is wrapped with *Cont*.

$$\textbf{type}\ ProxyRep\ a'\ a\ b'\ b\ m = \forall r.PCPar\ a\ a'\ (m\ r) \rightarrow \quad \text{-- request}$$
$$PCPar\ b'\ b\ (m\ r) \rightarrow \quad \text{-- respond}$$
$$m\ r$$

Then, we can proceed with defining the merge function for *ProxyRep* and the *Cont*-wrapped version similar to *Result$_R$*.

$$merge_{ProxyRep} :: (c' \rightarrow ProxyRep\ a'\ a\ c'\ c\ m) \rightarrow ProxyRep\ c'\ c\ b'\ b\ m \rightarrow$$
$$ProxyRep\ a'\ a\ b'\ b\ m$$
$$merge_{ProxyRep}\ fc'\ q = \lambda req\ res \rightarrow$$
$$\textbf{let}\ p'\ c' = fc'\ c'\ req$$
$$q' = flip\ q\ res$$
$$\textbf{in}\ q'\ (PCPar\ p')$$
$$\textbf{newtype}\ ContPr\ a'\ a\ b'\ b\ m\ r = ContPr\ \{\ unContPr ::$$
$$(r \rightarrow ProxyRep\ a'\ a\ b'\ b\ m) \rightarrow ProxyRep\ a'\ a\ b'\ b\ m\}$$
$$merge_{ContPr} :: (c' \rightarrow ContPr\ a'\ a\ c'\ c\ m\ Void) \rightarrow$$
$$ContPr\ c'\ c\ b'\ b\ m\ Void \rightarrow ContPr\ a'\ a\ b'\ b\ m\ r$$
$$merge_{ContPr}\ fc'\ (ContPr\ q) = ContPr\ (\lambda k \rightarrow$$
$$merge_{ProxyRep}\ (\lambda c' \rightarrow unContPr\ (fc'\ c')\ absurd)\ (q\ absurd))$$

6   Benchmarks

Figure 1 shows the results of Spivey's *primes* benchmark, which calculates the first n primes. The benchmarks are executed using the `criterion` library [9] on an Intel Core i7-6600U at 2.60 GHz with 8 GB memory running Ubuntu 16.04 and GHC 8.4.3, with -O2 enabled.[2]

The figure compares the `pipes` (v4.3.9) and `conduit` (v1.3.0.3) libraries to Spivey's original implementation (`contpipe`) and our generalized form (`proxyrep`).

We can see that the former two libraries, which use an ADT representation, both show the quadratic performance behaviour for a use case with a high amount of merge steps. On the other hand, the latter two show the improved performance behaviour. The slight overhead of `proxyrep` compared to `contpipe` can be explained by the specialization to IO () in the latter type.

The appendix contains the results of some additional microbenchmarks.

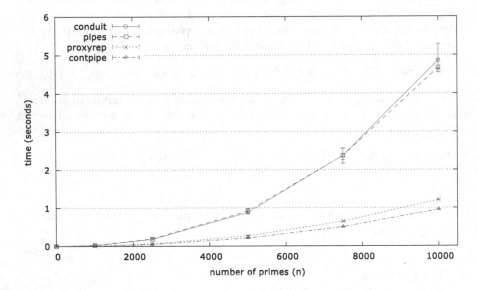

Fig. 1. Results of the *primes* benchmark.

7   Related Work

We have covered the main related works of Spivey [12], Shivers and Might [10] and the `pipes` library [5] in the body of the paper. Below we discuss some additional related work.

Encodings. The Church [1,2] and Scott [8] encodings encode ADTs using functions. The encoding derived in this paper has a close connection to the Scott encoding. The Scott encoding for *Producer* and *Consumer* are *ScottP* and *ScottC*. By moving the quantified variable a to the definition, we obtain *SP* and *SC*.

---

[2] The benchmarks are at https://github.com/rubenpieters/orth-pipes-bench.

$\textbf{newtype } ScottP \ o = ScottP \ (\forall a.(o \to ScottP \ o \to a) \to a)$
$\textbf{newtype } ScottC \ i = ScottC \ (\forall a.((i \to ScottC \ i) \to a) \to a)$
$\textbf{newtype } SP \ o \ a = SP \ ((o \to SP \ o \ a \to a) \to a)$
$\textbf{newtype } SC \ i \ a = SC \ (((i \to SC \ i \ a) \to a) \to a)$

Then, $\forall a.SP \ o \ a$ is representationally equivalent to $Producer_{Alt}$ and similarly for $\forall a.SC \ i \ a$ and $Consumer_{Alt}$ (see the appendix).

If we look at the Scott encoding $ScottPipe_\infty$ for $Pipe_\infty$, we can obtain an equivalent representation to $Result_R$ by using SP and SC instead of $ScottPipe_\infty$ in the parameter corresponding to their operations.

$\textbf{newtype } ScottPipe_\infty \ i \ o = ScottPipe_\infty$
$\quad (\forall a.(o \to ScottPipe_\infty \ i \ o \to a) \to ((i \to ScottPipe_\infty \ i \ o) \to a) \to a)$
$\textbf{type } SP_\infty \ i \ o = \forall a.(o \to SP \ o \ a \to a) \to ((i \to SC \ i \ a) \to a) \to a$

We dubbed this the *orthogonal encoding* due to the separation of the operations.

Conduit. The `conduit` library [11] is another popular choice for Haskell stream processing. The two main differing points of `conduit` with `pipes` is a built-in representation of leftovers and detection of upstream finalization. Leftovers are operations representing unprocessed outputs. For example in a *takeWhile* pipe, which takes outputs until a condition is matched, the first element not matching the condition will also be consumed. This element can then be emitted as a leftover, which will be consumed by the downstream with priority. Detecting upstream finalization is handled by *input* returning *Maybe* values, where *Nothing* represents the finalization of the upstream.

Parsers. Spivey mentioned in his work [12] that the *ContPipe* approach might be adapted to fit the use case of parallel parsers [3]. However, after gaining more insight into *ContPipe*, it does not seem that the merging operation for parsers immediately fits the pattern presented in this paper. One of the problematic elements is the *fail* operation, which is not passed as-is to the newly merged structure, but given a non-trivial interpretation. Namely, an interpretation dependent on the other structure during the recursive merge process.

Shallow To Deep Handlers. The handlers framework by Kammar et al. [6] supports both shallow handlers, based on case analysis, and deep handlers, based on folds. They cover an example of transforming a producer and consumer merging function from shallow handlers to deep handlers. This example is related to our simplified setting in Sect. 3. To do this they introduce *Prod* and *Cons*, which are equivalent to our *ProdPar* and *ConsPar*. Compared to their example, we take a more step-by-step explanatory approach and additionally move to more complicated settings in our further sections.

Multihandlers. The Frank language [7] is based on shallow handlers and supports a feature called multihandlers. These handlers operate on multiple inputs which have uninterpreted operations, much like pattern matching on multiple free structures. The patterns we have handled in this paper are concerned with pattern matching on multiple data structures and a mutual relation between these functions. This seems like an interesting connection to investigate further.

8   Conclusion

We have given an in-depth explanation of the principles behind the fast merging of the three-continuation approach. We have given a series of steps to derive this fast implementation from the less efficient one.

We apply this pattern to the setting of bidirectional pipes, as in the `pipes` library. This results in a more general version of this representation, but still has the same performance due to its efficient merge implementation.

We apply Spivey's benchmarks [12] to check that our generalized encoding retains similar performance. We also include the `pipes` library in the benchmark to compare with a commonly used implementation of bidirectional pipes.

This pipes encoding has been made available as a library on github[3].

Acknowledgements. We would like to thank Nicolas Wu, Alexander Vandenbroucke and the anonymous PADL reviewers for their feedback. This work was partly funded by the Flemish Fund for Scientific Research (FWO).

References

1. Böhm, C., Berarducci, A.: Automatic synthesis of typed lambda-programs on term algebras. Theor. Comput. Sci. **39**, 135–154 (1985). https://doi.org/10.1016/0304-3975(85)90135-5
2. Church, A.: The Calculi of Lambda-Conversion. Princeton University Press, Princeton (1941)
3. Claessen, K.: Parallel parsing processes. J. Funct. Program. **14**(6), 741–757 (2004). https://doi.org/10.1017/S0956796804005192
4. Ghani, N., Uustalu, T., Vene, V.: Build, augment and destroy, universally. In: Chin, W.-N. (ed.) APLAS 2004. LNCS, vol. 3302, pp. 327–347. Springer, Heidelberg (2004). https://doi.org/10.1007/978-3-540-30477-7_22
5. Gonzalez, G.: Haskell Pipes library (2012). http://hackage.haskell.org/package/pipes
6. Kammar, O., Lindley, S., Oury, N.: Handlers in action. In: Proceedings of the 18th ACM SIGPLAN International Conference on Functional Programming, ICFP 2013, pp. 145–158. ACM, New York (2013) https://doi.org/10.1145/2500365.2500590
7. Lindley, S., McBride, C., McLaughlin, C.: Do be do be do. In: Proceedings of the 44th ACM SIGPLAN Symposium on Principles of Programming Languages, POPL 2017, pp. 500–514. ACM, New York (2017). https://doi.org/10.1145/3009837.3009897

---

[3] https://github.com/rubenpieters/Orthogonal-Pipes.

8. Mogensen, T.: Efficient self-interpretation in lambda calculus. J. Funct. Program. **2**(3), 345–364 (1992). https://doi.org/10.1017/S0956796800000423
9. O'Sullivan, B.: Haskell Criterion library (2009). http://hackage.haskell.org/package/criterion
10. Shivers, O., Might, M.: Continuations and transducer composition. In: Proceedings of the 27th ACM SIGPLAN Conference on Programming Language Design and Implementation, PLDI 2006, pp. 295–307. ACM, New York (2006). https://doi.org/10.1145/1133981.1134016
11. Snoyman, M.: Haskell Conduit library (2011). http://hackage.haskell.org/package/conduit
12. Spivey, M.: Faster coroutine pipelines. In: Proceedings of the ACM Programming Languages, 1(ICFP), 5:1–5:23, August 2017. https://doi.org/10.1145/3110249

Classes of Arbitrary Kind

Alejandro Serrano[✉] and Victor Cacciari Miraldo[✉]

Department of Information and Computing Sciences,
Utrecht University, Utrecht, Netherlands
{A.SerranoMena,V.CacciariMiraldo}@uu.nl

Abstract. The type class system in the Haskell Programming language
provides a useful abstraction for a wide range of types, such as those that
support comparison, serialization, ordering, between others. This system
can be extended by the programmer by providing custom instances to
one's custom types. Yet, this is often a monotonous task. Some notions,
such as equality, are very regular regardless if it is being encoded for a
ground type or a type constructor. In this paper we present a technique
that unifies the treatment of ground types and type constructors whenever possible. This reduces code duplication and improves consistency.
We discuss the encoding of several classes in this form, including the
generic programming facility in GHC.

Keywords: Haskell · Type classes · Generic programming

1 Introduction

Type classes [16] are a widely used abstraction provided by the Haskell programming language. In their simplest incarnation, a type class defines a set of
methods which every *instance* must implement, for instance:

$$\textbf{class } Eq \ a \textbf{ where}$$
$$(\equiv) :: a \to a \to Bool$$

Where we are stating that a type a can be an instance of Eq as long as it
implements $(\equiv)$. This is a very useful mechanism, as it allows a programmer
to write polymorphic functions but impose some restrictions on the types. For
instance, consider the type of the nub function below:

$$nub :: (Eq \ a) \Rightarrow [a] \to [a]$$

It receives a list of arbitrary a's, as long we can compare these values for
equality. It returns a list of the same type, but removes every duplicate element.

Supported by NWO project 612.001.401.

J. J. Alferes and M. Johansson (Eds.): PADL 2019, LNCS 11372, pp. 150–168, 2019.
https://doi.org/10.1007/978-3-030-05998-9_10

The base library comes pre-packaged with instances for built-in types, such as integers, Booleans and lists. But the programmer is also allowed to extend this set of instances. For example, here is a data type representing binary trees with values in the internal nodes:

$$\text{data } Tree\ a = Leaf\ |\ Node\ (Tree\ a)\ a\ (Tree\ a)$$

Its corresponding instance for the Eq class is defined as:

$$\text{instance } Eq\ a \Rightarrow Eq\ (Tree\ a)\ \text{where}$$

$Leaf$	$\equiv Leaf$	$= True$
$(Node\ \ell_1\ x_1\ r_1)$	$\equiv (Node\ \ell_2\ x_2\ r_2)$	$= x_1 \equiv x_2 \wedge \ell_1 \equiv \ell_2 \wedge r_1 \equiv r_2$
$\_$	$\equiv \_$	$= False$

This example highlights one of the important features of the type class system: the availability for an instance of $Tree\ a$, in this case, depends on the availability of an instance for the type a. In other words, in order to compare a $Tree\ a$ for equality, we must also be able to compare values of type a, since these are the elements in the nodes of our tree. That way, we know that equality is defined for $Tree\ Bool$ — since $Bool$ is a member of the Eq type class — but not for $Tree\ (Int \rightarrow Bool)$ — since functions cannot be compared for equality.

Our $Tree$ data type is also an instance of the $Functor$ class, which states that we can change a $Tree\ a$ into a $Tree\ b$ as long as we can change one a into one b. We do so by applying this transformation uniformly in the nodes of the tree. In Haskell, we would say:

$$\text{class } Functor\ f\ \text{where}$$
$$fmap :: (a \rightarrow b) \rightarrow f\ a \rightarrow f\ b$$

$$\text{instance } Functor\ Tree\ \text{where}$$

$fmap\ \_\ Leaf$	$= Leaf$
$fmap\ f\ (Node\ \ell\ x\ r)$	$= Node\ (fmap\ f\ \ell)\ (f\ x)\ (fmap\ f\ r)$

There is a subtle difference between Eq and $Functor$ that is central to our work. The Eq class receives ground types, such as Int and $Tree\ Bool$; whereas the $Functor$ receives type constructors, such as $Tree$. In Haskell we distinguish between those by the means of *kinds*. The intuition is that a kind is the "type of types". By convention, ground types have kind $\star$. Therefore, our $Tree$ type is of kind $\star \rightarrow \star$, that is, given a ground type as an argument, it produces a ground type. The *kind system* prevents us from writing nonsensical statements such as $Functor\ Int$, since $Functor$ expects something of kind $\star \rightarrow \star$ and Int has kind $\star$.

There are several extensions to the type class mechanism, such as functional dependencies [7], and associated types [4]. For the purpose of this paper, though, we shall consider only the simpler version described above, with the occasional appearance of multi-parameter type classes [11].

1.1 Concepts of Arbitrary Kind

We can declare that lists support equality provided that their elements do so:

> instance $(Eq\ a) \Rightarrow Eq\ [a]$ where ...

However, lists support an even stronger notion of comparison: if we provide a comparison function between elements of types a and b, we can uniformly lift this operation to act over $[a]$ and $[b]$. This concept is captured by the $Eq1$ type class, which can be found in GHC's base library:

> class $Eq1\ (f :: \star \to \star)$ where
> $liftEq :: (a \to b \to Bool) \to f\ a \to f\ b \to Bool$

Following the same line of thought, we might be inclined to derive a similar notion for the $Either\ a\ b$ type. This is a type constructor with *two* arguments that can be compared in a similar way, but this time we would need two comparison functions in order to compare a $Either\ a\ b$ with a $Either\ c\ d$. Alas, we need to introduce yet another type class, since $Eq1$ only works for types of kind $\star \to \star$:

> class $Eq2\ (f :: \star \to \star \to \star)$ where
> $liftEq2 :: (a \to b \to Bool) \to (c \to d \to Bool)$
> $\to f\ a\ c \to f\ b\ d \to Bool$

> instance $Eq2\ Either$ where
> $liftEq2\ p\ \_\ (Left\quad x)\ (Left\quad y) = p\ x\ y$
> $liftEq2\ \_\ q\ (Right\ x)\ (Right\ y) = q\ x\ y$
> $liftEq2\ \_\ \_\ \_ \qquad\qquad \_ \qquad = False$

The notion of lifting equality makes sense for arbitrary kinds: Eq, $Eq1$, $Eq2$, and so on. Where Eq is seen as the $Eq0$ member of this sequence, where we do not take any equality function as argument because the type in question has no type parameters.

We can witness the same pattern for the *Monoid* and *Alternative* type classes, provided in the base library:

> class $Monoid\ (m :: \star)$ where
> $mempty\ :: a$
> $mappend :: a \to a \to a$

> class $Alternative\ (f :: \star \to \star)$ where
> $empty :: f\ a$
> $(\langle | \rangle)\quad :: f\ a \to f\ a \to f\ a$

A monoid is a type embodied with a way to combine two elements, *mappend*, which satisfies associativity and for which *mempty* acts as neutral element. An instance of *Alternative* for a type constructor C essentially states that $C\ a$ can be used as a monoid, regardless of the element a contained in the structure.

The relationship between *Monoid* and *Alternative* is different from that between *Eq* and *Eq1*: in the latter case we lift a growing sequence of functions, whereas in the former the type has the same shape regardless of the kind at play. Nevertheless, the programmer has to write a new class for every different kind, even though this might be a very regular notion.

1.2   Contributions

The main contribution of this paper is a pattern to define "once and for all" type classes to encompass notions such as *Eq* and *Monoid* which extend to arbitrary kinds. We borrow a technique from recent developmens in generic programming [14], enabling us to represent type applications uniformly (Sect. 2) and showcase its usage in the definition of type classes (Sect. 3). As it turns out, the ability of handling type applications on the term level has far more use than solely generic programming.

We also discuss an extension of the generic programming mechanism in GHC [8] to represent types of arbitrary kinds (Sect. 4). Our approach can be seen as a translation from the techniques introduced by Serrano and Miraldo [14] to the world of pattern functors.

2   Representing Type Application

The core issue is the inability to represent a type that is applied to n type variables. For the *Eq* case, we ultimately want write something in the lines of:

$$\textbf{class } Eq^n \ (f :: \star \to ... \to \star) \textbf{ where}$$
$$liftEq^n :: (a_1 \to b_1 \to Bool) \to ... \to (a_n \to b_n \to Bool)$$
$$\to f \ a_1 \ ... \ a_n \to f \ b_1 \ ... \ b_n \to Bool$$

Yet, simple Haskell without any extension does not allow us to talk about a type variable f applied to "as many arguments as it needs". In fact, we require some of the later developments on the Haskell language to be able to uniformly talk about types of arbitrary kinds. These developments include data type promotion [21] and partial support for dependent types [18].

The key idea is to split a type application such as $f \ a \ b \ c$ in two parts: the *head* f, and the *list of types* $\langle a, b, c \rangle$. Afterwards, we define an operator (: @@ :) which applies a list of types to a head. For example, we should have:

$$f : @@ : \langle a, b, c \rangle \approx f \ a \ b \ c$$

where the $\approx$ denotes isomorphism.

Naturally, we want to rule our incorrect applications of the (: @@ :) operator. For example, $Int : @@ : \langle Int \rangle$. should be flagged as wrong, since Int is not a type constructor, and thus cannot take arguments. In a similar fashion, $Tree : @@ : \langle Tree \rangle$ should not be allowed, because $Tree$ needs a ground type as argument. The required information to know whether a list of types can be applied to a head must be derived from the *kind* of the head. The solution is to add an index to the type Γ that keeps track of the *kind* of such environment. The definition is written as a Generalized Algebraic Data Type, which means that we give the type of each constructor explicitly:

infixr 5 : & :
data Γ k where
$\quad \epsilon \qquad\qquad :: \qquad\qquad\qquad \Gamma\ (\star)$
$\quad (:\&:) :: k \rightarrow \Gamma\ ks \rightarrow \Gamma\ (k \rightarrow ks)$

An empty list of types is represented by ϵ. If we apply such a list of types with a goal of getting a ground type, this implies that the kind we started with was already $\star$, as reflected in the index of this constructor. The other possibility is to attach a type of kind k to a list of types with kind ks, represented by the constructor $(:\&:)$. Here are some examples of lists of types with different indices:

$\quad Int\ :\&: \epsilon \qquad\qquad\qquad :: \Gamma\ (\star \rightarrow \star)$
$\quad Int\ :\&: Bool :\&: \epsilon :: \Gamma\ (\star \rightarrow \star \rightarrow \star)$
$\quad Tree :\&: Bool :\&: \epsilon :: \Gamma\ ((\star \rightarrow \star) \rightarrow \star \rightarrow \star)$

The next step is the definition of the $(:@:)$ operator.

data $(f :: k) :@: (tys :: \Gamma\ k) :: \star$ where
$\quad A0 :: f \qquad\qquad \rightarrow f :@: \epsilon$
$\quad Arg :: f\ t :@: ts \rightarrow f :@: (t :\&: ts)$

We abstain from using type families [13] since defining functions whose arguments are applied families is hard in practice. For instance, if we had defined $(:@:)$ as follows:

type family $(f :: k) :@:_{\mathsf{fam}} (tys :: \Gamma\ k) :: \star$ where
$\quad f :@:_{\mathsf{fam}} \epsilon \qquad\qquad = f$
$\quad f :@:_{\mathsf{fam}} (a :\&: as) = (f\ a) :@:_{\mathsf{fam}} as$

Then writing a simple function that is polymorphic on the *number*, such as:

$\quad g :: f :@:_{\mathsf{fam}} tys \rightarrow String$
$\quad g\ _ = $ "*Hello, PADLers!*"

Would be rejected by the compiler with the following error message:

```
Couldn't match type 'f :@: tys' with 'f0 :@: tys0'
Expected type: f :@: tys -> String
Actual type: f0 :@: tys0 -> String
NB: '(:@:)' is a non-injective type family
The type variables 'f0', 'tys0' are ambiguous
```

The problem is that type families are not necessarily injective. That is, the result of $f : @@ :_{\mathsf{fam}} tys$ is not sufficient to fix the values of the type variables f and tys in the type of g. This is not a problem with the type checking algorithm; these three different choices of f and tys are all equal to the same type:

$$
\begin{aligned}
Either : @@ :_{\mathsf{fam}} (Int :\&: Bool :\&: \epsilon) &\equiv Either\ Int\ Bool \\
Either\ Int : @@ :_{\mathsf{fam}} (Bool :\&: \epsilon) &\equiv Either\ Int\ Bool \\
Either\ Int\ Bool : @@ :_{\mathsf{fam}} \epsilon &\equiv Either\ Int\ Bool
\end{aligned}
$$

Hence, we stick with GADTs, which allows us to write the g function above. However, when we *call* the function we need to wrap the argument with constructor $A0$ and Arg. The amount of Arg constructors expresses how many of the arguments go into the list of types. For example:

$$
\begin{aligned}
g\ (A0\ (Left\ 3)) &\rightsquigarrow f = Either\ Int\ Bool, tys = \epsilon \\
g\ (Arg\ (Arg\ (A0\ (Left\ 3)))) &\rightsquigarrow f = Either, tys = Int :\&: Bool :\&: \epsilon
\end{aligned}
$$

This need to be explicit about the amount of type variables is definitely cumbersome. In Sect. 3.2 we define a type class which allows us to convert easily between uses of $(:@@:)$ and $(:@@:_{\mathsf{fam}})$.

Better Pattern Matching. A related problem with the usage of $(:@@:)$ is the need of nested Arg constructors, both in building values and pattern matching over them. Fortunately, we can reduce the number of characters by using *pattern synonyms* [12].

For the purposes of this paper, it is enough to provide synonyms from nested sequences of Arg up to length 2:

> pattern $A1\ x = Arg\ (A0\ x)$
> pattern $A2\ x = Arg\ (A1\ x)$

This means that we could have written the latest example using g as simply $g\ (A2\ (Left\ 3))$.

3   Arbitrary-Kind Type Classes

With the necessary tools at hand, we are ready to discuss how to define type classes for notions which exist in arbitrary kinds. Being able to access the type application structure on the term level, with $(:@@:)$, is essential. In what follows, we look at this construction by a series of increasingly complex type classes which generalize the well-known *Show*, *Eq*, and *Functor*.

Generalizing Show. In its bare bones version, *Show* specifies how to turn a value into a string. One could define a simplistic[1] version of *Show* as:

> class *Show* t where
>   *show* :: t → *String*

To specify that we want *Show* to work on arbitrary kinds, we need to add a kind signature to its definition, and change the type of the *show* method to apply a list of types:[2]

> class *Show*° (f :: k) where
>   *show*° :: f :@@: tys → *String*

We can define an instance for integers by piggybacking on the usual version of *Show* provided in Haskell's base library:

> instance *Show*° *Int* where
>   *show*° (A0 n) = *show* n

Note that since we are dealing with values of the data type (:@@:), we need to pattern match on *A0* to obtain the integer value itself.

If we try to write similar code for the *Maybe* type constructor, we will bump into an error. Consider the following *Show*° *Maybe* instance:

> instance *Show*° *Maybe* where
>   *show*° (Arg (A0 Nothing)) = "Nothing"
>   *show*° (Arg (A0 (Just x))) = "Just (" ++ *show*° (A0 x) ++ ")"

The compiler complains with:

```
Could not deduce (Show° t) arising from a use of 'show°'
```

The problem is in the call *show*° (A0 x) and stems from the fact that we have not provided any proof that the *contents* inside the *Just* constructor can be "shown". Let us recall the *Show* instance for *Maybe a*:

> instance *Show* a ⇒ *Show* (Maybe a) where ...

Note how this instance *requires* a proof that a is also an instance of *Show*. We therefore need a mechanism to specify that the arguments of *Maybe* :@@: tys, that is, tys, can be shown. That is, we need to specify some *constraint* over tys. This will allow us to call *show*° with a list of types tys whenever every element of this list is also member of *Show*°. In order to define this constraint we require

---

[1] The actual Haskell definition contains functions to deal with operator precedence and efficient construction of *Strings*.

[2] We use the notation f° to refer to the generalized version of f.

ConstraintKinds [1] GHC extension. In summary, this extension enables the manipulation of everything that appears before the ⇒ arrow in a Haskell type as if it was a regular type. The only difference is in the kind: normal arguments to functions must be of a type of kind $\star$, implicit arguments, to the left of the ⇒, must be of kind *Constraint*.

We will now define a constraint that depends on the types *tys* that are applied to a type constructor with $f : @@ : tys$. This definition will proceed by induction on the structure of *tys*. For the specific *Show*° case we define the following *AllShow*° constraint. Note here that the syntax for an empty constraint is () in GHC, and the conjunction of constraints is represented by tupling:

> **type family** *AllShow*° (*tys* :: Γ *k*) :: *Constraint* **where**
> $AllShow° \ \epsilon \qquad\qquad = ()$
> $AllShow° \ (t : \& : ts) = (Show° \ t, AllShow° \ ts)$

Finally we introduce this constraint in the type of *show*°:

> **class** *Show*° (*f* :: *k*) **where**
> $show° :: AllShow° \ tys \Rightarrow f : @@ : tys \rightarrow String$

The *Show*° instance for *Maybe* shown above is now accepted, since *AllShow*° applied to a list of types of the form $t : \& : \epsilon$ reduces to a constraint *Show*° *t*.

Generalizing Eq. The generalized equality class is slightly more complicated; the number of arguments to the *liftEq* function changes between classes:

> $(\equiv) \quad :: \qquad\qquad\qquad\qquad\qquad\qquad\qquad a \quad\;\rightarrow b \quad\;\rightarrow Bool$
> $liftEq \ :: (a \rightarrow b \rightarrow Bool) \qquad\qquad\qquad\qquad \rightarrow f \ a \ \rightarrow f \ b \ \rightarrow Bool$
> $liftEq2 :: (a \rightarrow b \rightarrow Bool) \rightarrow (c \rightarrow d \rightarrow Bool) \rightarrow f \ a \ c \rightarrow f \ b \ d \rightarrow Bool$

Hence, the number of arguments in this case is dictated by the kind of the type constructor *f*: one per appearance of $\star$. We will use a similar technique to *Show*°, and define a data type by induction on the structure of the type applications. This new data type, *Predicates*, will require a function $a \rightarrow b \rightarrow Bool$ for every pair of types obtained from the corresponding lists:

> **data** *Predicates* (*as* :: Γ *k*) (*bs* :: Γ *k*) **where**
> $P\epsilon \quad :: Predicates \ \epsilon \ \epsilon$
> $P\& \quad :: (a \rightarrow b \rightarrow Bool) \rightarrow Predicates \ as \ bs$
> $\qquad \rightarrow Predicates \ (a : \& : as) \ (b : \& : bs)$

Using this data type we can chain as many predicates as we need:

> $P\& \ f \ P\epsilon \qquad\qquad :: Predicates \ (a : \& : \epsilon) \qquad (b : \& : \epsilon)$
> $P\& \ f \ (P\& \ g \ P\epsilon) :: Predicates \ (a : \& : c : \& : \epsilon) \ (b : \& : d : \& : \epsilon)$

The final step to generalize the *Eq* notion is to use the explicit application operator (: @@:) in the definition of the type class. The result in this case is:

> class *Eq*° (*f* :: *k*) where
>   *eq*° :: *Predicates as bs* → *f* : @@ : *as* → *f* : @@ : *bs* → *Bool*

Here are the instances for integers and the instance for *Either*:

> instance *Eq*° *Int* where
>   *eq*° *P*ϵ (*A0 x*) (*A0 y*) = *x* ≡ *y*

> instance *Eq*° *Either* where
>   *eq*° (*P& l* (*P& r P*ϵ)) (*A2* (*Left x*)) (*A2* (*Left y*)) = *l x y*
>   *eq*° (*P& l* (*P& r P*ϵ)) (*A2* (*Right x*)) (*A2* (*Right y*)) = *r x y*
>   *eq*° _   _   _   = *False*

3.1   You-Name-It-Functors

As the final example of our approach, we are going to generalize several notions of functoriality, including those present in GHC's base library. With access to the structure of type applications available through (: @@:), we are able to unify the *Functor*, *Contravariant*, *Profunctor* and *Bifunctor* classes with many others. Recall the *Functor* type class, which describes how to lift a function into a container *f*:

> class *Functor f* where
>   *fmap* :: (*a* → *b*) → *f a* → *f b*

Many types, such as lists, *Maybe*, or binary trees, are examples of *Functors*. But now take the following data type, which describes a logical predicate:

> data *Pred a* = *Pred* (*a* → *Bool*)

It is not possible to write a *Functor* instance for this type. However, we can write one for *Contravariant*, a variation of *Functor* in which the function being lifted goes "in the opposite direction":

> class *Contravariant f* where
>   *contramap* :: (*b* → *a*) → *f a* → *f b*
> instance *Contravariant Pred* where
>   *contramap f* (*Pred p*) = *Pred* (*p* ∘ *f*)

These notions generalize to higher kinds. For example, the type *Either a b* behaves as a functor for both *a* and *b*. That is, if you give a function mapping *a* to *c*, if can be lifted to a function between *Either a b* to *Either c b*; and the same holds for the other type variable. We say that *Either* is a *bifunctor*. The type of functions, *a → b*, is slightly trickier, because it works as a contravariant functor in the source type, and as a usual functor in the target type. The name for this kind of structure is a *profunctor*. Both structures exist in the base libraries:

> class *Bifunctor f* where
> $\quad bimap :: (a \to b) \to (c \to d) \to f\ a\ c \to f\ b\ d$
>
> class *Profunctor f* where
> $\quad dimap :: (b \to a) \to (c \to d) \to f\ a\ c \to f\ b\ d$

With our techniques, we can develop a *unified* type class for all of these notions. The recipe is analogous: we need to specify some information for each type argument *tys* in $f : @@ : tys$. Here we need to know whether each position maps in the "same" or "opposite" way – we call this the *variance* of that position. This is essentially a list of flags whose length must coincide with the number of type arguments to the type. We copy the approach of Γ and *Predicates*, and define a new data type indexed by a kind:

> data *Variance k* where
> $V\epsilon ::$ $\qquad\qquad$ *Variance* $(\star)$
> $\Rrightarrow :: Variance\ ks \to Variance\ (\star \to ks)$
> $\Lleftarrow :: Variance\ ks \to Variance\ (\star \to ks)$
> $\curvearrowright :: Variance\ ks \to Variance\ (k \to ks)$

For the sake of generality, we have also included a $\curvearrowright$ flag which states that a type variable is not used in any constructor of the data type, and thus we can skip it in the list of functions to be lifted. Using this *Variance* type, we can express the different ways in which *Functor*, *Contravariant*, and *Bifunctor* operate on their type variables as $\Rrightarrow V\epsilon$, $\Lleftarrow V\epsilon$, and $\Rrightarrow (\Rrightarrow V\epsilon)$, respectively.

In contrast to the previous examples, to obtain the generalized version of the *Functor* we need an extra parameter: we must attach the corresponding *Variance*. Given a type constructor its variance is fixed, therefore, it can be uniquely determined. This is represented by a *functional dependency* [7]:

> class *Functor°* $(f :: k)\ (v :: Variance\ k)\ |\ f \to v$ where ...

The next step is defining lists of functions that we will need in order to map a $f : @@ : tys$ into a $f : @@ : txs$. This is done in the same fashion as in the previous examples: by induction on the structure of tys and txs. This time, however, in addition to the list of types for the source and the target, we also use the *Variance* to know which is the direction in which the function should operate:

$$
\begin{aligned}
&\mathrm{data}\ Mappings\ (v :: Variance\ k)\ (as :: \Gamma\ k)\ (bs :: \Gamma\ k)\ \mathrm{where}\\
&\quad M\epsilon ::\qquad\qquad\qquad Mappings\ V\epsilon\quad \epsilon\qquad\qquad \epsilon\\
&\quad M^{\Rightarrow} :: (a \rightarrow b) \rightarrow Mappings\quad vs\qquad\quad as\qquad\qquad bs\\
&\qquad\qquad \rightarrow Mappings\ (\Rightarrow vs)\ (a :\&: as)\ (b :\&: bs)\\
&\quad M^{\Leftarrow} :: (b \rightarrow a) \rightarrow Mappings\quad vs\qquad\quad as\qquad\qquad bs\\
&\qquad\qquad \rightarrow Mappings\ (\Leftarrow vs)\ (a :\&: as)\ (b :\&: bs)\\
&\quad M^{\frown} ::\qquad\qquad\qquad Mappings\quad vs\qquad\quad as\qquad\qquad bs\\
&\qquad\qquad \rightarrow Mappings\ (\frown vs)\ (a :\&: as)\ (b :\&: bs)
\end{aligned}
$$

We are now ready to write the definition of $Functor^{\diamond}$, by using a list of mappings as an argument to the generalize $fmap^{\diamond}$ function:

$$
\begin{aligned}
&\mathrm{class}\ Functor^{\diamond}\ (f :: k)\ (v :: Variance\ k)\ |\ f \rightarrow v\ \mathrm{where}\\
&\quad fmap^{\diamond} :: Mappings\ v\ as\ bs \rightarrow f : @@ : as \rightarrow f : @@ : bs
\end{aligned}
$$

What follows are two $Functor^{\diamond}$ instances for types of different kinds, namely, one for *Pred* and one for *Either*.

$$
\begin{aligned}
&\mathrm{instance}\ Functor^{\diamond}\ Pred\ (\Leftarrow V\epsilon)\ \mathrm{where}\\
&\quad fmap^{\diamond}\ (M^{\Leftarrow} f\ M\epsilon)\ (A1\ (Pred\ p)) = A1\ (Pred\ (p \circ f)))
\end{aligned}
$$

$$
\begin{aligned}
&\mathrm{instance}\ Functor^{\diamond}\ Either\ (\Rightarrow (\Rightarrow V\epsilon))\ \mathrm{where}\\
&\quad fmap^{\diamond}\ (M^{\Rightarrow} f\ (M^{\Rightarrow} \_\ M\epsilon))\ (A2\ (Left\ x))\ \ = A2\ (Left\ (f\ x))\\
&\quad fmap^{\diamond}\ (M^{\Rightarrow} \_\ (M^{\Rightarrow} g\ M\epsilon))\ (A2\ (Right\ y)) = A2\ (Right\ (g\ y))
\end{aligned}
$$

Note how the $Functor^{\diamond}$ *Pred* $(\Leftarrow\ V\epsilon)$ instance is equivalent to *Contravariant Pred* and similarly $Functor^{\diamond}$ *Either* $(\Rightarrow (\Rightarrow V\epsilon))$ is equivalent to *Bifunctor Either*. In fact, as a final touch, we can regain the old type classes by giving names to certain instantiations of the *Variance* parameter in $Functor^{\diamond}$:

$$
\begin{aligned}
&\mathrm{type}\ Functor\qquad\quad f = Functor^{\diamond}\ f\ (\Rightarrow V\epsilon)\\
&\mathrm{type}\ Contravariant\ f = Functor^{\diamond}\ f\ (\Leftarrow V\epsilon)\\
&\mathrm{type}\ Bifunctor\qquad\ f = Functor^{\diamond}\ f\ (\Rightarrow (\Rightarrow V\epsilon))\\
&\mathrm{type}\ Profunctor\qquad f = Functor^{\diamond}\ f\ (\Leftarrow (\Rightarrow V\epsilon))
\end{aligned}
$$

3.2 From Families to Data, and Back Again

The two ways of defining type application, $(:@@:_{fam})$ and $(:@@:)$, have dual advantages. In the case of the type family, the caller of the function does not have to wrap the arguments manually, but the compiler rejects the function if no further information is given. When using a data type, the compiler accepts defining functions without further problem, at the expense for the caller having to introduce $A0$ and Arg constructors.

The distinction does not have to be that sharp, though. It is simple to write a type class $Ravel$ which converts between the data type encoding and the type family encoding:

$$\text{class } Ravel \ (t :: \star) \ (f :: k) \ (tys :: \Gamma \ k) \mid f \ tys \to t \text{ where}$$
$$\quad unravel \ :: f : @@: tys \to f : @@:_{fam} tys$$
$$\quad ravel \quad :: f : @@:_{fam} tys \to f : @@: tys$$

$$\text{instance } Ravel \ t \ t \ \epsilon \text{ where}$$
$$\quad unravel \ (A0 \ x) = \quad x$$
$$\quad ravel \quad x \quad = A0 \ x$$
$$\text{instance } Ravel \ t \ (f \ x) \ tys \Rightarrow Ravel \ t \ f \ (x :\&: tys) \text{ where}$$
$$\quad unravel \ (Arg \ x) = unravel \ x$$
$$\quad ravel \quad x \quad = Arg \ (ravel \ x)$$

This way, we can pattern match in elements using $(:@@:)$ when defining function – and thus working around the problems of ambiguity discussed above – but at the same time provide an external interface with simpler types by means of the $unravel$ and $ravel$ conversion functions.

An immediate application of this type class is the definition of specialized versions of $fmap^\circ$ for the different variances with a name. Here is the $dimap$ function from the $Profunctor$ type class:

$$dimap :: Profunctor \ f \Rightarrow (b \to a) \to (c \to d) \to f \ a \ c \to f \ b \ d$$
$$dimap \ f \ g = unravel \circ fmap^\circ \ (M^{\Leftarrow} f \ (M^{\Rightarrow} g \ M\epsilon)) \circ ravel$$

We first map the given value of type $f \ a \ c$ into $f : @@: (a :\&: c :\&: \epsilon)$. At that point we can apply the generic operation $fmap^\circ$, we need to wrap the operations f and g into the $Mappings$ type. We get a result of type $f : @@: (b :\&: d :\&: \epsilon)$, which we map back to $f \ b \ d$ by means of $unravel$.

4 Generics for Arbitrary Kinds

As a final note on the applicability of $(:@@:)$, we would like to show how it immediatly helps in providing support for more types in the already existing GHC.Generics framework. In this section, we provide a direct translation of the work of Serrano and Miraldo [14] reusing most of the machinery already available in GHC instead of relying on complicated type level constructions, as in the original work. These extensions are available as part of the kind-generics library in Hackage.

Haskell compilers provide facilities to automatically write instances for some common classes, including *Eq* and *Show*. This mechanism is syntactically lightweight, the programmer is just required to add a deriving clause at the end of a data type definition:

$$\text{data } \textit{Either } a \ b = \textit{Left } a \mid \textit{Right } b \text{ deriving } (\textit{Eq}, \textit{Show})$$
$$\text{data } \textit{Pair} \quad a \ b = \textit{Pair } a \ b \qquad \text{deriving } (\textit{Eq}, \textit{Show})$$

GHC extends this facility with a mechanism to write functions which depend solely on the structure of the data type, but follow the same algorithm otherwise. This style is called *generic programming*.

The core idea of generic programming is simple: map data types to a uniform *representation*. Every function which operates on this representation is by construction generic over the data type. There are several ways to obtain the uniform representation in a typed setting; the main ones being codes [9,14,15], and pattern functors [8,10,20]. The latter is the one used by GHC, and the one we extend in this section.

In the pattern functor approach, the structure of a data type is expressed by a combination of the following functors, which act as building blocks:

$$\text{data } \textit{U1} \qquad a = \textit{U1}$$
$$\text{data } \textit{K1 } p \qquad a = \textit{K1 } a$$
$$\text{data } (f :*: g) \ a = f \ a :*: g \ a$$
$$\text{data } (f :+: g) \ a = \textit{L1 } (f \ a) \mid \textit{R1 } (g \ a)$$

Let us look at the representation of the aforementioned *Either* and *Pair*:

$$\textit{Rep } (\textit{Either } a \ b) = \textit{K1 } R \ a :+: \textit{K1 } R \ b$$
$$\textit{Rep } (\textit{Pair} \quad a \ b) = \textit{K1 } R \ a :*: \textit{K1 } R \ b$$

The *Either* type provides a choice between two constructors. This fact is represented by using the *coproduct* functor (:+:). The *Pair* type, on the other hand, requires two pieces of information. The *product* functor (:*:) encodes this information. In both cases, each field is represented by the *constant* functor *K1 R*.[3] The remaining block, *U1*, represents a constructor with no fields attached, like the empty list [].

---

[3] The first argument to *K1* was used in the past to encode some properties of the field. However, it has fallen into disuse, and GHC always sets its value to *R* in any automatically-derived representation.

Besides the structure of a type, we also need a map between *values* in the original type and its representation. The *Generic* type class bridges this gap:

```
class Generic a where
    type Rep a :: ⋆ → ⋆
    from :: a → Rep a x
    to   :: Rep a x → a
```

To define an instance of *Generic*, you need three pieces of information: (1) the representation *Rep*, which is a functor composed of the building blocks described above, (2) how to turn a value of type *a* into its representation – this is the function *from* –, and (3) how to map back – encoded as *to*. Writing these instances is mechanical, and GHC automates them by providing a *DeriveGeneric* extension.

Due to space limitations, we gloss over how to define functions which work on the generic representations. The interested reader is referred to the work of Magalhães *et al.* [8], and the documentation of GHC.Generics.

The first step towards generalizing the *Generic* type class is to extend its building blocks for the representations. In the case of the original *Rep*, we encode a type of kind ⋆ by a functor of kind ⋆ → ⋆; now we are going to encode a type of kind k by a representation of kind $\Gamma\ k → ⋆$. The use of a list of types Γ here is essential, because otherwise we cannot express arbitrary kinds. This approach deviates from the one taken by GHC, in which type constructors of kind ⋆ → ⋆ are also represented by functors of kind ⋆ → ⋆. In fact, all we need to do is define a new *K1* since the other combinators are readily compatible.

We solve this problem by introducing a separate data type to encode the structure of the type of a field [14, 17]. This is nothing more than the applicative fragment of λ-calculus, in which references to type variables are encoded using de Bruijn indices:

```
data TyVar d k where
    VZ ::                    TyVar (x → xs) x
    VS :: TyVar xs k →  TyVar (x → xs) k
data Atom d k where
    Var :: TyVar d k → Atom d k
    Kon :: k            → Atom d k
    (:@:) :: Atom d (k1 → k2) → Atom d k1 → Atom d k2
```

A value of *Atom d k* represents a type of kind k in an environment with type variables described by the kind d. *TyVar* refers to a type variable in the kind d using Peano numerals, starting from the left-most variable. For example, the type of the single field of the *Right* constructor is represented as *Var (VS VZ)*.

By itself, *Atom d k* only *describes* the shape of a type. In order to obtain an actual type, we need to *interpret* it with known values for all the type variables. If one thinks of *Atom*s as expressions with variables, such as $x^2 + x + 1$, interpreting the *Atom* boils down to obtaining the value of the expression given a value for each variable, like $x \mapsto 5$. This interpretation can be defined by recursion on the structure of the *Atom*:

```
type family Ty (t :: Atom d k) (tys :: Γ d) :: k where
  Ty (Var VZ)      (t :&: ts) = t
  Ty (Var (VS v)) (t :&: ts) = Ty (Var v) ts
  Ty (Kon x)       tys        = x
  Ty (f :@: x)     tys        = (Ty f tys) (Ty x tys)
```

Note that by construction an *Atom d k* is always interpreted to a type of kind k.

With these ingredients, we can encode the missing building block. In Haskell, it is required that fields in a data type have a type with kind $\star$. This is visible in the definition of F, where t must describe a type with that specific kind:

$$\text{data } F \ (t :: Atom \ d \ (\star)) \ (x :: \Gamma \ d) = F \ (Ty \ t \ x)$$

The representations of *Either* and *Pair* look as follows:

$$Rep^\diamond \ Either = F \ (Var \ VZ) :+: F \ (Var \ (VS \ VZ))$$
$$Rep^\diamond \ Pair \ \ = F \ (Var \ VZ) :*: F \ (Var \ (VS \ VZ))$$

Note the change in the arguments to $Rep^\diamond$. We are no longer defining a family of representations for every possible choice of type arguments to *Either* and *Pair*, as we did in the case of *Rep*. Here we encode precisely the polymorphic structure of the data types.

Finally, we can wrap it all together with a type class that declares the isomorphism between values and their generic representation.

```
class Generic° (f :: k) where
  type Rep° f :: Γ k → ⋆
  from° ::          f :@@: x → Rep° f x
  to°   :: Γs x → Rep° f x → f :@@: x
```

One part of the isomorphism, $from^\diamond$, has a straightforward type. The converse operation is harder to define though. The problem is that we need to match over the structure of the list of types, but this information is apparent from the kind itself. The solution is to use a *singleton* [5], that is, to introduce a new data type that completely mimics the shape of the type level information:

```
data Γs (tys :: Γ k) where
  εs ::             Γs ε
  &s :: Γs ts → Γs (t :&: ts)
```

By inspecting this singleton value, the compiler gains enough information about the shape of *tys* to know that the result is well-formed.

We can finally give the *Generic$^\circ$* instance for *Either*:

> instance *Generic$^\circ$ Either* where
> > type *Rep Either* = *F* (*Var VZ*) :+: *F* (*Var* (*VS VZ*))
> > *from$^\circ$* (*A2* (*Left x*)) = *InL* (*F x*)
> > *from$^\circ$* (*A2* (*Right y*)) = *InR* (*F y*)
> > *to$^\circ$* (&$_s$ (&$_s$ ϵ_s)) (*InL* (*F x*)) = *A2* (*Left x*)
> > *to$^\circ$* (&$_s$ (&$_s$ ϵ_s)) (*InR* (*F y*)) = *A2* (*Right y*)

4.1   Representing Constraints and Existentials

One advantage of this new representation is that it becomes simple to describe more complicated structures for data types. In particular, it enables us to represent constructors with constraints and existentials, key ingredients of Generalized Algebraic Data Types [19] available in Haskell and OCaml, among others.

The case of constraints is very similar to that of regular fields. As we have discussed several times already, a constraint is seen by GHC as a regular type of a specific kind *Constraint*. Since our language of types, *Atom*, works regardless of the kind it represents, we can still use it in this new scenario:

> data ($\Rightarrow$:) (*c* :: *Atom d Constraint*) (*f* :: Γ *d* $\to$ $\star$) (*x* :: Γ *d*) where
> > *C* :: *Ty c x* $\Rightarrow$ *f x* $\to$ (*c* $\Rightarrow$: *f*) *x*

The definition of ($\Rightarrow$:) wraps a representation *f* with an additional *implicit* parameter. This means that by merely pattern matching on the constructor we make this information available. For example, here is the usual definition of the *Equality* data type and its *Generic$^\circ$* instance:

> data *Equals a b* where
> > *Refl* :: *a* $\sim$ *b* $\Rightarrow$ *Equals a b*

> instance *Generic$^\circ$ Equals* where
> > type *Rep$^\circ$ Equals* = (*Kon* ($\sim$) :@: *Var VZ* :@: *Var* (*VS VZ*)) $\Rightarrow$: *U1*
> > *from$^\circ$* (*A2 Refl*) = *C U1*
> > *to$^\circ$* (&$_s$ (&$_s$ ϵ_s)) (*C U1*) = *A2 Refl*

Introducing existentials requires more involved types, however.

> data *E k* (*f* :: Γ (*k* $\to$ *d*) $\to$ $\star$) (*x* :: Γ *d*) where
> > *E* :: forall *k* (*t* :: *k*) *d* (*f* :: Γ (*k* $\to$ *d*) $\to$ $\star$) (*x* :: Γ *d*)
> > . *f* (*t* :&: *x*) $\to$ *E k f x*

The *E* type above provides us with the required kind Γ *d* $\to$ $\star$ given another representation with the kind Γ (*k* $\to$ *d*) $\to$ $\star$. In other words, the argument to *E* is another representation where we have an *additional* type variable available in the environment. This new type variable refers to the existential introduced.

The following data type, *Exists*, keeps a value of any type we want, but this type is not visible as an index to the type. Using E we can describe its representation in this generic framework:

> data *Exists* where
>   *Exists* :: $a \to$ *Exists*
>
> instance *Generic*$^\diamond$ X where
>   type *Rep*$^\diamond$ *Exists* = E $(\star)$ $(F$ $(Var$ $VZ))$
>   *from*$^\diamond$ $(A0$ $(Exists$ $x)) = E$ $(F$ $x)$
>   *to*$^\diamond$ ϵ_s $(E$ $(F$ $x)) = A0$ $(Exists$ $x)$

In conclusion, the introduction of the $(:@@:)$ construction provides a basis for more expressive generic programming. By defining only one new building block, F, we are readily able to represent types of arbitrary kind directly. Once these foundations are laid down, we can accommodate descriptions of types using constraints and existentials in our generic programming framework.

5   Related Work

Weirich and Casinghino [17] discuss how to encode arity and data type-generic operations in Agda. There are two main differences between that work and ours. First, the language of implementation is Agda, a language with full dependent types, as opposed to Haskell. Second, whereas their goal is to define arity-generic operations such as *map*, our goal is to describe notions which exist regardless of the arity, such as $Eq^\diamond$ and $Functor^\diamond$. As a result, we are less concerned about the implementation of the instances.

The work of Hinze [6] tackles poly-kinded generic programming from a different point of view. There generic functions defined over representations of the $\star$ are automatically lifted to data types of higher kinds. It is an interesting avenue to investigate how much of his method can be translated into our setting.

Quantified class constraints [2] allow the programmer to define type classes for constructors, such as *Show1*, by quantification over the constraints for ground types. However, the ability to define the class for arbitrary kinds is still missing. We foresee that a combination of $(:@@:)$ with quantified constraints is possible.

Our representation of types as a type constructor and a list of arguments resembles the applicative fragment of the spine calculus of [3]. In contrast we do not impose any restriction about the shape of the head.

6   Conclusion

In this paper we have presented a way to encode the generalities between types of possibly different kinds by means of polymorphic type classes. The key ingredient being the definition of the $(:@@:)$ data type, which turns n-ary applications into the application of one head and a list of types.

We have discussed generalizations of the well-known *Show*, *Eq*, and *Functor* type classes. In the latter case, we have also discussed how to represent the variance of a type variable as part of the type class. We have also shown how one could extend the *Generic* framework present in GHC to work over types of arbitrary kind with minimal fuss.

References

1. Bolingbroke, M.: Constraint Kinds (2011). http://blog.omega-prime.co.uk/?p=127
2. Bottu, G.J., Karachalias, G., Schrijvers, T., Oliveira, B.C.d.S., Wadler, P.: Quantified class constraints. In: Proceedings of the 10th International Symposium on Haskell, Haskell 2017. ACM (2017)
3. Cervesato, I., Pfenning, F.: A linear spine calculus. J. Log. Comput. **13**(5), 639–688 (2003)
4. Chakravarty, M.M.T., Keller, G., Peyton Jones, S., Marlow, S.: Associated types with class. In: Proceedings of the 32nd Symposium on Principles of Programming Languages, POPL 2005. ACM (2005)
5. Eisenberg, R.A., Weirich, S.: Dependently typed programming with singletons. In: Proceedings of the 2012 Haskell Symposium, Haskell 2012. ACM (2012)
6. Hinze, R.: Polytypic values possess polykinded types. In: Backhouse, R., Oliveira, J.N. (eds.) MPC 2000. LNCS, vol. 1837, pp. 2–27. Springer, Heidelberg (2000). https://doi.org/10.1007/10722010_2
7. Jones, M.P.: Type classes with functional dependencies. In: Smolka, G. (ed.) ESOP 2000. LNCS, vol. 1782, pp. 230–244. Springer, Heidelberg (2000). https://doi.org/10.1007/3-540-46425-5_15
8. Magalhães, J.P., Dijkstra, A., Jeuring, J., Löh, A.: Ageneric deriving mechanism for haskell. In: Proceedings of the 3rd Symposium on Haskell, Haskell 2010. ACM (2010)
9. Miraldo, V.C., Serrano, A.: Sums of products for mutually recursive datatypes: the appropriationist's view on generic programming. In: Proceedings of the 3rd International Workshop on Type-Driven Development, TyDe 2018. ACM (2018)
10. Noort, T.v., Rodriguez, A., Holdermans, S., Jeuring, J., Heeren, B.: A lightweight approach to datatype-generic rewriting. In: Proceedings of the Workshop on Generic Programming, WGP 2008. ACM (2008)
11. Peyton Jones, S., Jones, M., Meijer, E.: Type classes: an exploration of the design space. In: Haskell Workshop, Amsterdam (1997)
12. Pickering, M., Érdi, G., Peyton Jones, S., Eisenberg, R.A.: Pattern synonyms. In: Proceedings of the 9th International Symposium on Haskell, Haskell 2016. ACM (2016)
13. Schrijvers, T., Peyton Jones, S., Chakravarty, M., Sulzmann, M.: Type checking with open type functions. In: Proceedings of the 13th International Conference on Functional Programming, ICFP 2008. ACM (2008)
14. Serrano, A., Miraldo, V.C.: Generic programming of all kinds. In: Proceedings of the 11th Symposium on Haskell, Haskell 2018. ACM (2018)
15. de Vries, E., Löh, A.: True sums of products. In: Proceedings of the 10th Workshop on Generic Programming, WGP 2014. ACM (2014)
16. Wadler, P., Blott, S.: How to make ad-hoc polymorphism less ad hoc. In: Proceedings of the 16th Symposium on Principles of Programming Languages, POPL 1989. ACM (1989)

17. Weirich, S., Casinghino, C.: Arity-generic datatype-generic programming. In: Proceedings of the 4th Workshop on Programming Languages Meets Program Verification, PLPV 2010. ACM (2010)
18. Weirich, S., Voizard, A., de Amorim, P.H.A., Eisenberg, R.A.: A specification for dependent types in haskell. In: Proceedings ACM Programming Languages 1(ICFP) (2017)
19. Xi, H., Chen, C., Chen, G.: Guarded recursive datatype constructors. In: Proceedings of the 30th Symposium on Principles of Programming Languages, POPL 2003. ACM (2003)
20. Yakushev, A.R., Holdermans, S., Löh, A., Jeuring, J.: Generic programming with fixed points for mutually recursive datatypes. In: Proceedings of the 14th International Conference on Functional Programming, ICFP 2009. ACM (2009)
21. Yorgey, B.A., Weirich, S., Cretin, J., Peyton Jones, S., Vytiniotis, D., Magalhães, J.P.: Giving haskell a promotion. In: Proceedings of the 8th Workshop on Types in Language Design and Implementation, TLDI 2012. ACM (2012)

Distributed Protocol Combinators

Kristoffer Just Arndal Andersen[1]([⊠]) and Ilya Sergey[2]

[1] Aarhus University, Aarhus, Denmark
kja@cs.au.dk
[2] Yale-NUS College and NUS School of Computing, Singapore, Singapore
ilya.sergey@yale-nus.edu.sg

Abstract. Distributed systems are hard to get right, model, test, debug, and teach. Their textbook definitions, typically given in a form of replicated state machines, are concise, yet prone to introducing programming errors if naïvely translated into runnable implementations.

In this work, we present *Distributed Protocol Combinators* (DPC), a declarative programming framework that aims to bridge the gap between specifications and runnable implementations of distributed systems, and facilitate their modeling, testing, and execution. DPC builds on the ideas from the state-of-the art logics for compositional systems verification. The contribution of DPC is a novel family of program-level primitives, which facilitates construction of larger distributed systems from smaller components, streamlining the usage of the most common asynchronous message-passing communication patterns, and providing machinery for testing and user-friendly dynamic verification of systems. This paper describes the main ideas behind the design of the framework and presents its implementation in Haskell. We introduce DPC through a series of characteristic examples and showcase it on a number of distributed protocols from the literature.

1 Introduction

Distributed fault-tolerant systems are at the heart of modern electronic services, spanning such aspects of our lives as healthcare, online commerce, transportation, entertainment and cloud-based applications. From engineering and reasoning perspectives, distributed systems are amongst the most complex pieces of software being developed nowadays. The complexity is not only due to the intricacy of the underlying protocols for multi-party interaction, which should be resilient to execution faults, packet loss and corruption, but also due to hard performance and availability requirements [2].

The issue of system correctness is traditionally addressed by employing a wide range of *whole-system* testing methodologies, with more recent advances in integrating techniques for formal verification into the system development process [5,8,20]. In an ongoing effort of developing a *verification* methodology enabling the *reuse* of formal proofs about distributed systems in the context of an open world, the DISEL logic, built on top of the Coq proof assistant [3], has

© Springer Nature Switzerland AG 2019
J. J. Alferes and M. Johansson (Eds.): PADL 2019, LNCS 11372, pp. 169–186, 2019.
https://doi.org/10.1007/978-3-030-05998-9_11

been proposed as the first framework for mechanised verification of distributed systems, enabling modular proofs about protocol composition [24,26].

The main construction of DISEL is a *distributed protocol* $\mathcal{P}$—an operationally described replicated *state-transition system* (STS), which captures the shape of the state of each node in the system, as well as what it *can* or *cannot* do at any moment, depending on its state. Even though a protocol $\mathcal{P}$ is not an executable program and cannot be immediately run, one can still use it as an *executable specification* of the system, in order to prove the system's intrinsic properties. For instance, reasoning at the level of a protocol, one can establish that a property I : SystemState $\rightarrow$ Prop is an inductive invariant *wrt.* a protocol $\mathcal{P}$.[1] A somewhat simplified main judgement of DISEL, $\mathcal{P} \vdash c$, asserts that an actual system implementation c will *not* violate the operational specification of $\mathcal{P}$. Therefore, if this holds, one can infer that any execution of a program c, will not violate the property I, proved for protocol $\mathcal{P}$. DISEL also features a full-blown program logic, implemented as a Hoare Type Theory [19], which allows one to ascribe pre- and post-conditions to distributed programs, enforcing them via Coq's dependent types, at the expense of frequently requiring the user to write lengthy proof scripts.

While expressive enough to implement and verify, for instance, a crash-recovery service on top of a Two-Phase Commit [24], unfortunately, DISEL, as a systems *implementation* tool, is far from being user-friendly, and is not immediately applicable for rapid prototyping of composite distributed systems, their testing and debugging. Neither can one use it for teaching without assuming students' knowledge of Coq and Separation Logic [21]. Furthermore, system implementations in DISEL must be encoded in terms of low-level send/receive primitive, obscuring the high-level protocol design.

In this work, we give a practical spin to DISEL's main idea—disentangling protocol *specifications* from runnable, possibly highly optimised, systems *implementations*, making the following contributions:

- We distil a number of high-level distributed interaction patterns, which are common in practical system implementations, and capture them in a form of a novel family of *Distributed Protocol Combinators* (DPC)—a set of versatile higher-order programming primitives. DPC allow one to implement systems concisely, while still being able to benefit from protocol-based specifications for the sake of testing and specification-aware debugging.
- We implement DPC in Haskell, providing a set of specification and implementation primitives, parameterised by a monadic interface, which allow for multiple interpretations of protocol-oriented distributed implementations.
- We provide a rich toolset for testing, running, and visual debugging of systems implemented via DPC, allowing one to state and dynamically check the protocol invariants, as well as to trace their execution in a GUI.
- We showcase DPC on a variety of distributed systems, ranging from a simple RPC-based cloud calculator and its variations, to distributed locking [10], Two-Phase Commit [7], and Paxos consensus [12,13].

---

[1] Examples of such properties include global-systems invariants, used, in particular, to reason about the whole system reaching a consensus [22,25].

2   Specifying and Implementing Systems with DPC

In this work, we focus on message-passing asynchronous distributed systems, where each node maintains its internal state while interacting with others by means of sending and receiving messages. That is, the messages, which can be sent and received at any moment, with arbitrary delays, drops, and rearrangements, are the only medium of communication between the nodes. DPC takes the common approach of thinking of message-passing systems as shared-memory systems, in which each message in transit is allocated in a virtual shared "message soup", where it lingers until it is delivered to the recipient [24,27].

The exact implementation of the *per-node* internal state might differ from one node to another, as it is virtually unobservable by other participants of the system. However, in order for the whole system to function correctly, it is required that each node's behaviour would be at least coherent with some notion of *abstract state*, which is used to describe the interaction protocol.

In the remainder of this section, we will build an intuition of designing a system "top-down". We will start from its specification in terms of a protocol that defines the abstract state and governs the message-passing discipline, going all the way down to the implementation that defines the state concretely and possibly combines several protocols together. For this, we use a standard example of a distributed calculator.

2.1   Describing Distributed Interaction

In a simple cloud calculator, a node takes one of two possible roles: of a *client* or of a *server*. A client may send a request along with data to be acted upon to the server (*e.g.*, a list of numbers [3, 100, 20]

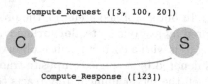

Compute_Request ([3, 100, 20])

Compute_Response ([123])

to compute the sum of), and the server in turn responds with the result of the computation, as shown on the diagram on the right. For uniformity of implementation, all messages, including the response of the server are lists of integers. Notice that this description does not restrict *e.g.*, the order in which a server must process incoming requests from the clients, which leaves a lot of room for potential optimisations on the implementation side.

In order to capture the behavioural contract describing the interaction between clients and servers, we need to be able to outlaw some unwelcome communication scenarios. For instance, in our examples, it would be out of protocol for the server to respond with a wrong answer (in general an issue of safety) or to the wrong client (in general an issue of security). A convenient way to restrict the communication rules between distributed parties is by introducing the *abstract state* describing specific "life stages" of a client and a server, as well as associated messages that trigger changes in this state—altogether forming an STS, a well-known way to abstractly describe and reason about distributed protocols [14,15].

Let us now describe our calculator protocol as a collection of coordinated transition systems. The client's part in the protocol originates in a state ClientInit containing the input it is going to send to the server, as well as the server's identity. From this state, it can send a message to server S with the payload [3, 100, 20]. It then must wait, in a blocking state, for a response from the server.[2] Upon having received the message, the client proceeds to a third and final state, ClientDone. From here, no more transitions are possible, and the client's part in the protocol is completed. A schematic outline of the client protocol is depicted in Fig. 1(a).

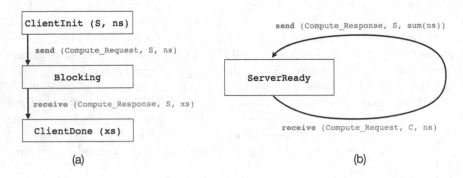

Fig. 1. State transitions for a client (a) and a server (b) in the calculator protocol.

In our simplified scenario, the protocol for the server (Fig. 1(b)) can be captured by just one state, ServerReady, so that receiving the request and responding to it with a correct result is observed as "atomic" by other parties, and hence, is denoted by a single composite transition. In other words, at the specification level, the server immediately reacts to the request by sending a response.

Notice that the protcol places no demands on the number of clients, servers or unrelated nodes in the network, nor does it restrict the number of instances of the protocol are running in a given network. The specification is "local" to the parties involved (which in general can number arbitrarily many).

This "request/respond" communication pattern is so common in distributed programming that it is worth making explicit. We will refer to this pattern as a pure *remote procedure call* (RPC) and take it as our first combinator for protocol-based implementation of distributed systems.

---

[2] Remember that this is a specification-level blocking, the implementation can actually do something useful in the same time, just not related to this protocol!

2.2 Specifying the Protocol

We can capture the RPC-shaped communication in DPC by first enumerating all possible states of nodes in the protocol in a single data type. For the calculator, the states can be directly translated from the description above to the following Haskell data type:

```
data S = ClientInit NodeID [Int]
       | ClientDone [Int]
       | ServerReady
```

NodeID is a type synonym for Int, but any type with equality would serve. ClientInit contains the name of the server and the list to sum. ClientDone contains the response from the server. Next, we describe the only kind of exchange that takes place in a network of clients and servers communicating by following the RPC discipline. We do so by specifying when a client can produce a request in a protocol, and how the server computes the response. Perhaps, a bit surprisingly, no more information is needed, as the pattern dictates that clients await responses from servers, and the server responds immediately. This is the reason why need only enumerate two states for the client, eliding the one for blocking, as per Fig. 1(a): the framework adds the third during execution by wrapping the states in a type with an additional Blocking constructor.[3] The following definition of compute outlines the specification of the protocol's STSs:

```
compute :: Alternative f ⇒ ([Int] → Int) → Protlet f S
compute f = RPC "compute" clientStep serverStep
  where
    clientStep s = case s of
      ClientInit server args → Just (server, args, ClientDone)
      _ → Nothing
    serverStep args s = case s of
      ServerReady → Just ([f args], ServerReady)
      _ → Nothing
```

As per its type, compute takes a client-provided function of type [Int] → Int, which is used by the server to perform calculations. The result of compute is of type Protlet f S, where S is the data type of our STS states defined just above and f is an instance encapsulating a possible non-determinism in a protocol specification. Later constructions will make integral use of non-determinism to, e.g., decide on the next transition depending on the external inputs, and the parameter f serves to restrict what notion of non-determinism is used in the definition of protocols.[4] For now, the result of compute is entirely deterministic.

Protlets (*aka* "small protocols") are the main building blocks of our framework. A distributed protocol can be thought of as a family of protlets, each of which corresponds to a logically independent piece of functionality and can be captured by a fixed interaction pattern between nodes. In a system, each node can act according to one or more protlets, executing the logic corresponding to

---

[3] See the discussion of executing specification in Sect. 3.
[4] One can think of any protocol, whose diagram has a fork, as non-deterministic.

them sequentially, or in parallel. For this example, there is just the one exchange of messages, so a single protlet makes for the complete protocol description.

Our framework provides several constructors to build protlets from the data type description for the protocol state space and the operational semantics of its transitions. In the example above, RPC is a data constructor, which encodes the protlet logic by means of two functions. Its first argument, clientStep, prescribes that from ClientInit state, a node can send args to node server, and the response payload is later wrapped via ClientDone to form the succesor state. The second argument, serverStep, says that the state ServerReady can serve a request in one step: receiving args and responding with f args in a singleton list, continuing in the same state. We have now completely captured the above intuitions and transition system of the calculator in less than ten lines of Haskell.

2.3 Executing the Specification

The immediate benefits of having an executable operational specification of a protocol is to be able to run it, locally and without needing full deployment across a network, ensuring that it satisfies basic sanity checks and more complex invariants.

The execution model for protlets is a small-step operational semantics, with the granularity of transitions being that of the involved protlets. We take as machine configurations the entire network of nodes and their abstract states.

In case several protlets of a similar shape are involved (e.g., a node is involved in two or more RPCs), we distinguish them by introducing protlet labels, a solution that is standard for program logics for concurrency [4,23]. Having introduced protlet labels, we can logically partition the local state of each node along the protlet instance space, maintaining a local state portion "per protlet", per node. We represent this operational machine configuration as the datatype SpecNetwork, which is a record data structure maintaining an environment of protlets (indexed by their associated labels) and a protlet state for each node and protocol instance, so that the operational semantics changes one node's one protlet's state at a time. The following code creates a network for the calculator protocol with two nodes (identified by 0 and 1), both running just one protlet (labelled with 0), for the input for the example from Sect. 2.1:

```
addNetwork :: Alternative f ⇒ SpecNetwork f S
addNetwork = initializeNetwork nodeStates protocols
  where
    nodeStates = [ (0, [(0, ServerReady)])
                 , (1, [(0, ClientInit 0 [3, 100, 20])]) ]
    protocols = [(0, [compute sum])]
```

In any given network configuration, many actions can be possible. A node may be ready to initiate an RPC, or it might be ready to receive a message—many such actions may be enabled and relevant at once.[5] As the purpose of

---

[5] And their abundance is precisely why reasoning about distributed systems is hard.

running the specification is to trace the possible behaviors in the protocol, we choose the next action to execute in the network by leaving the resolution to the *user* of the semantics. To do so, we implement the executable small-step relation as a monad-parameterised function capturing the possibility of non-determinism (hence `Alternative f`). This makes the implementation of the operational semantics simple, yet general, as it just needs to describe an `f`-ary choice or `f`-full collection of transitions at each step:

```
step :: (Monad f, Alternative f) ⇒ SpecNetwork f s → f (SpecNetwork f s)
```

The network can be "run" by iterating this small-step execution function with a suitable instance of `f`, a standard construction in implementation of a non-determinism in monadic interpreters.

For example, we can instantiate the non-determinism to the classic choice of the list monad [17], which leads to enumerating every possible action. We can then iterate the function `step` by choosing a random possible transition, as in the following interaction with the library, where we explore the "depth" of a single run of the protocol.

```
> length <$> simulateNetworkIO addNetwork
4
```

This is coherent with the first example we envisioned *wrt.* the protocol: there is (1) the initial state; (2) the state with the client awaiting response, but the message undelivered; (3) the state with the client waiting and the server having sent a response; and finally, (4) a terminal state with the client done.

The non-determinism can be similarly resolved by enumerating all possible paths through a protocol, up to a certain trace length if the execution space is not finite. If the state space of a network is finite, this can yield actual finite-space model checking procedures. In the following subsection, we will explore another alternative to resolving the non-determinism, yielding an unusual yet very useful execution method.

2.4   Interactive Exploration with GUI

By delegating the decision of which transition to follow to the user of an application that performs this simulation, we can allow the client of the framework to explore the network behaviour interactively. The DPC library provides a command-line GUI application facilitating interactive

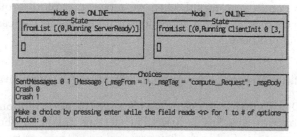

Fig. 2. The interactive exploration tool, loaded with the calculator protocol.

exploration of distributed networks step-by-step. Provided an initial network specification like the one described previously, one can start the session by typing the following:

```
> runGUI addNetwork
```

This yields the interface displayed in Fig. 2. By choosing specific transitions in sequence, the user can evolve and inspect the network at each step of execution. This is useful for protocol design and debugging, and can help understand the dynamics of a protocol, and the kinds of communication patterns it describes

For example, in Fig. 3 we show the subsequent prompt after showing the selection of Option 1:

```
SentMessages 0 1 [Message {_msgFrom = 1, _msgTag = "compute__Request",...
```

SentMessages is a human readable piece of data that represents the option of sending in protocol instance 0, from node 1 the message with sender 1 of tag "compute__Request". Here, the recipient and message content is elided for issues of screenspace, but as the window is enlarged, so is the depth of information provided.

The state view is then shows that Node 0 now has said message waiting for it in the soup, and Node 1 is now blocking. The user is then presented with subsequent possible choices, here the option for the calculator to receive the request and send the response in one atomic action, as dictated by the protocol.

Additionally, as can be seen in Fig. 2, in the interactive tool we enrich the possible transitions at every step with the possibility of a node to go off-line. In effect, it means it will stop processing messages, modelling a benign (non-byzantine) fault. Other nodes cannot

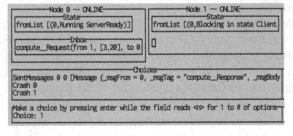

Fig. 3. Choosing option 1 in the prompt from Fig. 2.

observe this and will "perceive" the node as not responding. This, however, becomes very useful when we move to explore protocols that allow for partial responses among a collection of nodes, as in the case of crash-resilient consensus protocols.

2.5   Protocol-Aware Distributed Implementations

Distributed systems protocols serve as key components of some of the largest software systems in use. The actions taken in the protocol are governed by programs outside the key protocol primitives, so it is vital that implementations can integrate with software components in real general-purpose languages. We here present such a language with primitives for sending and receiving messages as an embedded domain-specific language (EDSL) in Haskell. This allows use of the entire Haskell toolkit in engineering efficient optimised implementations relying on distributed interaction.

Naturally, as implementations deviate from the protocols (in the way they, *e.g.*, implement internal state), we want to ensure that the they still adhere to the protocol as specified. To achieve this, we introduce primitives for *annotating* implementations with protocol-specific assertions. These annotations can be ignored by execution-oriented interpretations aiming for efficiency rather than verification guarantees.

The following code implements a calculator server in plain Haskell using do-notation to sequence effectful computations. The effects are described by type class constraints: `MessagePassing` provides a `send` and `receive` primitive, and `ProtletAnnotations` providing the `enactingServer` primitive, explained below.

```
addServer :: (ProtletAnnotations S m, MessagePassing m) ⇒ Label → m a
addServer label = loop
  where
    loop = do
      enactingServer (compute sum) $ do
        Message client _ args _ _ ← spinReceive [(label, "Compute__Request")]
        send client label "Compute__Response" [sum args]
      loop
```

By using type classes describing operations, we allow for several different interpretations of this code. For instance, by interpreting the `send` and `receive` as POSIX Socket operations, we obtain a subroutine in the IO Monad, Haskell's effectful fragment, that we can integrate into any larger development with no interpretive overhead. The `spinReceive` operation is defined using recursion and a primitive `receive` operation that attempts to receive an incoming message with a tag from amongst a list of canididate message tags in a non-blocking manner.

The body of `addServer` is annotated with a (`compute sum`) protlet, enforcing that the server responds to the client atomically (in terms of message passing) and to perform the `sum` function (or something observationally equivalent) on the supplied arguments. By bracketing the `receive` and `send` in the `enactingServer` primitive, the implementation declares its intent to conform to the server role of the RPC, as dictated by the protocol. Once we have a client to play the other role in the protocol, we will demonstrate how this intent can be checked dynamically. The message tags that appear in the code are *by convention* the tags used in the RPC protocol, *i.e.*, the name of the protocol with a suffix indicating the role in the RPC that the message plays.

In contrast DISEL and other static verification frameworks that enforce protocol adherence via (dependent) type systems (embedded in Coq or other proof assistants) [11,24], we verify protocol properties dynamically. The tradeoff is that of coverage versus annotation and proof overhead. We can, through exploiting executable specifications, check that *a single run of a program* adheres to a protocol. Notice that `addServer` is, like the specification of the `compute` protlet, agnostic in the number and kinds of other nodes in the network. Its behaviour is locally and completely described by its implementation, and is segregated from interfering with unrelated protlets via the `label` parameter. We refer the reader to the development for a number of client component implementations.

Let us now reap the benefits of protocol-aware distributed programming enabled by DPC and *dynamically check* that the implementations do indeed follow the abstract protocols. We achieve this by interpreting the EDSL into a datatype of abstract syntax trees (AST) that makes it possible to inspect their evaluations at run time. We give a small-step structural operational semantics to this language, and, precisely like the exectuable specifications, lift the evaluation of a single program to that of an entire network of programs, by assigning each program a node identifier in the network. Here, the global state (of type ImplNetwork m Int, with m constrained as in addServer/addClient) is just the message soup, and the node-local state is the program itself. Such an evaluation is implemented by the following function.

```
runPure :: ImplNetwork (AST s) a →
[(TraceAction s, ImplNetwork (AST s) a)]
```

Here, the AST data type is the HOAS AST for message-passing implementations to be interpreted. The result of running the network is a (possibly infinite) list of TraceActions and the network configurations they lead to. We can simulate a full run of the network by taking the last network in this list, provided the network terminates. Messages can be examined by considering the soup component at every step of evaluation.

We can verify that our implementation indeed adheres to the desired protocol by the trace produced by runPure on a network configuration, ensuring that (a) every observable action is compatible with the state that the node is supposed to be in, and (b) checking the messages expected from these states. For this, we implement yet another operational semantics, where the machine configuration is a protocol state for every node id, and the program is a trace of primitive actions. The interpreter faults if the current action is not applicable to the state, or sends or receives messages not prescribed by the specification. We can run the adherence checker on a *prefix* (*e.g.*, of length 15) of the infinite trace as follows:

```
> checkTrace addNetwork $ fmap fst . take 15 $ runPure addConf
  Right ()
```

The result of Right () indicates success: the trace did indeed conform to the protlet annotations of the program, assuming the initial state of the implementations in addConf assumed an initial abstract state corresponding to the the network state of addNetwork.

What happens if we introduce a mistake in the implementation? For instance, if we erroneously annotate the server as intending to serve a product function (instead of sum), we will fail protocol adherence, because the specification does not agree on the content of the messages. In a different scenario, if we run the client implementation *twice*, the checker would report an error, as this is not allowed by the protocol: the client would have brought itself to the terminal state ClientDone by the first RPC, and, hence, cannot proceed. By enriching dynamic testing with protocol adherence checks we believe we can achieve greater assurances of the correctness of our implementations without resorting to use full-blown verification frameworks [8,24].

3   Framework Internals

3.1   The Specification Language

A full distributed system specification consists of a collection of nodes, each assigned a unique node identifier, and a collection of protlets for each instance label. A node owns local state, partitioned according to protocol instance labels. A protlet describes one exchange pattern between parties. A collection of protlets over the same state space then describe an entire protocol.

In the overview we saw the simplest protlet, the pure RPC, but through exploration of examples and case studies, we have discovered a number of such patterns, each more general than the previous. These are implemented as extensions to the `Protlet` data type. One such is the broadcast protlet, integral for describing multi-party protocols.[6]

```
data Protlet f s =
  | RPC         String (ClientStep s) (ServerStep s)
  | Broadcast   String (Broadcast s)  (Receive s) (Send f s)
  | ...
```

The component functions of the protlets reuse a number of common type abbreviations, here `ClientStep`, `Send` etc. All are at work in the above listing. This common structure unifies their implementation in the operational semantics. The expansion of, *e.g.*, the `Broadcast` synonym is as follows:

```
type Broadcast s = s →
Maybe ([(NodeID, [Int])], [(NodeID, [Int])] → s)
```

This models a "partial" function on states s, saying under which conditions a node can initiate a broadcast, by enumerating the recipients and the body of the messages to them, along with a continuation processing the received answers with their associated senders. This continuation is stored in the implicit blocking state during actual execution of the specification.

The specification language is given a non-deterministic operational semantics as described in Sect. 2.3. Recall the network step function:

```
step :: (Monad f, Alternative f) ⇒
SpecNetwork f s → f (SpecNetwork f s)
```

It is implemented by computing an f-full of possible transitions for every node in the network and combining the result of taking all possible transitions on the current network. The key operation of `step` is a dispatch on the current protocol state of a node:

```
case state of
  BlockingOn _ tag f nodeIDs k →
    resolveBlock label tag f nodeID inbox nodeIDs k
  Running s → do
    protlet ← fst <$> oneOf (_globalState Map.! label)
    stepProtlet nodeID s inbox label protlet
```

---

[6] We elide the other protlet constructors, which can be found in our implementation.

The constructors BlockingOn and Running are supplied by the framework. The first is used to track the terms under which a node is blocking: what message(s) it needs to continue and from whom. resolveBlock computes whether the conditions are met for the current node to continue.

Here, _globalState is the mapping of collections of protlets (*i.e.*, a protocol) from instance labels. We then choose between protlets using oneOf :: [a]→f a. stepProtlet dispatches control based on a case distinction on the protlet constructor: for example, here is the branch for the Broadcast protlet:

```
stepProtlet :: (Monad m, Alternative m) ⇒
  NodeID → s → [Message] → Label → Protlet m s →  m (Transition s)
stepProtlet nodeID state inbox label protlet = case protlet of
  ...
  Broadcast name broadcast receive respond →
    tryBroadcast label name broadcast nodeID state inbox <|>          -- (1)
    tryReceive label (name ++ "__Broadcast") receive nodeID state inbox <|>   -- (2)
    trySend label respond nodeID state inbox                          -- (3)
  ...
```

A node attempting to advance a protocol using the Broadcast protlet can do so if it is (1) a client ready to perform a broadcast; (2) a server ready to receive such a broadcast; or (3) a server that is ready to respond to a broadcast. The try functions all follow the same structure: check that the user-provided protlet component functions apply, and if so, generate an appropriate transition. For instance, here is the signature of one such function for Broadcast:

```
tryBroadcast :: Alternative f ⇒ Label → String → Broadcast s →
                NodeID → s → [Message] → f (Transition s)
```

Interpretations of Protocols. As described in Sect. 2.3, the operational semantics of protocols can be instantiated to obtain different interpretations. We here look at bounded model checking mentioned in passing in the overview. We can use the List monad to enumerate all execution paths in a breadth-first manner:

```
simulateNetworkTraces :: SpecNetwork [] s → [[SpecNetwork [] s]]
```

This yields a list-of-lists where the nth list contains all possible states after n steps of execution, in a breadth first enumeration of the state space. Each constituent list of states is necessarily finite, but the list-of-lists need not be in the case of infinite network executions. By virtue of Haskell's lazy evaluation, such a computational object is useful. We can then write a procedure that, given a trace, applies a boolean predicate at every step of the trace.

```
checkTrace :: Invariant m s Bool → m → [SpecNetwork f s] → Either Int ()
```

The Invariant data type is an abbreviation for a boolean predicate on the type s that additionally takes some "meta-data" m, like "roles" in a protocol, needed to express the invariant. The procedure checkTrace returns Right () to signify that there were no violations of the invariant, while it returns Left n to report that the nth state was the first state to violate the invariant. With this language of predicates we can build invariants and with the aforementioned checking procedure we can perform (bounded) checking that an invariant is in fact inductive (*i.e.*, holds for each state). In the case of a finite state space, this amounts to real verification of inductive invariants. The most sophisticated example we have successfully specified is an inductive invariant for a Two-Phased Commit protocol [24], for which we refer the curious reader to the implementation.

3.2 The Implementation Language

The monadic language for message-passing programs is implemented as an EDSL in Haskell. This has the benefit of providing all the standard tools for writing Haskell programs; all the abstraction mechanisms and organisational principles are at hand to write sophisticated software, including lazy evaluation, higher-order functions, algebraic data types and more. By virtue of the modularity offered by the approach of EDSLs, it is straightforward to give multiple interpretations of such programs.

At the time of this writing DPC's implementation fragment came with three interpretations of the monadic interface:

1. The AST monad used for dynamic verification of implementation adherence of the implementations to protocols, and covered in detail in Sect. 2.5.
2. A shared-memory based interpretation where nodes are represented as threads, and message passing is performed by writing to shared message queues using non-blocking concurrency primitives.
3. An interpretation for distributed message passing.

In the third case (true distribution), we give an interpretation into IO computations performing message passing through POSIX Sockets. For this, each computation needs an "address book" mapping NodeIDs to physical addresses (concretely, IP adresses and ports). Additionally, each program will have access to a local mailbox, represented by a message buffer being filled by a local thread whose only function is to listen for messages. These two pieces of data are collected in a record of type NetworkContext. Computations running in such a context are captured in a type synonym over the ReaderT monad transformer:

```
newtype SocketRunnerT m a = SocketRunnerT {
  runSocketRunnerT :: ReaderT NetworkContext m a }
```

What follows is the implementation of the send primitive in this particular instance of the message-passing interface:

```
instance (MonadIO m) => MessagePassing (SocketRunnerT m) where
  send to lbl tag body = do
    thisID <- this
    let p = encode $ Message thisID tag body to lbl
    peerSocket <- (!to) <$> view addressBook
    void . liftIO $ Socket.send peerSocket p mempty
```

The code for sending messages is, thus, implemented in a form of a Reader-like computation over an IO-capable monad m as indicated by the MonadIO constraint. It starts by building a Message containing the supplied tag, body, receiver (to) and label, along with the executing nodes ID, as supplied by another primitive, this. It then uses `encode` to serialize this message into bytestring `p`. `p` is then sent to the appropriate `peerSocket`, as resolved by the `addressBook`, using the `System.Socket.Send` operation from the POSIX Socket library for Haskell. The monadic glue code (and the rest of the Haskell toolkit) is interpreted by choosing an appropriate base monad for the interpretation, *e.g.*, the `IO` monad. Ultimately, we build the following function for running the system:

```
defaultMain :: NetworkDescription → NodeID → SocketRunner a → IO ()
```

It takes a `NetworkDescription`, which maps `NodeID`s to physical addresses, a `NodeID` with which to identify this node, and a computation in the above described interpretation of message passing programs. The result is an `IO()` computation that establishes (if run on each machine) a fully connected mesh network with every node in the supplied network description, and then proceeds to run the supplied computation, passing messages accordingly. This interpretation can be used to facilitate integration of DPC-based implementations with real Haskell code once they have been assured to comply with their protocols.

4   Evaluation

The implementation of DPC is publicly available online for extensions and experimentation.[7] We now report on our experience of using DPC for implementing and validating some commonly used distributed systems.

4.1   More Examples

In order to evaluate the framework, we have encoded a number of textbook distributed protocols, translating their specifications to the abstractions of DPC. By doing so, we were aiming to answer the following research questions:

1. Are our `Protlet`-based combinator sufficiently expressive to capture a variety of distributed systems from the standard literature in a natural way?
2. Is it common to have realistic protocols that require *more than one* combinator, *i.e.*, can be efficiently decomposed into multiple `Protlet`s?
3. What is the implementation burden for encoding systems using DPC?

The statistics for our experiments is summarised in Table 1.

The framework has been shaped by the explorations of protocols that we have made, but we believe that the answer to Q1 is affirmative, supported by the variety of protocols we have so far explored. The answer to Q2 is also affirmative. Complex protocols from literature decompose into interactions shaped as RPCs, notifications, *etc*, and we manage to capture all of them in protlets. Simply put, for every arrow in a diagram of the network indicating a communication channel, the protocol has a protlet detailing the exchanges occuring across that channel. For instance the two-phase protocols like Paxos and Two-Phase Commit (2PC)

---

[7] https://github.com/kandersen/dpc.

Table 1. A summary for implemented systems: protocol, runnable implementation, count of constituent protlets, size of encoding (lines of code), employed combinators.

Protocol	Impl	Protlets	LOC	RPC	ARPC	Notif	Broad	OneOf	Quorum
Calculator	✓	1	10	✓	✓			✓	
Lock Server		4	73	✓	✓	✓			
Concurrent Database		3	23	✓					
Two-Phase Commit		2	43				✓		
Paxos	✓	2	42						✓

naturally decompose into two broadcast/quorum phases, while more asymmetric protocols like distributed locking [10] requires as many as four protlets.

Regarding Q3, the lines of code versus complexity of protocol are indicative of a positive relationship between complexity and effort to encode a protocol, which is desireable. That is, a lot of complexity is encapsulated by the treatment of combinators, so the coding effort in the framework is very light.

The nature of the verification that the framework enables is naturally not strictly sound (as it is dynamic), but techniques like bounded model checking are readily explorable. With it, we have been able to validate, *e.g.*, correctness for the 2PC protocol [24], a not an insignificant proof burden.

The framework also affords exploration in other directions than we have mentioned so far. We have experimented with enriching the message passing language with operations for shared-memory concurrency and thread-based parallelism. The database example in the table uses *node-local* threads to maintain a database that is served by two different threads. Our approach to dynamic checking of protocol adherence scales to concurrency, and we have a concurrent Calculator server serving *multiple* arithmetic functions *in parallel*.

4.2 A Case Study: Constructing and Running Paxos Consensus

For a representative exploration of the capabilities of DPC we turn to a study of the Paxos Consensus [2,6,12]. Paxos solves a problem of reaching a consensus on a single value agreed upon across multiple nodes, of which a subset acts as proposers (who suggest the values) and another, complementary subset acts as acceptors (who reach an agreement). The nature of the Paxos algorithm lends itself well to interactive exploration and the specification should be robust to issues that appear specifically in distributed systems, like arbitrary interleaving of messages, message reorderings, and nodes going offline. The tools we have developed so far are enough to explore these aspects of the protocol.

We can specify this protocol in DPC with relatively little code. We further generalise the `Broadcast` combinator to "quorums"—broadcasts that await only a certain number of responses before proceeding. We introduce another entry in our `Protlet` datatype for capturing this pattern.

```
data Protlet f s = ...
  | Quorum String Rational (Broadcast s) (Receive s) (Send f s)
```

The `Quorum` protlet is and acts identical to the Broadcast protlet, but it is further instrumented by a rational number indicating the number of responses to await before proceeding. We encode the dissection of nodes into proposers and acceptors directly in the state of the protocol, similar to how we dissected the state space of the cloud server along Client/Server lines. The proposer starts in (`ProposerInit b v as`) with the desire to propose to acceptors as the value v with priority (*ballot*) b. We encode this with a quorom protlet:

```
prepare :: Alternative f ⇒ Label → Int → Protlet f PState
prepare label n = Quorum "prepare" ((fromIntegral n % 2) + 1) propositionCast ...
  where
    propositionCast = λcase
      ProposerInit b v as → Just (zip as (repeat [b]), propositionReceive b v as)
      _ → Nothing
```

Here, `prepare` is parameterised by the number of participants. Hence, the protlet dictates we should wait for a majority quorum, to avoid ties in the system. The listing shows the initiation of the first broadcast as representative of the rest of the implementation. The proposer starts in an `ProposerInit` state, in which it initiates a broadcast poll of all `as` acceptors, sending its ballot b.

The second phase of the protocol is encoded as another `Quorum` protlet, where the proposers react to the outcome of the responses on the first polling. The interactive exploration tool can be used to explore, for instance, the robustness of the protocol with respect to crashing participants versus crashing proposers, and why a quorum size of $\left(\frac{n}{2} + 1\right)$ acceptors is sufficient for reaching consensus.

The explored implementation demonstrates use of the *state* monad to organise the acceptor as an effectful program, and a *callback* to provide the ballot to the proposer, using features of Haskell, while retaining the benefits of the framework. Neither effect is possible to express at the protocol specification level.

5   Related Work

Declarative programming for distributed systems. In the past five years, several works were published proposing mechanised formalisms for scalable verification of distributed protocols, both in synchronous [5] and asynchronous setting [24,27]. All those verification frameworks allow for executable implementations, yet the encoding overhead is prohibitively high, and no abstractions for specific interaction patterns are provided in any of them. Most of the DSLs for distributed systems we are aware of are implemented by means of extracting code rather than by means of a shallow DSL embedding [9,16,18]. MACE [9], a C++ language extension and source-to-source compiler, provides a suite of tools for generating and model checking distributed systems. DISTALGO [18] and SPLAY [16] extract implementations from protocol descriptions.

In a recent work, Brady has described a discipline of protocol-aware programming in IDRIS [1], in which adherence of an implementation to a protocol is ensured by the host language's dependent type system, similarly to DISEL, but in a more lightweight form. That approach provides strong static safety guarantees; however, it does not provide dedicated combinators for specific protocol patterns, *e.g.*, broadcasts or quorums.

DPC's protlets adapt DISEL's protocols, that are phrased exclusively in terms of *low-level* send/receive commands, which should be instrumented with protocol-specific logic for each new construction. While it is possible to derive DPC's protlets in DISEL, extracting them and ascribing them suitable types requires large annotation overhead.

6 Conclusion and Future Work

Declarative programming over distributed protocols is possible and, we believe, can lead to new insights, such as better understanding on how to structure systems implementations. Even though there are several known limitations to the design of DPC (for instance, in order to define new combinators, one needs to extend `Protlet`), we consider our approach beneficial and illuminating for the purposes of prototyping, exploration, and teaching distributed system design.

In the future, we are going to explore the opportunities, opened by DPC, for randomised protocol testing and lightweight verification with refinement types.

Acknowledgements. We thank PADL'19 referees for their many helpful suggestions. The authors' work on this project has been supported by the grant by UK Research Institute in Verified Trustworthy Software Systems (VeTSS).

References

1. Brady,E.: Type-driven development of concurrent communicating systems. Comput. Sci. (AGH), **18**(3) (2017)
2. Chandra, T., Griesemer, R., Redstone, J.: Paxos made live: an engineering perspective. In: PODC (2007)
3. Coq Development Team. The Coq Proof Assistant Reference Manual (2018)
4. Dinsdale-Young, T., Dodds, M., Gardner, P., Parkinson, M.J., Vafeiadis, V.: Concurrent abstract predicates. In: D'Hondt, T. (ed.) ECOOP 2010. LNCS, vol. 6183, pp. 504–528. Springer, Heidelberg (2010). https://doi.org/10.1007/978-3-642-14107-2_24
5. Dragoi, C., Henzinger, T.A., Zufferey,D.: PSync: a partially synchronous language for fault-tolerant distributed algorithms. In: POPL (2016)
6. García-Pérez, Á., Gotsman, A., Meshman, Y., Sergey, I.: Paxos consensus, deconstructed and abstracted. In: Ahmed, A. (ed.) ESOP 2018. LNCS, vol. 10801, pp. 912–939. Springer, Cham (2018). https://doi.org/10.1007/978-3-319-89884-1_32

7. Gray, J.N.: Notes on data base operating systems. In: Operating Systems (1978)
8. Hawblitzel, C., et al.: IronFleet: proving practical distributed systems correct. In: SOSP (2015)
9. Killian, C.E., Anderson, J.W., Braud, R., Jhala, R., Vahdat, A.M.: Mace: language support for building distributed systems. In: PLDI (2007)
10. Kleppmann, M.: How to do distributed locking, 08 February 2016. https://martin.kleppmann.com/2016/02/08/how-to-do-distributed-locking.html
11. Krogh-Jespersen, M., Timani, A., Ohlenbusch, M.E., Birkedal, L.: Aneris: a logic for node-local, modular reasoning of distributed systems (2018, unpublished draft)
12. Lamport, L.: The part-time parliament. ACM Trans. Comput. Syst. **16**(2), 133–169 (1998)
13. Lamport, L.: Paxos made simple (2001)
14. Alford, M.W., et al.: Formal foundation for specification and verification. In: Paul, M., Siegert, H.J. (eds.) Distributed Systems: Methods and Tools for Specification. An Advanced Course. LNCS, vol. 190, pp. 203–285. Springer, Heidelberg (1985). https://doi.org/10.1007/3-540-15216-4_15
15. Lampson, B.W.: How to build a highly available system using consensus. In: WDAG (1996)
16. Leonini, L., Riviere, E., Felber, P.: SPLAY: distributed systems evaluation made simple (or how to turn ideas into live systems in a breeze). In: NSDI (2009)
17. Liang, S., Hudak, P., Jones, M.P.: Monad transformers and modular interpreters. In: POPL (1995)
18. Liu, Y.A., Stoller, S.D., Lin, B., Gorbovitski, M.: From clarity to efficiency for distributed algorithms. In: OOPSLA (2012)
19. Nanevski, A., Morrisett, G., Shinnar, A., Govereau, P., Birkedal, L.: Ynot: dependent types for imperative programs. In: ICFP (2008)
20. Newcombe, C., Rath, T., Zhang, F., Munteanu, B., Brooker, M., Deardeuff, M.: How Amazon web services uses formal methods. Commun. ACM **58**(4), 66–73 (2015)
21. O'Hearn, P., Reynolds, J., Yang, H.: Local reasoning about programs that alter data structures. In: Fribourg, L. (ed.) CSL 2001. LNCS, vol. 2142, pp. 1–19. Springer, Heidelberg (2001). https://doi.org/10.1007/3-540-44802-0_1
22. Pîrlea, G., Sergey, I.: Mechanising blockchain consensus. In: CPP (2018)
23. I. Sergey, A. Nanevski, and A. Banerjee. Mechanized verification of fine-grained concurrent programs. In PLDI, 2015
24. Sergey, I., Wilcox, J.R., Tatlock, Z.: Programming and proving with distributed protocols. In: PACMPL(POPL), vol. 2 (2018)
25. van Renesse, R., Altinbuken, D.: Paxos made moderately complex. ACM Comp. Surv. **47**(3), 42 (2015)
26. Wilcox, J.R., Sergey, I., Tatlock, Z.: Programming language abstractions for modularly verified distributed systems. In: SNAPL (2017)
27. Wilcox, J.R., et al.: Verdi: a framework for implementing and formally verifying distributed systems. In: PLDI (2015)

Creating Domain-Specific Languages by Composing Syntactical Constructs

Viktor Palmkvist[✉] and David Broman

KTH Royal Institute of Technology, Stockholm, Sweden
{vipa,dbro}@kth.se

Abstract. Creating a programming language is a considerable undertaking, even for relatively small domain-specific languages (DSLs). Most approaches to ease this task either limit the flexibility of the DSL or consider entire languages as the unit of composition. This paper presents a new approach using syntactical constructs (also called syncons) for defining DSLs in much smaller units of composition while retaining flexibility. A syntactical construct defines a single language feature, such as an `if` statement or an anonymous function. Each syntactical construct is fully self-contained: it specifies its own concrete syntax, binding semantics, and runtime semantics, independently of the rest of the language. The runtime semantics are specified as a translation to a user defined target language, while the binding semantics allow name resolution *before* expansion. Additionally, we present a novel approach for dealing with syntactical ambiguity that arises when combining languages, even if the languages are individually unambiguous. The work is implemented and evaluated in a case study, where small subsets of OCaml and Lua have been defined and composed using syntactical constructs.

1 Introduction

Designing and implementing user friendly *domain-specific languages (DSLs)* requires both extensive programming language knowledge and domain expertise. Instead of implementing a DSL compiler or interpreter from scratch, there are several approaches for developing new DSLs more efficiently. For instance, a language can be defined by compiler construction [8] or preprocessing template tools [3,20] that translate a DSL program into another language with well defined syntax and semantics. Another alternative is to *embed* [14] the DSL into another host language, thus reusing the language constructs directly from the host language. Such an approach, often referred to as *embedded DSLs*, has been used in various domains [1,2,11,24,27].

New language constructs can, for instance, be implemented using host language constructs that lifts programs into data [4,19], or by using various forms of *macro systems* [23]. A macro defines a new construct by expanding code into the host language, thus giving the illusion of a new language construct without the need to redefine the underlying language. The sophistication of a macro system

© Springer Nature Switzerland AG 2019
J. J. Alferes and M. Johansson (Eds.): PADL 2019, LNCS 11372, pp. 187–203, 2019.
https://doi.org/10.1007/978-3-030-05998-9_12

varies from simple text expansion systems to systems using hygienic macros that enable correct name bindings [6,9] and macro systems with static types [13,16].

Macro systems enable rapid prototyping of language constructs, but the concrete syntax of a macro tends to be limited to the syntax of the language, e.g., Lisp macros look like Lisp. On the other hand, compiler construction tools, such as parser generators and transformation frameworks, enable a higher degree of flexibility in terms of syntax, but do not directly give the same composability properties; the smallest unit of reuse tends to be a language, in contrast with macros, which are more fine-grained.

In this paper, we develop the concept of *syntactical constructs* (also called *syncons* for short) that enables both *composable language constructs* and *syntactic freedom*. In contrast to current state-of-the-art techniques, the composability is fine-grained, at the language construct level. That is, instead of composing complete DSLs, syncons enable composability of individual language constructs. A syncon defines a single language feature, such as an if statement or an anonymous function. Each syncon specifies its own syntax, binding semantics, and runtime semantics, independently of the rest of the language. The semantics are defined using a translation into another target language, similar to macros.

However, fine-grained composability introduces further challenges regarding unambiguous parsing. For instance, composing two individual language constructs picked from two different languages may create an ambiguous language as a result, even if the two languages are individually unambiguous. The approach presented in this paper uses general context-free grammars for syntactical flexibility, which presents a problem: static ambiguity checking for context-free grammars is undecidable [5]. A novel aspect of our approach is dynamic ambiguity checking, which means that errors are encountered and reported at parse time, similarly to how dynamically typed languages present type errors at runtime.

As part of our work, we have designed and implemented a prototype system for creating languages using the *syncon approach*. We make no assumptions about the target language, but for the purposes of evaluation, we have implemented a small interpreted language to fill this role. Figure 1 shows a high-level overview of our approach, where the different Sects. 2, 3 and 4 are highlighted with dashed lines. More specifically, we make the following main contributions:

- We explain the key idea of the *syncon* concept, as well as how the concrete syntax of a composed language is constructed. All parsing operations are performed by first constructing a context-free grammar, which is then handed to a general parser (Sect. 2).
- We motivate why dynamic ambiguity checking is, in some cases, preferable to fully unambiguous languages, and explain our approach. Specifically, when an ambiguity is encountered, the parser produces multiple parse trees, which are examined in order to present a useful error message (Sect. 3).
- We implement name resolution and expansion (Sect. 4), and evaluate the whole approach using a case study, where small subsets of OCaml and Lua are defined using syncons. We show how language constructs in one language can be extracted and composed into the other language (Sect. 5).

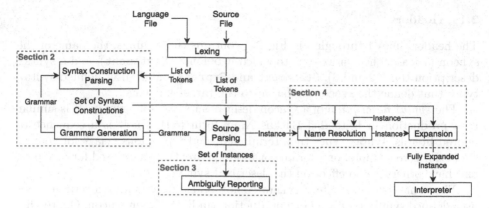

Fig. 1. An overview of the various components of the system, and the sections that explain them.

2 Defining Syncons

The central component in the approach presented in this paper is a *syncon*, short for syntactical construct. Each syncon belongs to a single *syntax type*, similar to how a value in a regular programming language belongs to a type. Figure 2a shows an example that defines a slightly simplified version of a local variable declaration in Lua. The definition consists of three parts: a header, a set of properties, and a body.

```
1  syntax local:Statement =          Header
2     "local" x:Identifier
3     ("=" e:Expression)?
4  {
5     #bind x after                   Properties
6     #scope (e)
7     BExpression'                     Body
8        defAfter 'id(x) =
9        (@ref (@deref
10          't(foldl e _ (e)
11             (BExpression' @unit))))
12 }                                          (a)
```

```
1  if true then
2     local a
3     local b = 1 + 2
4     return b
5  else
6     return 3
7  end                    (b)

syntax if:Statement =
   "if" c:Expression
   "then" b:Block
   ... "end"
{ #scope (b) ... }        (c)
```

Fig. 2. (a) A syncon implementing a basic form of a local variable declaration in Lua. (b) Code in Lua with two local declarations that can be parsed using this syncon. (c) A syncon implementing **if**, with most details elided.

2.1 Header

The header (lines 1 through 3 in Fig. 2a) contains three things: the name of the
syncon (`local`), the syntax type to which it belongs (`Statement`), and a syntax
description (lines 2 and 3). `Statement` and `Expression` are user-defined syntax
types that define the syncon's relation to the target language.

The *syntax description* of a syncon describes its concrete syntax. It is similar
to a production in Extended Backus Naur form (EBNF): it is a sequence of
quoted literals, syntax types (non-terminals), and repetitions (via ? for zero or
one, * for zero or more, or + for one or more). Parentheses are used for grouping
and have otherwise no effect on the described syntax.

The context-free grammar generated for parsing has one non-terminal per
user-defined syntax type, and one production (in EBNF) per syncon. Quoted literals and a few builtin syntax types (`Identifier`, `String`, `Integer`, and `Float`)
are terminals.

2.2 Properties

The properties of `local` (lines 5 and 6 in Fig. 2a) specify its binding semantics,
i.e., which names it introduces, and how they are available to other code. A
syncon can specify its binding semantics in two essentially orthogonal ways:

- As an *adjacent* binding; for instance, `#bind x before` or `#bind x after`. This
  binds the identifier x in code appearing before or after the current syncon,
  respectively. Line 5 of Fig. 2a states that x (from the syntax description on
  line 2) is available only after the end of the local declaration. For example, b,
  introduced on line 3 in Fig. 2b, is bound on line 4, but not on line 2 or 3.
  The extent of an adjacent binding can be limited by a parent syncon specifying
  a scope; for instance, `#scope (e1 e2)`. This ensures that no adjacent binding
  in subtrees e1 or e2 can be seen from the outside, while allowing both e1 and
  e2 access to the bindings introduced in the other. The `#scope` declaration in
  Fig. 2c ensures that no bindings introduced in the **then** branch are accessible
  outside it.
- As a *nested* binding; for instance, `#bind x in e`. This binds identifier x in the
  subtree represented by e.

Figure 3 shows the AST for the code in Fig. 2b. The dashed boxes denote the
regions covered by **before** and **after** in `local` b on line 3 in Fig. 2b. The region
in shows which regions *could* be covered by a `#bind x in e` declaration. The
horizontal bars represent scopes, which limit the extent of the adjacent bindings,
showing that **if** introduces a scope around each of its two branches. Had these
not been there, then **before** would have included **true** as well, while **after**
would have included the right-most **block** and all its descendants (i.e., the **else**
branch) as well.

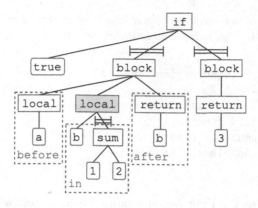

Fig. 3. The AST of the code in Fig. 2b.

Note that a single syncon may use any number of adjacent and nested binding declarations, though usually with different identifiers. Adjacent bindings are, to the best of our knowledge, novel, and give two advantages over purely nested bindings:

1. Syncons may introduce bindings that can be used in a mutually recursive way. For example, a pair of mutually recursive functions require the other function to be in scope in its own body, but purely nested bindings can only accomplish this for one of the functions.
2. The binding constructs common in imperative languages can be modeled more simply. For example, the `local` declaration defined in Fig. 2a does not contain the statements that follow it, which would be required if only nested bindings were available.

The remaining properties are associativity and precedence, similar to most parser generators, that transform the generated context-free grammar appropriately.

2.3   Body

The body of `local`, found on lines 7 through 11 in Fig. 2a, specifies how it is translated to the underlying target language. The expansion is specified in a small DSL with three kinds of constructs: variable references, folds, and syntax literals. Variables are most commonly introduced in the syntax description in the header (x and e on lines 2 and 3 in Fig. 2a, respectively). Folds are used to reduce a sequence of syntax trees to a single syntax tree. For example, the fold on lines 10 and 11 in Fig. 2a has the following form:

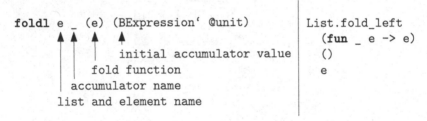

The OCaml code to the right has the same meaning, but with more familiar syntax. It is a left-fold, folding over the sequence e (which has length 0 or 1, since it was introduced by ?). The accumulator is given the name "_" (i.e., it is ignored), while the current element in the sequence reuses the name e. The folding function is merely e, i.e., it ignores the accumulator and returns the element as is. The initial value of the accumulator is a @unit value, which models Lua's nil. The end result is e if it is non-empty, and @unit otherwise. If * or + is used in the syntax description, folds can also be done over longer lists.

A syntax literal is introduced by a syntax type and a backtick (BExpression' on lines 7 and 11 in Fig. 2a) followed by code with that syntax type. Code to be run at expand-time can be spliced into a literal using one of several forms: 't() for a user-defined syntax type (line 10 in Fig. 2a), 'id() for an identifier (line 8 in Fig. 2a), 'str() for a string, 'int() for an integer, and 'float() for a float.

BExpression is a syntax type in the target language, while defAfter, @ref, @deref, and @unit are constructs in that language. The workings of these are not relevant to the syncon approach, and are thus omitted.

The need to specify the syntax type of the syntax literal stems from a lack of context. The issue is that the meaning of some pieces of syntax depend on their context, even in a context-free language. For example, in OCaml,

```
let example [1] = [1]
```

contains the syntax "[1]" twice, first as a pattern, then as an expression. In a syntax literal this context is absent, thus we require the language implementer to specify the syntax type using, e.g., BExpression'. Similarly, each spliced expression must be tagged by syntax type.

3   Ambiguity Reporting

This section first argues that a dynamic check is in some cases preferable to an unambiguous grammar, which is followed by an explanation of our approach.

3.1 Motivation

Consider the following nested `match`-expression in OCaml:

```
1  let result = match 1 with
2    | 1 -> match "one" with
3        | str -> str
4    | 2 -> "two"
```

The compiler reports a type error, stating that line 4 matches a value of type `int`, but expects a value of type `string`. The compiler sees the `match`-arm on line 4 as belonging to the `match` on line 2, rather than the one on line 1, which is what the programmer intended. This happens because OCaml has no layout rules—the indentation has no impact on the semantics of the program—and the compiler assigns every `match`-arm to the closest `match`, resulting in a type error. Instead, the appropriate solution is to surround the inner `match`-expression with parentheses, which has nothing to do with the types of the patterns. Dynamic ambiguity checking can instead detect this case as an ambiguity and present it as such, yielding a clearer error message. We return to this example in the evaluation in Sect. 5.

3.2 Finding Ambiguities

In the case of ambiguous source code, the parser will produce multiple parse trees, a so called *parse forest*. This is a programmer error, so the system must produce a useful error message. In particular, it is insufficient to merely say "the source code is ambiguous" since the ambiguity likely involves a very limited portion of the code. Additionally, once we have isolated the truly ambiguous portions of the source code, we must present the different interpretations in an understandable way. This subsection considers the former problem, while Sect. 3.3 deals with the latter.

To aid in our discussion, consider the following parse forest, produced by parsing "1 + 2 * 3 * 4" when we have defined precedence but not associativity:

$$\text{add}_{1:7}(1_1, \text{mul}_{3:7}(2_3, \text{mul}_{5:7}(3_5, 4_7)))\mid \quad \text{add}_{1:7}(1_1, \text{mul}_{3:7}(\text{mul}_{3:5}(2_3, 3_5), 4_7))$$

The subscripts signify the source code area covered (henceforth referred to as the *range* of the parse tree). We see that the two parse trees share some structure: both have the form $\text{add}_{1:7}(1_1, \text{mul}_{3:7}(\_, \_))$. The addition is thus unambiguous and we wish to report only the multiplication as ambiguous. In particular, we can find a parse forest for the range 3 : 7 whose parse trees appear as descendants in the full parse forest:

$$\text{mul}_{3:7}(2_3, \text{mul}_{5:7}(3_5, 4_7))\mid \quad \text{mul}_{3:7}(\text{mul}_{3:5}(2_3, 3_5), 4_7)$$

We will refer to such a parse forest as a *subforest*.

Finding an ambiguity is now equivalent to finding a subforest whose parse trees differ, while the full ambiguity report selects a set of such subforests.

We require three helper functions before the actual algorithm. First, we will consider two parse trees to be shallowly equal (written $=_s$) if they only differ in their children (or do not differ at all). For example, $\mathrm{add}_{1:3}(1,2) =_s \mathrm{add}_{1:3}(4,5)$, but $\mathrm{add}_{1:4}(1,2) \neq_s \mathrm{add}_{1:3}(4,5)$ (different range) and $\mathrm{add}_{1:3}(1) \neq_s \mathrm{add}_{1:3}(1,2)$ (different number of children). Second, $children(t)$ denotes the children of the syntax tree t, while $children(t)_i$ is the ith child of t, going left to right. Third, $range(t)$ is the range of the syntax tree t. The algorithm involves three steps, starting with the complete parse forest as the input F:

function AMBIGUITIES(F)
  if $\exists t_1, t_2 \in F.\ t_1 \neq_s t_2$ **then**
    return $\{F\}$
  end if   Step 1
  If all $t \in F$ are shallowly equal, then they have
  the same number of children. Call this number n.
  $S \leftarrow \{\{children(t)_i \mid t \in F\} \mid 1 \leq i \leq n\}$
  if $\exists S' \in S.\ \exists t_1, t_2 \in S'.\ range(t_1) \neq range(t_2)$ **then**
    return $\{F\}$
  end if   Step 2
  return $\bigcup_{S' \in S}$ AMBIGUITIES(S')   Step 3
end function

The first step checks that all trees are shallowly equal, the second step extracts all direct subforests, and the third recurses on those subforests. If either of the first two steps fail, then we can find no smaller subforest for the current range, thus we return F.

Applying this to the example, we quickly find that the forest only contains trees that are shallowly equal (step 1), and it has two subforests: $\{1_1\}$ and $\{\mathrm{mul}_{3:7}(2_3, \mathrm{mul}_{5:7}(3_5, 4_7)), \mathrm{mul}_{3:7}(\mathrm{mul}_{3:5}(2_3, 3_5), 4_7)\}$ (step 2). The former is trivially unambiguous, but the latter is not: while the trees are shallowly equal (step 1), we cannot extract subforests (step 2), since the children do not cover the same range.

3.3 Reporting Ambiguities

With the ambiguities found, in the form of subforests, they must be presented to the user. Each contained parse tree could be arbitrarily large, thus presenting them in their entirety is likely to be more noise than valuable information. It is our hypothesis that merely presenting two levels of the trees (the root and its children) is sufficient information to begin addressing the problem and includes very little noise.

For example, the ambiguity in the previous section is presented as follows:

$$\texttt{mul}_{3:7}(\texttt{integer}_3, \texttt{mul}_{5:7}) | \quad \texttt{mul}_{3:7}(\texttt{mul}_{3:5}, \texttt{integer}_7)$$

Furthermore, the range information can be used to highlight the corresponding regions of the source code.

As a final point, in the presence of a grouping operation (e.g., parentheses) ambiguities involving operators can be presented in a more natural way, even if our prototype implementation does not yet support it.

4   Binding Semantics and Expansion

Once we have parsed a syntactically unambiguous program and produced an AST we now turn our attention to its semantics, in particular, its binding semantics. The name resolution pass (Sect. 4.1) discovers the connections between binders and bound identifiers, as well as any binding errors that may be present, while expansion (Sect. 4.2) transforms the AST in the parsed language to an AST in the target language.

4.1   Name Resolution

The name resolution pass is implemented as a relatively simple tree-traversal that collects adjacent and nested bindings, and checks for binding errors. This can be done without expanding any syncon since they all include their binding semantics. The details of this traversal are tedious and not particularly relevant for this paper and are thus not included, but can be found in the first author's Master's thesis [18]. Two kinds of binding errors are considered:

- An identifier is reported as unbound if it is not part of a binding construct (i.e., if it does not appear in a #bind declaration) and is not already bound in its context.
- If a binding for an identifier is introduced twice in the same scope *and* the ranges of the bindings overlap, then they are reported as duplicate. The former requirement allows shadowing, but only in nested scopes, while the latter allows multiple definitions in the same scope, but only if no references could be ambiguous.

Finally, if there are no binding errors, name resolution performs a reference-preserving renaming of all identifiers in the AST, such that no identifier is introduced in a binding more than once. This simplifies writing a correct expansion, since the programmer can now assume that no rearranging of the children of a syncon instance can cause accidental name capture or a duplicate binding.

4.2 Expansion

Expanding a single syncon instance consists of running a simple interpreter for the DSL described in Sect. 2.3, with one important thing to mention: identifiers that appear in syntax literals must be different between different expansions, to prevent accidental name capture. In practice this is accomplished by tagging each such identifier with a number that is unique per expansion (e.g., the first expansion has number 1, the second number 2, etc.). Note that while the expansion may assume that no rearranging of the instance's children can cause a duplicated binding (as mentioned in the previous section), it does not need to ensure that this is true *after* the expansion.

Expanding an AST repeats this process until no remaining syncon instances have expansions, i.e., until all remaining syncons are part of the base language. However, we do need to maintain the invariant. Since an adjacent binding may affect the AST arbitrarily far away from its introduction (depending on which parents introduce scopes), we cannot simply perform renaming only on the result of the expansion. Instead, we perform another name resolution pass, but only when needed; most syncons do not duplicate children when they expand, in which case there is no possibility of a duplicated binding.

5 Evaluation

The approach presented in this paper has been evaluated through an implementation of the system as a whole, and then creating two language subsets using syncons to evaluate their expressiveness. Note that the language subsets are of general-purpose programming languages, rather than DSLs. Having pre-existing, well-defined semantics gives a ground truth that simplifies evaluation, and the approach being useful for general purpose programming languages suggests that it would be useful for a DSL as well.

5.1 Implementation

To evaluate our approach, we have written an interpreter[1] in Haskell, containing the phases described in Sects. 2, 3 and 4. The general parser used is an off-the-shelf implementation[2] of the Earley parsing algorithm [7]. We have also implemented a simple interpreter for a small, mostly functional, base language. The language subsets in Sect. 5.2 expand to this base language, which thus gives us the ability to run programs and compare the syncon language implementations with the original implementations.

The base language features include anonymous functions, mutable references, continuations, and several builtin values (e.g., primitives for arithmetic, list manipulation, and printing).

---

[1] Available at https://github.com/miking-lang/syncon.
[2] http://hackage.haskell.org/package/Earley.

5.2 Case Studies

To evaluate the expressiveness of syncons, we have implemented small subsets of two common programming languages:

OCaml. We have implemented a (dynamically typed) subset of OCaml to test that syncons can express a relatively standard functional programming language, with additional focus on pattern matching. The OCaml subset implementation consists of 32 syncons, spread over 3 syntax types.

Lua. We have implemented a subset of Lua to test that syncons can express the control flow common in imperative language. It is worth noting here that tables and coroutines, arguably the more particular features of Lua, are not implemented, since they are not the reason for choosing Lua as a test language. The Lua subset implementation consists of 29 syncons, spread over 5 syntax types.

To test the correctness of these subset implementations, we have written several small programs:

- `fib.ml` and `fib.lua`. These programs implement functions for finding the nth fibonacci number, one with the quadratic recursive definition, and a linear version. They test most binding constructs, some control flow, and basic arithmetic.
- `fizzbuzz.ml` and `fizzbuzz.lua`. These programs implement fizzbuzz, an (in)famous interview problem, and test more control flow and comparisons.
- `misc.ml`. This program tests the various remaining syntax constructions in the OCaml subset, for example, boolean literals, anonymous functions and cons patterns.
- `misc.lua`. This program tests the various remaining syntax constructions in the Lua subset, for example, grouping by parentheses, **break**, and multiplication.

The programs are chosen to ensure that between them, each syncon is used at least once, and that some non-trivial control flow is used, e.g., recursion, mutual recursion, and (in Lua) iteration.

   We then compare the output of running each program in the subset implementation and the canonical implementation. One additional complexity is that the subset implementations do not support the standard libraries for the languages, nor importing of modules. In particular, printing is a builtin primitive in the subset implementations. To cover this difference we prepend a small prelude to each program before running. With the exception of this prelude, the programs are identical between the implementations.

To test language construct composability, we extend Lua in two ways: we add destructuring to existing binding constructs, and we add a new `match`-statement. Both of these are accomplished by reusing syncons from the OCaml subset.

5.3   Analysis and Discussion

This section examines the result of extending the Lua subset with syncons from OCaml, a few ambiguity errors in the OCaml subset, the effects of contextual information on syncon independence, and a brief summary of other results.

```
syntax local:Statement =              syntax local:Statement =
  "local" x:Identifier                  "local" x:Pattern
  ("=" e:Expression)?                   ("=" e:Expression)?
{                                     {

  #bind x after
  #scope (e)                            #scope (e)
  BExpression'                          BExpression'
    defAfter 'id(x) =                     't(x) (fun _. @crash)
    (@ref (@deref                         (@ref (@deref
        't(foldr e _ (e)                      't(foldr e _ (e)
            (BExpression' @unit))))               (BExpression' @unit))))
}                                     }
```

Fig. 4. The change required to make a `local`-declaration in Lua support destructuring.

Cross-Language Reuse. Figure 4 shows the example from Sect. 2, to the left as it was then, and to the right extended to handle destructuring using arbitrary patterns. The patterns are defined in the OCaml subset, but can be reused in Lua by merely importing them. Patterns are implemented as anonymous macros that take two arguments: a function to call if the pattern match fails, and the value to match against. We thus require three changes: switch `Identifier` for `Pattern`, remove `#bind x after`, and switch `defAfter` with an invocation of `x`. However, the binding semantics are slightly different, the right version allows e to use names introduced by x, i.e., we allow recursive bindings, although the system should be extended to be more conservative and disallow such bindings.

To add `match` we must accommodate for syntactic and semantic differences between the two languages; sensible syntax in OCaml does not necessarily fit in Lua, and Lua has a distinction between statements and expressions while OCaml does not. We thus create a new syncon that expands to the `match`-syncon from OCaml, which we import. This choice mirrors one from regular programming: do you use an external library directly, or do you wrap it in an interface that is more convenient for the current application? Different situations will produce different answers.

Ambiguity Errors. Consider the following OCaml code:

```
1  let result = match 1 with
2    | 2 -> match "two" with
3         | str -> str
4    | 4 -> "four"
5  let list = [a; b]
```

Lines 1 through 4 are the example from Sect. 3.1. Our prototype produces the following ambiguity errors. Since this is a pure research prototype, little effort has been spent on the presentation of the errors, only on what information is presented.

```
Ambiguity: "1:14-4:16"
(("match", "1:14-4:16"),
 [("intLit", "1:20-1:21"),
  ("intPat", "2:5-2:6"),              Ambiguity: "5:12-5:18"
  ("match", "2:10-3:22"),            (("list", "5:12-5:18"),
  ("intPat", "4:5-4:6"),              [("seqComp", "5:13-5:17")])
  ("stringLit", "4:10-4:16")])      (("list", "5:12-5:18"),
(("match", "1:14-4:16"),             [("variable", "5:13-5:14"),
 [("intLit", "1:20-1:21"),            ("variable", "5:16-5:17")])
  ("intPat", "2:5-2:6"),
  ("match", "2:10-4:16")])
```

The first ambiguity covers the match expression on lines 1 through 4, and has two interpretations. Both are `match`-expressions and contain an integer literal (1) and an integer pattern (2). Then comes the difference: either there is a nested `match` ending on line 3, then an integer pattern and a string literal (i.e., another `match`-arm), or a single nested `match` that ends on line 4. This agrees with the conclusion in Sect. 3.1: the match-arm on line 4 could belong to either `match`.

The second error states that the right hand side of line 5 is either (i) a list of one element (a sequential composition), or (ii) a list of two elements (two variables). The rewrite required to handle this case in our prototype as in the canonical implementation is possible, but requires duplicating syncons. An automatic method to perform the rewrite without duplication seems plausible, but is left for future work.

Note that the errors highlight only the ambiguous parts, `let result =` and `let list =` are not included, since they are unambiguous.

Contextual Information. Certain syncons require information from their context, e.g., a pattern needs the value being matched, and `return` needs to know which function to return from. There are two intuitive ways we might attempt to provide this information:

- Have a parent syncon bind a name which the child uses. This does not work because the system prevents all forms of name capture.
- Have the child syncon produce a function, which the parent syncon then applies to the information required. This works, but the function introduces a scope, which hides any adjacent bindings exposed by the child.

To work around this, our base language contains a form of anonymous macros; functions that do not introduce a scope, must be applied immediately, and take an opaque piece of syntax as an argument.

However, using anonymous macros in this fashion introduces coupling between syncons: if one syncon requires contextual information, then all syncons of the same syntax type must produce an anonymous macro and the information must be threaded to children, even if the syncon itself does not require it.

Other Considerations and Limitations. This work introduces the new syncon approach, which enables both fine-grained composability and syntactic freedom. There are, however, a few limitations with the work presented so far. Specifically, (i) the binding semantics for syncons have no concept of modules or namespaces, and (ii) syncons cannot be disambiguated by whether their contained identifiers are bound or not, which precludes, e.g., pattern match and unification as done in Prolog. We consider these limitations as future work. Additionally, we wish to evaluate the approach on complete languages, rather than the subsets here, as well as more common language compositions, e.g., HTML and JavaScript.

6   Related Work

Macros in the Lisp family of languages provide a small unit of composition, but are limited in their syntax; a Lisp macro still looks like Lisp. Racket [10], a Lisp language oriented towards language creation, allows a language designer to supply their own parser, circumventing this limitation. However, such a parser loses the small unit of composition; the syntax is defined as a whole rather than as a composition of smaller language constructs. λ_m [13] introduces a type system that prevents macros from introducing binding errors, thus providing an automated expansion checker that our approach currently lacks. However, λ_m only supports nested bindings, adjacent bindings are not expressible. Romeo [22] goes further and allows procedural macros, as opposed to pattern-based ones, and thus features a more powerful macro system than both λ_m and this paper. Binding safety is again ensured by a type system, with what amounts to algebraic data types describing the abstract syntax trees that are processed. However, this system runs into the expression problem; old macros cannot be reused if new constructs are added to the language being transformed. Additionally, both λ_m and Romeo are still constrained to Lisp syntax.

SoundX [16] takes a different approach to macros: they rewrite type derivation trees instead of syntax trees. The resulting macros can be checked to introduce neither binding errors nor type errors. As an additional benefit, they can also use type information present in the derivation but not explicitly present in the source code. However, the concrete syntax (specified with a context free grammar using SDF [12]) of a language described with SoundX has no guarantees on ambiguity, nor a way to deal with any ambiguity that shows up.

Compared to various embedded approaches to DSLs [1,2,4,11,14,24,27], our approach gives greater syntactical flexibility, but less convenient expressive power due to the limited nature of the DSL for specifying the expansion. Wyvern [17] gives a pragmatic alternative to specifying complete new languages; new types can be given custom literal syntax, but the rest of the language is fixed. Silkensen et al. [21] provide an approach for parsing composed grammars efficiently using what amounts to type information for bound identifiers.

JastAdd [8] allows modularly defining languages using an attribute grammar-based system, but requires an external parser. The system allows smaller units of composition than a language, namely modules. However, extra care must be taken to produce features that can be reused with granularity. Silver [25] (a more concise description and example of use can be found in [15]), also based on attribute grammars, includes a parser (Copper [26]) and gives more guarantees under composition: the composed concrete syntax is unambiguous and no attributes are missing. However, syntax is limited to LALR(1) and each extension construct must start with a distinguishing terminal, to signal the transition from core language to extension language.

The work presented in this paper is based on the first author's Master's thesis [18], which has not been formally published before.

7   Conclusion

In this paper, we introduce the concept of a syntactical construct (syncon) that enables both fine-grained composability of language constructs and syntactic freedom for the syntax of the defined language. As a consequence of this flexibility, we show how dynamic ambiguity detection is an alternative to static ambiguity checking. The syncon approach is implemented in Haskell, and evaluated by specifying small subsets of OCaml and Lua using syncons, where certain language constructs are imported from the other language. Although the current implementation has certain limitations, we contend that dynamic ambiguity checking and fine-grained language construct composition can be good complements to pure static and more restrictive approaches. Combining the benefits of both static and dynamic detection—using a form of hybrid detection and reporting—can be an interesting direction for future work.

Acknowledgements. The authors would like to thank Elias Castegren, Mads Dam, Philipp Haller, Daniel Lundén, Saranya Natarajan, Oscar Eriksson, and Rodothea Myrsini Tsoupidi for valuable input and feedback. This project is financially supported by the Swedish Foundation for Strategic Research (FFL15-0032).

References

1. Augustsson, L., Mansell, H., Sittampalam, G.: Paradise: a two-stage dsl embedded in haskell. In: Proceedings of the 13th ACM SIGPLAN International Conference on Functional Programming, ICFP 2008, pp. 225–228. ACM (2008)
2. Bjesse, P., Claessen, K., Sheeran, M., Singh, S.: Lava: hardware design in Haskell. In: Proceedings of the Third ACM SIGPLAN International Conference on Functional Programming, pp. 174–184. ACM Press, New York (1998)
3. Bravenboer, M., Kalleberg, K.T., Vermaas, R., Visser, E.: Stratego/XT 0.17. A language and toolset for program transformation. Sci. Comput. Program. **72**(1), 52–70 (2008)
4. Broman, D., Siek, J.G.: Gradually typed symbolic expressions. In: Proceedings of the ACM SIGPLAN Workshop on Partial Evaluation and Program Manipulation, PEPM 2018, pp. 15–29. ACM, New York (2018)
5. Cantor, D.G.: On the ambiguity problem of backus systems. J. ACM **9**(4), 477–479 (1962)
6. Dybvig, R.K., Hieb, R., Bruggeman, C.: Syntactic abstraction in scheme. LISP Symb. Comput. **5**(4), 295–326 (1993)
7. Earley, J.: An efficient context-free parsing algorithm. Commun. ACM **13**(2), 94–102 (1970)
8. Ekman, T., Hedin, G.: The JastAdd system – modular extensible compiler construction. Sci. Comput. Program. **69**(1), 14–26 (2007)
9. Flatt, M.: Binding as sets of scopes. In: Proceedings of the 43rd Annual ACM SIGPLAN-SIGACT Symposium on Principles of Programming Languages, POPL 2016, pp. 705–717. ACM, New York (2016)
10. Flatt, M., PLT: Reference: Racket. Technical report PLT-TR-2010-1, PLT Design Inc. (2010)
11. Giorgidze, G., Nilsson, H.: Embedding a functional hybrid modelling language in haskell. In: Scholz, S.-B., Chitil, O. (eds.) IFL 2008. LNCS, vol. 5836, pp. 138–155. Springer, Heidelberg (2011). https://doi.org/10.1007/978-3-642-24452-0_8
12. Heering, J., Hendriks, P.R.H., Klint, P., Rekers, J.: The syntax definition formalism SDF–reference manual–. ACM SIGPLAN Not. **24**(11), 43–75 (1989)
13. Herman, D., Wand, M.: A theory of hygienic macros. In: Drossopoulou, S. (ed.) ESOP 2008. LNCS, vol. 4960, pp. 48–62. Springer, Heidelberg (2008). https://doi.org/10.1007/978-3-540-78739-6_4
14. Hudak, P.: Building domain-specific embedded languages. ACM Comput. Surv. **28**, 196 (1996)
15. Kaminski, T., Kramer, L., Carlson, T., Van Wyk, E.: Reliable and automatic composition of language extensions to C: the ableC extensible language framework. Proc. ACM Program. Lang. **1**(OOPSLA), 98:1–98:29 (2017)
16. Lorenzen, F., Erdweg, S.: Sound type-dependent syntactic language extension. In: Proceedings of the 43rd Annual ACM SIGPLAN-SIGACT Symposium on Principles of Programming Languages (POPL), vol. 51, pp. 204–216. ACM Press (2016)
17. Omar, C., Kurilova, D., Nistor, L., Chung, B., Potanin, A., Aldrich, J.: Safely composable type-specific languages. In: Jones, R. (ed.) ECOOP 2014. LNCS, vol. 8586, pp. 105–130. Springer, Heidelberg (2014). https://doi.org/10.1007/978-3-662-44202-9_5
18. Palmkvist, V.: Building Programming Languages, Construction by Construction. Master's thesis, KTH Royal Institute of Technology (2018)

19. Rompf, T., Odersky, M.: Lightweight modular staging: a pragmatic approach to runtime code generation and compiled DSLs. In: Proceedings of the Ninth International Conference on Generative Programming and Component Engineering, GPCE 2010, pp. 127–136. ACM, New York (2010)
20. Sheard, T., Jones, S.P.: Template meta-programming for Haskell. In: Haskell 2002: Proceedings of the 2002 ACM SIGPLAN Workshop on Haskell, pp. 1–16. ACM Press, New York (2002)
21. Silkensen, E., Siek, J.: Well-typed islands parse faster. In: Loidl, H.-W., Peña, R. (eds.) TFP 2012. LNCS, vol. 7829, pp. 69–84. Springer, Heidelberg (2013). https://doi.org/10.1007/978-3-642-40447-4_5
22. Stansifer, P., Wand, M.: Romeo. In: Proceedings of the 19th ACM SIGPLAN International Conference on Functional Programming - ICFP 2014, vol. 49, pp. 53–65. ACM Press, New York (2014)
23. Steele, Jr., G.L.: An overview of COMMON LISP. In: Proceedings of the 1982 ACM Symposium on LISP and Functional Programming, LFP 1982, pp. 98–107. ACM, New York (1982)
24. Sujeeth, A.K., et al.: Delite: a compiler architecture for performance-oriented embedded domain-specific languages. ACM Trans. Embed. Comput. Syst. (TECS) 13(4s), 134:1–134:25 (2014)
25. Van Wyk, E., Bodin, D., Gao, J., Krishnan, L.: Silver: an extensible attribute grammar system. Sci. Comput. Program. 75(1–2), 39–54 (2010)
26. Van Wyk, E.R., Schwerdfeger, A.C.: Context-aware scanning for parsing extensible languages. In: Proceedings of the 6th International Conference on Generative Programming and Component Engineering - GPCE 2007, p. 63. ACM Press, New York (2007)
27. Wan, Z., Hudak, P.: Functional reactive programming from first principles. In: PLDI 2000: Proceedings of the ACM SIGPLAN 2000 Conference on Programming Language Design and Implementation, pp. 242–252. ACM Press, New York (2000)

Proof-Carrying Plans

Christopher Schwaab[1], Ekaterina Komendantskaya[2], Alasdair Hill[2(✉)],
František Farka[1,2], Ronald P. A. Petrick[2], Joe Wells[2], and Kevin Hammond[1]

[1] School of Computer Science, University of St Andrews, St Andrews, UK
{cjs26,ff32,kh8}@st-andrews.ac.uk
[2] Department of Computer Science, Heriot-Watt University, Edinburgh, UK
{ek19,ath7,rpp6,jbw}@hw.ac.uk

Abstract. It is becoming increasingly important to verify safety and
security of AI applications. While declarative languages (of the kind
found in automated planners and model checkers) are traditionally used
for verifying AI systems, a big challenge is to design methods that generate verified executable programs. A good example of such a *verification to implementation"* cycle is given by automated planning languages
like PDDL, where plans are found via a model search in a declarative language, but then interpreted or compiled into executable code
in an imperative language. In this paper, we show that this method
can itself be verified. We present a formal framework and a prototype
Agda implementation that represent PDDL plans as executable functions that inhabit types that are given by formulae describing planning
problems. By exploiting the well-known Curry-Howard correspondence,
type-checking then automatically ensures that the generated program
corresponds precisely to the specification of the planning problem.

Keywords: AI planning · Curry-Howard correspondence
Constructive logic · Verification · Dependent types

1 Motivation

Declarative programming languages have long provided convenient formalisms
for knowledge representation and reasoning, ranging from Lisp and Prolog in the
1960s-1980s to modern SMT solvers [2,3], model checkers [13], and automated
planners [4,11]. Common features of such languages typically include a clear
logic-based syntax, a well-understood declarative semantics, and an inference
engine that produces sound results with respect to the semantics.

As AI applications become increasingly deployed in the real world, e.g. in self-
driving vehicles or autonomous robots, so safety and security issues are becoming
increasingly important. Existing ad-hoc software development approaches do not
provide the strong confidence levels that the public expects from such applications. It is tempting to envisage that declarative languages will play an increasingly important role in verifying the safety and security of real-world AI applications. Ideally, such languages could become vehicles for *proof-carrying code*,

© Springer Nature Switzerland AG 2019
J. J. Alferes and M. Johansson (Eds.): PADL 2019, LNCS 11372, pp. 204–220, 2019.
https://doi.org/10.1007/978-3-030-05998-9_13

an approach in which all relevant verification properties are directly embedded in the source code [12]. To make this possible, we must supplement the ability to prove that a property A holds in a theory T (denoted $T \vdash A$) with robust mechanisms that can generate a program p that executes according to the specification A, together with a proof that p satisfies A (denoted $T \vdash p : A$). Such an approach would embed verification directly as an integral part of the implementation cycle for AI applications.

The well-known *Curry-Howard correspondence* [19,20], tells us, of course, that some proofs in intuitionistic first-order logic can be represented as computable functions. In this case, first-order formulae are seen as *types*, and proofs are seen as terms that inhabit those types. For example, when we write $T \vdash p : A$, we mean that a *proof term p* is an *executable program* that satisfies proposition A, and moreover that this inference is sound, i.e. that $T \vdash p : A$ holds in some formal system.

Until recently, the significance of the Curry-Howard correspondence has been predominantly theoretical. The main impediment to its practical application has been the immaturity of programming languages that could fully implement this idea. For example, in order to express verification properties of AI applications, a language that could infer $T \vdash p : A$ must possess at least first-order types. Moreover, it should ideally also possess *dependent types*. Several dependently-typed languages have now become available and increasingly practical, e.g., Coq, Agda, and Idris. This development has made it possible to re-open the discussion of the actual practical value of the *Curry-Howard correspondence*. For example, in [6,7] Fu et al. have given a Curry-Howard interpretation for first-order Horn clauses and the resolution algorithm; and Urzyczyn and Schubert [16] have given a constructive semantics for answer set programming.

In this paper, we turn our attention to AI Planning languages [4,11] – a rapidly growing research and engineering area that develops methods and tools for generating plans from declarative problem specifications. We show that the Planning Domain Definition Language (PDDL) [11] is a natural domain for the Curry-Howard implementation of declarative reasoning. In particular, specifications of planning problems that are usually written in first-order logic can be expressed naturally as types, and executable plans that are generated by PDDL can be formalised as programs that inhabit those types. Type checking thus verifies that correct executable programs are generated from specifications *via* the automated planning tool. We provide a proof-of-concept implementation [17] in the dependently-typed language Agda.

2   Example: Proof-Carrying PDDL

Figure 1 shows a snippet of PDDL code that describes the classic Blocksworld domain, a simple planning task for a robot assembling a tower from bricks. It defines a set of predicates (`handEmpty`, `holding`, `onTable`, `on`, `clear`) and an action `pickup_from_table` that must satisfy certain pre- and post-conditions ("effects") that are expressed using those predicates. Several such actions are usually defined as part of a planning domain. In addition, a grounded problem will also be supplied to the planner, e.g., to form a stack of blocks a on b on c, given that a, b and c are initially on the table (but not on each other). Given the domain and problem definitions, an automated planner will initiate an algorithm (e.g., a search procedure) to generate a sequence of actions that satisfy the specification and the goal. In our case, one possible solution is:

```
Plan1 = pickup_from_table b; putdown_on_stack b c;
  pickup_from_table a; putdown_on_stack a b.
```

```
Definition of a Planning Domain:      Definition of a Planning Problem:

(define (domain blocksworld)
    (:requirements :strips)
     (:predicates
         (handEmpty)
         (holding ?x)
         (onTable ?x)                  (define (problem blocksworld1)
         (on ?x ?y)                        (:domain blocksworld)
         (clear ?x) )                      (:objects a b c)
                                           (:init (onTable a)
     (:action pickup_from_table                  (onTable b)
         :parameters                             (onTable c)
         (?x)                                     (clear a)
         :precondition                            (clear b)
         (and (handEmpty)                         (clear c)
              (onTable ?x)                        (handEmpty) )
              (clear ?x) )              (:goal (and (on a b)  (on b c))))
         :effect
         (and (not (handEmpty))
              (not (onTable ?x))
              (holding ?x) )))
```

Fig. 1. The Blocksworld: a code snippet defining the planning domain and a planning problem.

We would like to have an implementation of this planning language where an executable function $plan_1$ is generated from the planning domain and problem, such that $plan_1$ corresponds to the actions of Plan1 and has a type onTable a $\wedge$ onTable b $\wedge$ onTable c $\wedge$ clear a $\wedge$ clear b $\wedge$ clear c $\wedge$ handEmpty $\rightsquigarrow$ on a b $\wedge$ on b c. If this judgement type-checks, then we will obtain a verified program $plan_1$ that can be later compiled and executed. As we will show in the rest of the paper, this task is far from trivial. Although the Curry-Howard correspondence tells us that, in principle, (intuitionistic) first-order proofs have a computational meaning, it is not enough for us to just formulate arbitrary proofs. Firstly, we need to formulate a generic and automatable approach to translate PDDL domains and problems into the dependently-typed setting. In addition, we need to devise our calculus in such a way as to ensure that the programs that inhabit the types give us the actual executable plans in the PDDL sense. In this paper, we therefore develop two parallel narratives. The first sets up the general method in mathematical notation independently of the concrete implementation. The second illustrates the important engineering aspect of this work, with reference to the intricacies of the Agda encoding that we give in [17]. The two parallel story lines merge when we come to the main result of this paper: the formal proof of soundness of the proof terms that implement the plans. We state this in standard mathematical notation, but delegate the proof checking to Agda. In time, we envisage that our Agda prototype will become a fully fledged program for generation of executable code from planners, while maintaining the guarantees of soundness of the generated code relative to the plan specification.

Atomic Formulae	$At \ni A$	$::= R\, C_1 \dots C_n$
Formulae	$Form \ni P, Q$	$::= A \mid \neg A \mid P \wedge Q$
Polarities	$Polarity \ni t$	$::= + \mid -$
States	$\mathcal{N} \ni M, N$	$::= [\,] \mid [A^t, N]$
Plans	$Plan \ni f$	$::= \text{halt} \mid \alpha; f$
Contexts	$\Gamma \ni \Gamma_1, \Gamma_2$	$::= \alpha : M \rightsquigarrow N$

Fig. 2. Definitions of Formulae, States, Plans and Actions, given a set of predicates $\mathcal{R} = \{R, R_1, R_2, ..., R_n\}$, a set of constants $\mathcal{C} = \{C_1, C_2, ..., C_k\}$, and a set of constant actions $\{\alpha, \alpha_1, \ldots, \alpha_m\} \cup \text{halt}$.

3   Planning Problems as Types

In their development of the STRIPS planner, Fikes and Nilsson presented an inference system for planning languages that is based on the notion of states, or possible *worlds*. The worlds are sets of atomic formulae, that interpret complex formula of the planning domain. Operators that are defined on the worlds interpret planning actions, and rewrite the worlds by adding and deleting the atomic formulae. The inference algorithm thus starts in an initial world and ends in a goal world by the repeated application of the operators. The system is sound in the sense that the resultant world model satisfies the goal. We now provide a show how to work with STRIPS predicates directly in a type-system, yielding proof obligations that will be fulfilled by plan execution.

3.1   Formal Language and Its Declarative Semantics

We assume a finite set of predicates $\mathcal{R} = \{R, R_1, R_2, ..., R_n\}$ each R_i of fixed arity, and a finite set $\mathcal{C} = \{C_1, C_2, ..., C_k\}$ of constants (also known as "objects").

The standard definition of first-order formulae is given in Fig. 2. It has two notable restrictions: the formulae do not admit variables, and only atomic formulae can be negated. The former restriction, together with the assumption that there are only finitely many constants, ensures that the set of all atomic formulae is finite, which makes it possible to take the *closed world assumption* [15], and ensure the decidability of set membership on possible worlds. The latter restriction means that disjunction is not definable in our language. In PDDL, two key restrictions apply to the use of disjunction. Firstly, all formulae are pre-compiled into disjunctive normal form. Secondly, no "actions" can have disjunctive "effects", i.e. they cannot give rise to disjunctive post-conditions. Thus, our second restriction actually adheres to the practice of PDDL plan specification and search.

```
module PCPlans                          module Blocksworld where
  {R : Set }
  {isDE : IsDecEquivalence              data C : Set where
          {A = R} (_≡_) }                 a b c : C
where
                                        data R : Set where
data Form : Set where                     handEmpty : R
  _∧_ : Form → Form → Form                onTable clear holding : C → R
  ¬_ : R → Form                           on : C → C → R
  atom : R → Form

                                        open import PCPlans {R} {isDE}
```

Fig. 3. Left: Module *PCPlans* giving a general-case Agda definition of a formula, following the set-up of Fig. 2. Right: Module *Blocksworld* giving specification of the particular Blocksworld domain from Fig. 1: listing its constants and predicates.

```
World : Set          data Polarity : Set where    neg : Polarity → Polarity
World = List R         + − : Polarity             neg + = −
                                                  neg − = +
```

Fig. 4. Agda definitions of worlds as lists of atomic formulae, polarities. (Module *PCPlans*)

Example 1. Given the syntax of Sect. 2, handEmpty ∧ ¬onTable a is a formula.

The inductive definitions of Fig. 2 are given as data type definitions in our Agda implementation (Fig. 3). We provide a generic Agda module, *PCPlans*, that is parametric in predicates and actions. For each planning problem, the set of predicates $\mathcal{R}$ may then be defined concretely, as in the *Blocksworld* module. Propositional equality on atomic formulae must be shown to be decidable for the particular planning problem. As we will show later, this property is needed in order to manipulate world representation. Since our implementation of the *PCPlans* module takes a generic approach, a proof that propositional equality $\_\equiv\_$ for $\mathcal{R}$ is decidable must also be provided as a module parameter. This explains the declaration of the main module:

module *PCPlans* $\{\mathcal{R} : Set\ \}\ \{isDE : IsDecEquivalence\ \{A = \mathcal{R}\}\ (\_\equiv\_)\ \}$

When we instantiate $\mathcal{R}$ with a finite set of predicates for each planning problem, we need to instantiate $isDE$ with a proof that propositional equality for this particular problem is indeed decidable. In [17] we show how to automate such "boilerplate" proofs for any given $\mathcal{R}$, using reflection.

Given a set w of atomic formulae (called a *world*), a formula F *is satisfied by* w if $w \models_+ F$ can be derived using the rules of Fig. 5. In Agda, we take advantage of the extensive library of list operations, and so define worlds as lists of atomic formulae, as shown in Fig. 4. Figure 7 gives an Agda definition of the entailment relation.

Example 2. Given the world $w_1 = \{\texttt{handEmpty}\}$, $w_1 \models_+ \texttt{handEmpty} \wedge\neg\ \texttt{onTable a}$.

It might be expected that the rule for conjunction with negative polarity to be given by two additional rules: $\dfrac{w \models_- P}{w \models_- P \wedge Q}$ and $\dfrac{w \models_- Q}{w \models_- P \wedge Q}$. However, our current rule is sound given the syntax restrictions, and it simplifies our reasoning on decidability of normalisation, which we define next.

$$\frac{w \models_t P \quad w \models_t Q}{w \models_t P \wedge Q} \qquad \frac{w \models_{-t} P}{w \models_t \neg P} \qquad \frac{A \in w}{w \models_+ A} \qquad \frac{A \notin w}{w \models_- A}$$

Fig. 5. Declarative interpretation of formulae. We define $-l$ by taking $-+ = -$ and $-- = +$.

```
data _⊨[_]_ : World → Polarity → Form → Set where
    flip : ∀{w t A} → w ⊨[ neg t ] (atom A) → w ⊨[ t ] ¬ A
    both : ∀{w t P Q} → w ⊨[ t ] P → w ⊨[ t ] Q → w ⊨[ t ] P ∧ Q
    somewhere : ∀{w a} → a ∈ w → w ⊨[ + ] atom a
    nowhere : ∀{w a} → a ∉ w → w ⊨[ - ] atom a
```

Fig. 6. Agda definition of the entailment relation given in Fig. 5. (Module *PCPlans*)

3.2   Operational Semantics, States and Types

Matching the declarative-style semantics of Fig. 5, we can define an operational semantics, given by a normalisation function that acts directly on formulae and computes lists of atomic formulae with polarities. A *state* is defined as a list of atomic formulae with polarities, as in Fig. 2. By a small abuse of notation, we will use $\in$ to denote list membership, as well as set membership. The function $\downarrow_t$ *normalises* a formula to a state:

$$(P \wedge Q) \downarrow_t N = Q \downarrow_t P \downarrow_t N$$
$$\neg A \downarrow_t N = A \downarrow_{-t} N$$
$$A \downarrow_t N = [A^t, N]$$

We write $P \downarrow_t$ to mean $P \downarrow_t [\,]$.

Example 3. Continuing with the previous examples, we have:
(handEmpty $\wedge \neg$onTable a) $\downarrow_+ = $ [handEmpty$^+$, onTable a$^-$]

As might be expected, while the definition of the entailment relation $\models_t$ is given as an inductive data type in Agda, the normalisation is defined as a function (Fig. 7). Note again that, in order to bring the disjunction into this language in any future extensions, normalisation function for minus could be amended, to allow for non-determinism. Normalisation is sound relative to the declarative interpretation of formulae. Given a state N, define a *well-formed world* w_N to contain all A such that $A^+ \in N$ and contain no A's such that $A^- \notin N$. Generally w_N is not uniquely defined, and we use the notation $\{w_N\}$ to refer to the (necessarily finite) set of all w_N. We then have the result:

$$NPred : Set$$
$$NPred = List\,(Polarity \times R)$$

$$\_\downarrow[\_] : Form \rightarrow Polarity \rightarrow NPred \rightarrow NPred$$
$$P \wedge Q \downarrow[\,t\,]\,N = Q \downarrow[\,t\,]\,P \downarrow[\,t\,]\,N$$
$$\neg\,x \downarrow[\,t\,]\,N = (neg\,t\,,x) :: N$$
$$atom\,x \downarrow[\,t\,]\,N = (t\,,x) :: N$$

Fig. 7. Agda definition of the normalisation function. (Module *PCPlans*)

Theorem 1 (Soundness and completeness of normalisation). *Given a formula P and a world w, it holds that $w \models_t P$ iff $w \in \{w_{P\downarrow_t}\}$.*

Proof. ($\Rightarrow$) is proven by induction on the derivation of $w \models_t P$. ($\Leftarrow$) follows by induction on the shape of P, cf. the attached Agda file [17] for the fully formalised proof.

Example 4. If $N =$(handEmpty $\wedge \neg$onTable a) $\downarrow_+$, then w_N may be given by e.g. $w_1 =$ {handEmpty}, or $w_2 =$ {handEmpty, onTable b}, or any other world containing handEmpty but not onTable a. The given formula will be satisfied by any such w_N.

Theorem 1 will allow us to work with states at the type level, while keeping the link to the standard PDDL formula syntax and declarative semantics.

We finally define actions and plans. Given a halting state halt, and a finite set of constant *actions* $\{\alpha, \alpha_1, \ldots, \alpha_m\}$, we define *plans* inductively as sequences of action names ending with halt, cf. Fig. 2. Once again, we show an instantiated version of the Agda definition of actions in Fig. 8, with actions specified as per the Blocksworld problem. In the Agda prototype [17], we first develop the code for an abstract set *Action*, and then instantiate it on the concrete examples. Figure 8 also shows the Agda function $plan_1$ that encodes **Plan1** given in Sect. 2 in PDDL syntax. Keeping in line with Sect. 2, a *planning domain (or a context)* Γ is a set of actions with effects, of the form $\alpha : N \rightsquigarrow M$, where α is a constant action, and N, M are states (see Fig. 2). Figure 9 shows an Agda implementation of both the general definition of a context Γ and one concrete Γ_1 that corresponds to the PDDL code snippet of Fig. 1.

```
data Plan : Set where                    plan₁ : Plan
  doAct : Action → Plan → Plan           plan₁ = doAct pickup_from_table_b
  halt : Plan                                     (doAct putdown_on_stack_b_c
                                                    (doAct pickup_from_table_a
data Action : Set where                             (doAct putdown_on_stack_a_b
  pickup_from_table_b : Action                        halt)))
  pickup_from_table_a : Action
  putdown_on_stack_b_c : Action
  putdown_on_stack_a_b : Action
```

Fig. 8. Agda abstract definition of a *Plan* according to Fig. 2, in module *PCPlans*. A concrete instantiation of the set of actions, a concrete plan $plan_1$ in module *Blocksworld*.

```
Γ : Set
Γ = Action → N Pred × N Pred

Γ₁ : Γ
Γ₁ pickup_from_table_b =
  (atom handEmpty ∧ atom (onTable b) ∧ atom (clear b)) ↓₊ ,
  ((¬ handEmpty ∧ ¬ (onTable b) ∧ atom (holding b)) ↓₊)
Γ₁ pickup_from_table_a = ...
Γ₁ putdown_on_stack_b_c =
  (atom (holding b) ∧ atom (clear c)) ↓₊ ,
  (¬ (holding b) ∧ ¬ (clear c) ∧ atom (on b c) ∧ atom handEmpty) ↓₊
Γ₁ putdown_on_stack_a_b = ...
```

Fig. 9. Agda definition of the concrete context Γ_1 in module *Blocksworld*.

We now move on to our main goal: to realise the Curry-Howard intuition and define a framework in which plans will inhabit normalised formulae seen as types. We wish to show that, proving that a certain (possibly composite) plan f satisfies pre- and post-conditions given by the formulae P and Q will be equivalent to typing the judgement

$$\Gamma \vdash f : P \downarrow_+ \rightsquigarrow Q \downarrow_+$$

We will say $P \downarrow_+$ is the initial state of the plan f, and $Q \downarrow_+$ is its final state. In the next section, we introduce typing rules that define derivations of these judgements.

4   Plans as Proof Terms

4.1   Typing Rules for Planning Problems

A naïve attempt to type plans introduces two problems. First, an action $f : M \rightsquigarrow N$ should not produce exactly N, but an extension of M by N. For example, picking up b from the table does not affect the fact that c is still on the table (this is known as the *STRIPS assumption* in planning [21]). To solve this problem, we introduce an override operator $M \sqcup N$:

$$M \sqcup [\,] = M$$
$$M \sqcup [A^t, N] = [A^t, M \backslash \{A^+, A^-\}] \sqcup N$$

The second problem involves applying $f : M \rightsquigarrow N$ in a state M' that is stronger (has more atomic formulae) than M. For example, if b is known to be on the table, knowing that c is also on the table should not preclude picking up b. This state-weakening action corresponds to sub-typing $M <: M'$ defined in Fig. 10. When we write $M <: M'$, we will say M' is a *sub-type* of M. This agrees with the usual convention that a sub-type is given by a stronger predicate. The rules of Fig. 11 define how a program $f : M \rightsquigarrow N$ can be typed given some planning domain Γ. A well-typed plan $\Gamma \vdash f : M \rightsquigarrow N$ "transports" an initial state M to a goal state N. The Agda code implements the typing relation as an inductive data type with two constructors, *halt* and *seq*, following verbatim Fig. 11 (see also the accompanying Agda file). To exemplify these rules, we refer again to the Blocksworld problem with the pre-condition $P_0 =$ onTable a $\wedge$ onTable b $\wedge$ onTable c $\wedge$ clear a $\wedge$ clear b $\wedge$ clear c $\wedge$ handEmpty and the post-condition $Q_0 =$ on a b $\wedge$ on b c. Suppose that the PDDL planner proposes Plan1, as given in Sect. 2. Let $plan_1$ be the corresponding version in the precise mathematical notation of Fig. 2 (cf. also its Agda version in Fig. 8):

$$plan_1 = \text{pickup\_from\_table\_b}; \text{putdown\_on\_stack\_b\_c};$$
$$\text{pickup\_from\_table\_a}; \text{putdown\_on\_stack\_a\_b}; \text{halt}$$

If $\Gamma_1 \vdash plan_1 : P_0 \downarrow_+ \rightsquigarrow Q_0 \downarrow_+$ yields a typing derivation by Fig. 11, then this typing derivation verifies that $plan_1$ correctly implements the given planning

$$\text{NilSub} \;\frac{}{[\,]\; <:\; N} \qquad \text{ASub}\; \frac{N <:\, M \quad A^t \in M}{A^t, N\; <:\, M}$$

Fig. 10. Sub-typing of normalised formulae.

$$\text{Halt}\;\frac{M' <:\, M}{\Gamma \vdash \text{halt}\,:\, M \rightsquigarrow M'} \qquad \text{Seq}\;\frac{M_1' <:\, M_1 \qquad (\alpha : M_1' \rightsquigarrow M_2) \in \Gamma \quad \Gamma \vdash f\,:\, M_1 \sqcup M_2 \rightsquigarrow M_3}{\Gamma \vdash \alpha; f\,:\, M_1 \rightsquigarrow M_3}$$

Fig. 11. Well-typing relation for plans.

problem in the planning domain Γ_1 (cf. also Agda code for Γ_1 in Fig. 9). To make our example more readable, we will use our mathematical notation. This gives the following definition of Γ_1, corresponding to the Agda code of Fig. 9:

$$\Gamma_1 = \{\texttt{pickup\_from\_table\_b} : \begin{array}{c} \texttt{handEmpty} \wedge \\ \texttt{onTable b} \wedge \\ \texttt{clear b} \end{array}\Big\downarrow_{+} \;\rightsquigarrow\; \begin{array}{c} \neg\texttt{handEmpty} \wedge \\ \neg(\texttt{onTable b}) \wedge \\ \texttt{holding b} \end{array}\Big\downarrow_{\!\!}$$

$$\texttt{pickup\_from\_table\_a} : \ldots$$

$$\texttt{putdown\_on\_stack\_b\_c} : \begin{array}{c} \texttt{holding b} \wedge \\ \texttt{clear c} \end{array}\Big\downarrow_{+} \;\rightsquigarrow\; \begin{array}{c} \neg(\texttt{holding b}) \wedge \\ \neg(\texttt{clear c}) \wedge \\ \texttt{on b c} \wedge \\ \texttt{handEmpty} \end{array}\Big\downarrow_{+}$$

$$\texttt{putdown\_on\_stack\_a\_b} : \ldots\}$$

Let us perform the typing derivation for $\Gamma_1 \vdash \text{plan}_1 : P_0 \downarrow_+ \rightsquigarrow Q_0 \downarrow_+$. Given $P_0 \downarrow_+$, then the first action that we can apply by the Seq rule is `pickup_from_table_b`. The application of Seq demands that $P_0 \downarrow_+$ is a sub-type of the initial state of the action `pickup_from_table_b` in Γ_1. A sub-typing derivation provides such a proof, selecting the required piece of evidence from $P_0 \downarrow_+$, i.e. $\texttt{handEmpty}^+, (\texttt{onTable b})^+, (\texttt{clear b})^+ <: (\texttt{onTable a})^+, (\texttt{onTable b})^+, (\texttt{onTable c})^+, (\texttt{clear a})^+, (\texttt{clear b})^+, (\texttt{clear c})^+, \texttt{handEmpty}^+$. We have thus verified that $\text{plan}_1 = \texttt{pickup\_from\_table\_b};\ f'$. To complete the proof of well-typedness and compute an action for f', we must show that the remainder of the plan is typeable. According to Seq, we now have a new state $P_1 = P_0 \downarrow_+ \sqcup \texttt{handEmpty}^-, (\texttt{onTable b})^-, (\texttt{holding b})^+ = (\texttt{onTable a})^+, (\texttt{onTable b})^-, (\texttt{onTable c})^+, (\texttt{clear a})^+, (\texttt{clear b})^+, (\texttt{clear c})^+, (\texttt{handEmpty})^-, (\texttt{holding b})^+$, as well as an obligation to prove f' : $P_1 \rightsquigarrow Q_0 \downarrow_+$. We can pick the next action from Γ_1: `putdown_on_stack_b_c`. Again P_1 is readily shown to be a sub-type of the pre-conditions of `putdown_on_stack_b_c`. Continuing in this way for each action in plan_1, the final state is $P_3 = (\texttt{onTable a})^-, (\texttt{onTable b})^-, (\texttt{onTable c})^+, (\texttt{clear a})^+, (\texttt{clear b})^-, (\texttt{clear c})^-, (\texttt{on b c})^+, \texttt{handEmpty}^+, (\texttt{holding b})^-, (\texttt{on a b})^+, (\texttt{holding a})^-$. However, this is not the same state as the goal state Q_0. To resolve such cases, we have the rule Halt, eliminating all unnecessary evidence from the current state by proof of sub-typing i.e. $\Gamma_1 \vdash$ halt : $P_3 \rightsquigarrow Q_0$. Clearly (on a b)$^+$, (on b c)$^+ <: P_3$ as required. We have thus verified that $\Gamma_1 \vdash$ plan$_1$: $P_0 \downarrow_+ \rightsquigarrow Q_0 \downarrow_+$. In Agda, the above derivation will amount to type-checking the function $Derivation$ as shown in Fig. 12. If it type-checks, then we know that $plan_1$ can be soundly executed as a function. Proving this property in general is the subject of the next section.

P_0 : *Form*
$P_0 = atom\,(onTable\,a) \wedge atom\,(onTable\,b) \wedge atom\,(onTable\,c) \wedge$
$atom\,(clear\,a) \wedge atom\,(clear\,b) \wedge atom\,(clear\,c) \wedge atom\,hand\,Empty$

Q_0 : *Form*
$Q_0 = atom\,(on\,a\,b) \wedge atom\,(on\,b\,c)$

$Derivation$: $\Gamma_1 \vdash plan_1$: $(P_0 \downarrow_+) \rightsquigarrow (Q_0 \downarrow_+)$
$Derivation = ...$

Fig. 12. Agda type-checking the derivation of $\Gamma_1 \vdash$ plan$_1$: $P_0 \downarrow_+ \rightsquigarrow Q_0 \downarrow_+$. We give the full code for $Derivation$ in [18] or [17].

4.2 Computational Characterisation of Plans: Soundness of Plan Execution

The proof of $\Gamma_1 \vdash$ plan$_1$: $P_0 \downarrow_+ \rightsquigarrow Q_0 \downarrow_+$ provides evidence that the *execution* of plan$_1$ on a world satisfying P_0 produces a new world satisfying Q_0. Generally, the inference of $\Gamma \vdash f$: $M \rightsquigarrow N$, with $f = \alpha_1; \ldots; \alpha_j$; halt corresponds to successively applying actions $\alpha_1 \ldots \alpha_j$ to states $M, M_1, \ldots M_j$ in a sequence of state transitions, satisfying $N <: M_j$. We now prove that the plan f thus inferred indeed has a computational meaning, i.e. can be *evaluated*, and that the result of its evaluation is sound. To state this, we need to define an *evaluation function* $[\![.]\!]$ that will interpret actions on worlds. Recall that every state N maps to a world w_N. Let us use notation σ for an arbitrary mapping (an *action handler*) that maps each action α : $M \rightsquigarrow N$ to insertions and deletions on the world w_M according to α's action on M. We then define the evaluation function $[\![]\!]_w^\sigma$ that *evaluates* a plan to a world (according to a given world w and action handler σ):

$$[\![halt]\!]_w^\sigma = w$$
$$[\![\alpha; f]\!]_w^\sigma = [\![f]\!]_{(\sigma\ \alpha\ w)}^\sigma$$

We say that an action handler σ is *well-formed* if, for any $w \in \{w_M\}$, $M' <: M$ and α : $M' \rightsquigarrow N$ in Γ it follows that $(\sigma\ \alpha\ w) \in \{w_{M \sqcup N}\}$. Figure 13 shows Agda definitions of an action handler and evaluation action.

Canonical Handler. In order to be constructive in our further claims, and to provide a practical solution to the quest for a well-formed handler, we first define

$ActionHandler : Set$
$ActionHandler = Action \rightarrow World \rightarrow World$

$[\![\_]\!] : Plan \rightarrow ActionHandler \rightarrow World \rightarrow World$
$[\![\ doAct\ \alpha\ f\ ]\!]\ \sigma\ w = [\![\ f\ ]\!]\ \sigma\ (\sigma\ \alpha\ w)$
$[\![\ halt\ ]\!]\ \sigma\ w = w$

$\sigma\alpha : NPred \rightarrow World \rightarrow World$
$\sigma\alpha\ []\ w = w$
$\sigma\alpha\ ((+,x) :: N)\ w = x :: \sigma\alpha\ N\ w$
$\sigma\alpha\ ((-,x) :: N)\ w = remove\ x\ (\sigma\alpha\ N\ w)$

$canonical\text{-}\sigma : \Gamma \rightarrow ActionHandler$
$canonical\text{-}\sigma\ \Gamma_1\ \alpha = \sigma\alpha\ (proj_2\ (\Gamma_1\ \alpha))$

Fig. 13. Agda code for an action handler, an evaluation function and a canonical handler.

a *canonical handler* for a given context (planning domain). Firstly, we define a function σ_α that constructs a world from a state:

$$\sigma_\alpha\ [\ ]\ w = w$$
$$\sigma_\alpha\ [A^+, N']\ w = \sigma_\alpha\ N'\ (w \cup \{A\})$$
$$\sigma_\alpha\ [A^-, N']\ w = \sigma_\alpha\ N'\ (w \setminus \{A\})$$

Next, given a context Γ, we apply σ_α to N for each $\alpha : M \rightsquigarrow N$ in Γ; thus obtaining a canonical mapping $\sigma_\alpha\ \Gamma$ from actions and worlds into worlds, as required. The resulting canonical action handler is well-formed, as long as the states to which it is applied are consistent, in the following sense:

Implicit consistency assumption: for every state N, if $A^t \in N$ then $A^{-t} \notin N$.

Proposition 1. *Given a context Γ, the canonical action handler $\sigma_\alpha\ \Gamma$ is well-formed.*

Proof. The proof starts with considering an arbitrary state M with $w \in \{w_M\}$, an arbitrary $A^t \in M$, and an arbitrary action α in Γ such that $M' <: M$ and $\alpha : M' \rightsquigarrow N$. It proceeds by considering two cases, when $t = +$ and $t = -$, and consequently when $A \in w$ or $A \notin w$. In each of these cases, it considers all possible effects of σ_α (i.e. formula deletions and insertions) in the process of constructing the world $w' = canonical\text{-}\sigma\ \alpha\ w$. The attached Agda file gives the full proof. It uses the implicit consistency assumption to eliminate the cases when states are inconsistent and hence when more than one choice for deletion/insertion are possible.

The next two theorems show that executing a well-typed plan f by the evaluation function $[\![f]\!]_w^\sigma$ is *sound*, for any well-formed handler σ.

Theorem 2. (Soundness of evaluation for normalized formulae). *Suppose $\Gamma \vdash f : M \rightsquigarrow N$. Then for any $w \in \{w_M\}$, and any well-formed handler σ, it follows that $[\![f]\!]_w^\sigma \in \{w_N\}$.*

Proof. The proof proceeds by structural induction on the typing derivation $\Gamma \vdash f : M \rightsquigarrow N$.

Case 1 (Halt). By assumption $w \in \{w_M\}$ and thus because $N <: M$, it follows $w \in \{w_N\}$. Since $[\![\text{halt}]\!]_w^\sigma = w$, we get $[\![\text{halt}]\!]_w^\sigma \in \{w_N\}$ as required.

Case 2 (Seq). Note that $f = \alpha; f'$ and therefore $\alpha : M' \rightsquigarrow M_2$ is in Γ and $\Gamma \vdash f' : M \sqcup M_2 \rightsquigarrow N$ by inversion on $\Gamma \vdash \alpha; f' : M \rightsquigarrow N$. Then by induction every $w' \in \{w_{M \sqcup M_2}\}$ gives $([\![f]\!]_{w'}^\sigma) \in \{w_N\}$ for any well-formed σ. However, by the well-formedness of σ and because $w \in \{w_M\}$, we have $(\sigma \ \alpha \ w) \in \{w_{M \sqcup M_2}\}$. Thus $[\![f']\!]_{(\sigma \ \alpha \ w)}^\sigma \in \{w_N\}$ and therefore $[\![f]\!]_w^\sigma \in \{w_N\}$.

Theorem 3 (Soundness of evaluation). *Suppose $\Gamma \vdash f : P \downarrow_+ \rightsquigarrow Q \downarrow_+$ then for any w such that $w \models_+ P$, and any well-formed σ it follows $[\![f]\!]_w^\sigma \models_+ Q$.*

Proof. By assumption $w \models_+ P$ and by the completeness of normalisation (Theorem 1), we have $w \in \{w_{P\downarrow_+}\}$. Then from Theorem 2, we have $[\![f]\!]_w^\sigma \in \{w_{Q\downarrow_+}\}$. Thus by the soundness of normalisation (Theorem 1), obtain $[\![f]\!]_w^\sigma \models_+ Q$.

Thus the derivation of a type for a plan f induces a proof that the execution of a plan in world w is correct. Although neither of the above theorems depends on the implicit consistency assumption for its proofs, the existence of a well-formed and canonical handler is predicated upon the consistency assumption. Our Agda implementation of a canonical handler (cf. Fig. 13) allows us to fully harness the computational properties of plans. For the Blocksworld example, we can directly evaluate $[\![\text{plan}_1]\!]_w^\sigma$ by plugging in:
- in place of w – the world resulting from computing $\sigma_\alpha(P_0 \downarrow_+ [\ ]) \varnothing$. (To see this, recall that P_0 is the formula that described the initial state in all examples of the previous section, and $P_0 \downarrow_+ [\ ]$ is the state resulting from normalising P_0.)
- and in place of σ – the canonical handler for Γ_1. (Recall that Γ_1 is the context that defined the given planning domain in the previous section.)

In Agda, we simply evaluate the term:

$$[\![\text{plan}_1]\!] \ (\text{canonical} - \sigma \ \Gamma_1) \ (\sigma \alpha \ (P_0 \downarrow [\ + \ ] \ [])\ [])$$

Evaluation of this term results, just as we manually computed in the last section, in a world $w' = \{\ \text{handEmpty}, \text{on a b}, \text{on b c}, \text{clear a}, \text{onTable c}\}$ (in Agda syntax: $handEmpty :: (on\ a\ b) :: (on\ b\ c) :: (clear\ a) :: (onTable\ c) :: [])$). That is, the world that corresponds to the state P_3 of the previous section. Observe that $w' = \sigma_\alpha \ P_3 \ \varnothing$.

5   Discussion, Conclusions, and Future Work

We have given a proof of concept formalisation of a subset of PDDL plans in type theory. In line with the Curry-Howard approach to first-order logic, we formulated an inference system that treats planning domains as types, and generated plans as functions that inhabit these types. Type-checking then ensures the soundness of these executable functions relative to the specifications given as types. This paper does not cover the whole PDDL syntax, nor does it implement the search and decision procedures of a usual automated planner e.g. the *Stanford Research Institute Problem Solver* STRIPS [4]. Rather, our contribution is in setting up the original design of a method of Curry-Howard approach to AI planning languages in general, as well as showing the feasibility of its successful implementation in a dependently typed language, such as Agda. This dual purpose has determined our style of presentation, in which the formal method has been given in parallel with, but independently from, the Agda code.

Further Experiments with Plans: In the accompanying implementation [17], we provide a second fully implemented example of a PDDL domain and plan checking in Agda: for a *Logistic* planning problem. The problem consists of finding the best route (airplanes, tracks, cities of call) to deliver a given parcel to a given office. The experiment showed that, once the main Agda implementation is set up, instantaiting it with various problems only takes a routine boilerplate code (such as e.g. proofs of decidability of equality on predicates). Generation of this boilerplate code can in future be fully automated using code reflection. Throughout our implementation, we have been working with plans generated by an on-line PDDL editor http://editor.planning.domains/. In the future, a parser can be added to convert PDDL syntax directly into Agda.

With the view to future extensions, our Agda code is designed in a modular way, as Sect. 3.1 illustrates: the main Agda file implementing the subset of PDDL syntax is fully generic, and its definitions are instantiated as required when a particular planning domain, such as *Blockworld* or *Logistic*, is presented. Proofs of decidability for objects and predicates for each given problem are obtained in a generic way, as well, see [17].

Computational Content of Plans and the Implicit Consistency Assumption: As Proposition 1 has shown, the existence of a canonical and well-formed handler depends crucially on the implicit consistency assumption. At the same time, the proofs of Theorems 2 or 3 do not depend on the consistency assumption. Thus, as we show in [18], it is possible in principle to construct planning domains and problems that violate the assumption but are accepted by the well-typedness relation of Fig. 11. However, if such examples are added to the system, the implicit consistency assumption needs to be removed (or else $\perp$ will become provable, as [18] shows). But without the assumption, we lose the existence of a well-formed and canonical handler and thus the ability to evaluate the plans. This situation is of course illustrative of the rigour and transparency that a constructive approach brings to verification. In our case, it dictates that any practical deployment of the presented prototype needs to enforce the consistency assumption. This can be done by either embedding additional state consistency checks or by implementing states as partial functions from formulae to Booleans.

Generating Executable Plans from Agda: The main advantage of the presented approach is the ability to generate executable code directly from plans verified in Agda. We show in [18] how first a Haskell code, and then an executable binary file, are automatically generated from the verified plan (*plan*$_1$ from our earlier example). Such binary files can then be directly deployed in applications such as e.g. robots. This is in contrast to the existing practices when verified plans are separately converted into C or Python code without any guarantees of compliance of that code to the verified plans.

Related Work: Verification of AI languages and applications is an active research field. In planning languages, two major trends exist. Firstly, PDDL is used to verify autonomous systems and applications, see e.g. [14]; and it has been successfully integrated within other similar languages, such as GOLOG [10], with the purpose of verifying plans written in the situation calculus [1,22]. Secondly, planning domains have been verified using model checkers [9], other automated provers such as Event-B [5], or planning support tools such as VAL [8]. The method that we have presented is complementary to these two trends. Its main difference lies in taking the perspective of *intrinsic*, rather than *external* verification. That is, the correctness of the generated plans is verified not by an external tool, such as a model checker, but is performed intrinsically within the code that implements the plans. At the same time, the code that implements the plans is inseparable from the language in which planning domains are specified. Furthermore, the executable binary files automatically extracted from Agda are not just ready for deployment, but also bear the verification guarantees provided by Agda proofs. To our knowledge, this is the first attempt to bring these benefits of the Curry-Howard approach to automated planning languages. Provisioning types for plans not only equips planners with certificates of correctness for inspection, but also provides a direct link to an implementation's type theory.

Current Limitations and Possible Improvements: First-Order Planning Domains and First-Order Types: Although the technical development of the code that we have presented takes full advantage of Agda's dependent types, the types that represent the predicates and formulae of the planning problems are given by simple types. This is because we propositionalised the planning domains. We however hope to extend this initial framework to the full first-order syntax of PDDL. This development will also involve the following extensions.

Beyond Consistency Assumptions; Constraints: We have discussed the implicit consistency assumption that our approach imposes. More generally, we note that PDDL lacks any general method of handling consistency as well as similar but more complex constraints and invariants, such as, for example, constraints saying that `handEmpty` and `holding x` are mutually exclusive. This is a complex problem, but one for which we anticipate that our dependently-typed setting will soon provide some useful solutions.

Functions and Higher-Order Plans: The design of this Agda prototype has revealed several limitations in state-of-the-art implementations of planning languages: e.g. their reliance on the closed word assumption and formulae grounding, the absence of functions, and the restricted use of disjunctions. Again, we see a potential of our method to overcome many of these limitations thanks to our general dependently-typed set-up, in which the use of functions, higher-order features, constraints and effect handling will be much more natural than in the current implementations.

Acknowledgements. This research has been generously supported by EPSRC Platform Grant EP/N014758/1 "The Integration and Interaction of Multiple Mathematical Reasoning Processes", EPSRC Doctoral Training Partnership, EPSRC grant EP/PP020631 "Discovery: Pattern Discovery and Program Shaping for Manycore Systems", and by EU Horizon 2020 grant ICT-779882 "TeamPlay: Time, Energy and security Analysis for Multi/Many-core heterogenous PLAtforms".

References

1. Claßen, J., Eyerich, P., Lakemeyer, G., Nebel, B.: Towards an integration of Golog and planning. In: Veloso, M.M. (ed.) IJCAI 2007, Proceedings of the 20th International Joint Conference on Artificial Intelligence, Hyderabad, India, 6–12 January 2007, pp. 1846–1851 (2007)
2. de Moura, L., Bjørner, N.: Z3: an efficient SMT solver. In: Ramakrishnan, C.R., Rehof, J. (eds.) TACAS 2008. LNCS, vol. 4963, pp. 337–340. Springer, Heidelberg (2008). https://doi.org/10.1007/978-3-540-78800-3_24
3. Dutertre, B., De Moura, L.: The Yices SMT solver. Technical report, August 2006. Tool paper at http://yices.csl.sri.com/tool-paper.pdf
4. Fikes, R., Nilsson, N.J.: STRIPS: a new approach to the application of theorem proving to problem solving. Artif. Intell. **2**(3/4), 189–208 (1971)
5. Fourati, F., Bhiri, M.T., Robbana, R.: Verification and validation of PDDL descriptions using Event-B formal method. In: 2016 5th International Conference on Multimedia Computing and Systems (ICMCS), pp. 770–776, September 2016
6. Fu, P., Komendantskaya, E.: Operational semantics of resolution and productivity in horn clause logic. Formal Asp. Comput. **29**(3), 453–474 (2017)
7. Fu, P., Komendantskaya, E., Schrijvers, T., Pond, A.: Proof relevant corecursive resolution. In: Kiselyov, O., King, A. (eds.) FLOPS 2016. LNCS, vol. 9613, pp. 126–143. Springer, Cham (2016). https://doi.org/10.1007/978-3-319-29604-3_9
8. Howey, R., Long, D., Fox, M.: VAL: automatic plan validation, continuous effects and mixed initiative planning using PDDL. In: 16th IEEE International Conference on Tools with Artificial Intelligence, pp. 294–301 (2004)
9. Khatib, L., Muscettola, N., Havelund, K.: Verification of plan models using UPPAAL. In: Rash, J.L., Truszkowski, W., Hinchey, M.G., Rouff, C.A., Gordon, D. (eds.) FAABS 2000. LNCS, vol. 1871, pp. 114–122. Springer, Heidelberg (2001). https://doi.org/10.1007/3-540-45484-5_9
10. Levesque, H.J., Reiter, R., Lespérance, Y., Lin, F., Scherl, R.B.: GOLOG: a logic programming language for dynamic domains. J. Logic Program. **31**(1), 59–83 (1997)

11. McDermott, D., et al.: PDDL - The Planning Domain Definition Language (Version 1. 2). Technical Report CVC TR-98-003/DCS TR-1165, Yale Center for Computational Vision and Control (1998)
12. Necula, G.C.: Proof-carrying code. In: POPL, pp. 106–119 (1997)
13. Ong, L.: Higher-order model checking: an overview. In: 30th Annual ACM/IEEE Symposium on Logic in Computer Science, LICS 2015, Kyoto, Japan, 6–10 July 2015, pp. 1–15 (2015)
14. Raimondi, F., Pecheur, C., Brat, G.: PDVer, a tool to verify PDDL planning domains. In: ICAPS 2009 Workshop on Verification and Validation of Planning and Scheduling Systems, Thessaloniki, Greece, 20 September 2009
15. Reiter, R.: On closed world data bases. In: Gallaire, H., Minker, J. (eds.) Logic and Data Bases, pp. 55–76. Plenum Press, New York (1978)
16. Schubert, A., Urzyczyn, P.: Answer set programming in intuitionistic logic. Indagationes Mathematicae **29**(1), 276–292 (2018). l.E.J. Brouwer, fifty years later
17. Scwaab, C., Hill, A., Farka, F., Komendantskaya, E.: Proof-Carrying Plans: Agda Implementation and Examples (2018). https://github.com/PDTypes
18. Scwaab, C., et al.: Proof-Carrying Plans: Extended Version of This Paper with Appendices (2018). https://github.com/PDTypes/PADL19/blob/master/padl-pddl-verification.pdf
19. Sorensen, M.H., Urzyczyn, P.: Lectures on the Curry-Howard Isomorphism, Studies in Logic, vol. 149. Elsevier, New York (2006)
20. Wadler, P.: Propositions as types. Commun. ACM **58**(12), 75–84 (2015)
21. Waldinger, R.J.: Achieving several goals simultaneously. Machine Intelligence 8 (1977)
22. Zarrieß, B., Claßen, J.: Decidable verification of GOLOG programs over non-local effect actions. In: Schuurmans, D., Wellman, M.P. (eds.) Proceedings of the Thirtieth AAAI Conference on Artificial Intelligence, Phoenix, Arizona, USA, 12–17 February 2016, pp. 1109–1115. AAAI Press (2016)

Static Partitioning of Spreadsheets for Parallel Execution

Alexander Asp Bock[✉][iD]

Computer Science Department, IT University of Copenhagen,
Copenhagen, Denmark
albo@itu.dk

Abstract. Spreadsheets are popular tools for end-user development and complex modelling but can suffer from poor performance. While end-users are usually domain experts they are seldom IT professionals that can leverage today's abundant multicore architectures to offset such poor performance. We present an iterative, greedy algorithm for automatically partitioning spreadsheets into load-balanced, acyclic groups of cells that can be scheduled to run on shared-memory multicore processors. A big-step cost semantics for the spreadsheet formula language is used to estimate work and guide partitioning. The algorithm does not require end-users to modify the spreadsheet in any way. We implement three extensions to the algorithm for further accelerating computation; two of which recognise common cell structures known as cell arrays that naturally express a degree of parallelism. To the best of our knowledge, no such automatic algorithm has previously been proposed for partitioning spreadsheets. We report a maximum 24-fold speed-up on 48 logical cores.

Keywords: Spreadsheets · Partitioning · Parallelism

1 Introduction

Spreadsheets are popular tools for end-user development, modelling and education. Spreadsheet end-users create and maintain large, complex spreadsheets over several years [14] and this complexity often leads to costly errors [10] and poor performance [19]. End-users are usually domain experts but are seldom IT professionals and may thus require help from experts to accelerate computation.

In recent years, multicore processors have become ubiquitous. For spreadsheet end-users to benefit from this powerful hardware, they should have a tool at their disposal to automatically identify and exploit parallelism in their spreadsheets. Spreadsheets lend themselves well to parallelization as they are both declarative and first-order functional languages.

In this paper, we present an iterative, greedy algorithm for automatically and statically partitioning a spreadsheet into load-balanced, acyclic groups of cells.

Supported by the Independent Research Fund Denmark.

J. J. Alferes and M. Johansson (Eds.): PADL 2019, LNCS 11372, pp. 221–237, 2019.
https://doi.org/10.1007/978-3-030-05998-9_14

Partitioning is guided by a big-step cost semantics to estimate the work of cells and to produce well-balanced partitions. We implement the algorithm in the research spreadsheet application Funcalc [18] written in C#, and we believe this is the first thorough investigation of static partitioning of spreadsheets.

2   Related Work

Spreadsheet research has primarily focused on error detection, handling and mitigation [6] and less on parallelization. In this section, we briefly discuss some of the research relevant to spreadsheet parallelism.

There exist multiple distributed systems for spreadsheet calculation like ActiveSheets [3], Nimrod [2] and HPC Services for Excel [16]. All three systems require manual modification of the spreadsheet which may take a substantial amount of time or require help from experts.

In his 1996 dissertation, Wack [21] investigated parallelization of spreadsheet programs using distributed systems and an associated machine model. He partitioned and scheduled a set of predefined patterns and parallelized them via message-passing in a network of work stations. Our algorithm does not rely on pre-defined patterns or an existing network of work stations but instead targets shared-memory multicore processors.

Biermann et al. [5] rewrote so-called *cell arrays* to higher-order, compiled function calls on arrays completely transparent to end-users. Their approach parallelized the internal evaluation of each rewritten array but evaluated disjoint cell arrays sequentially.

LibreOffice Calc automatically compiled data-parallel expressions into OpenCL kernels that execute on AMD GPU's [20]. They reported a 500-fold speed-up for a particular spreadsheet.

In recent work [4], we presented a task-based parallel spreadsheet interpreter, dubbed Puncalc, that automatically discovers parallelism and finds cyclic references in parallel. The system targets shared-memory multiprocessors and does not require modification of the spreadsheet. The algorithm obtained roughly a 16-fold speed-up on 48 cores on the same set of benchmark spreadsheets used in this paper. Puncalc is a dynamic algorithm that may not distribute work as well as the static approach presented here.

Our static partitioning algorithm is primarily inspired by the work of Sarkar et al. [17] on the first-order functional language SISAL which was intended to supersede Fortran as the primary language for scientific computing. Sarkar worked on an optimising compiler that automatically extracted parallelism by analysing an intermediate graph representation of the program. The program was then partitioned at compile-time and scheduled onto available processors at runtime. SISAL programs were shown to run on par with Fortran programs on a contemporary supercomputer [8].

3 Contributions

We present the following key contributions:

1. A cost model based on a big-step cost semantics for Funcalc's formula language (Sect. 5).
2. An algorithm for statically partitioning spreadsheets and scheduling them on shared-memory multicore processors (Sect. 6).
3. Three extensions to the algorithm for further accelerating execution of the partitioned spreadsheet. Two of the extensions exploit common cell structures known as *cell arrays* that naturally express some degree of parallelism (Sects. 7.1 to 7.3).

4 Background: Spreadsheet Concepts

We now introduce some basic spreadsheet concepts deemed necessary for reading this paper. Readers already familiar with the subject can skip this section while those interested in learning more are encouraged to read [18].

4.1 Formulas and Cell References

A cell can contain either a constant, such as a number, string or error (e.g. #NA or #DIV/0!); or a formula expression denoted by a leading equals character (e.g. =1+2). Each cell has a unique address denoted by its column and row where columns start at A and rows at 1. Formulas can refer to other cells by using their addresses, or they can refer to an area of cells using the addresses of two corner cells separated by a colon. For example, cell C1 in Fig. 1a refers to cells A1 and A2 while cell C3 refers to the cell area spanned by cells A1 and B2.

Cell references may be relative or absolute in each dimension. Relative references refer to other cells using offsets, so the referenced cell depends on the position of the referring cell. Absolute references do not change and are prefixed by a dollar sign. For example, the formula =$A2 in cell C2 refers absolutely to column A but relatively to row 2, so copying it to cell C3 would change the cell reference to $A3, but it would remain unchanged if copied it to D2 since the column is absolute. This reference scheme is called the A1 format. Relative references are more clearly expressed in the R1C1 format where relative references are denoted by square brackets containing an offset, and absolute references are denoted by the absence of square brackets and an absolute row or column number. The same spreadsheet is shown in Fig. 1b in R1C1 format.

4.2 The Support and Dependency Graphs

Cell references establish a cell *dependency graph*. Its inverse, the *support graph*, captures cell support and is analogous to a dataflow graph where nodes are cells and data flows along the edges from dependencies to supported cells. Cell C1 in Fig. 1a depends on A1 and A2 while both A1 and A2 support C1. Both the dependency and support graphs may be cyclic.

	A	B	C
1	10	20	=A1+A2
2	30	40	=$A2
3			=A1:B2

(a)

	A	B	C
1	10	20	=R[+0]C[-2]+R[+1]C[-2]
2	30	40	=R[+0]C1
3			=R[+0]C[-3]:R[+1]C[-2]

(b)

Fig. 1. An example spreadsheet in A1 and R1C1 reference formats.

4.3 Recalculation

There are two major types of recalculation. *Full recalculation* unconditionally reevaluates all formula cells. *Minimal recalculation* only reevaluates the transitive closure of cells reachable, via the support graph, from cells modified by the user. In Fig. 1a, whenever a user edits the value in A1, cells C1 and C3 must be updated to reflect the change. The static partitioning algorithm considers all cells in the spreadsheet and thus performs a full recalculation.

4.4 Cell Arrays

Also known as copy-equivalent formulas [12] or cp-similar cells [1], cell arrays [9] denote a contiguous rectangular area of formulas that share the same formula expression in R1C1 format and thus the same computational semantics [9]. A 3 rows by 1 column cell array in column B is shown in Fig. 2a in A1 format and in Fig. 2b in R1C1 format. The latter format clearly shows that the formulas in the cell array share a common expression.

Cell arrays are common in spreadsheets because they describe bulk operations on collections of cells similar to e.g. `map` and `reduce` on arrays in functional programming. These bulk operations can usually be parallelized as we shall see later. For example, the cell array in Fig. 2a effectively describes a `map` operation on column A. Dou et al. [9] found that 69% (7416 out of 10754) of spreadsheets containing formulas from the EUSES [11] and Enron [13] corpora also contained cell arrays, and that they contained on average 80 cell arrays each. The benchmark spreadsheets from LibreOffice Calc used in this paper are also mainly comprised of large cell arrays.

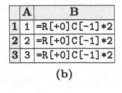

	A	B
1	1	=A1*2
2	2	=A2*2
3	3	=A3*2

(a)

	A	B
1	1	=R[+0]C[-1]*2
2	2	=R[+0]C[-1]*2
3	3	=R[+0]C[-1]*2

(b)

	A	B
1	1	=R[+5]C[+0]*2
2	2	=R[+5]C[+0]*2
3	3	=R[+5]C[+0]*2

(c) Transitive cell array.

	A	B
1	1	=R[+0]C[-1]*2
2	2	=R[+0]C[-1]*2
3	3	=R[+0]C[-1]*2

(d) Intransitive cell array.

Fig. 2. Each cell in the cell array of column B in Fig. 2a takes the corresponding value in column A and multiplies it by two.

Cell arrays can be classified as either *transitive* (Fig. 2c) or *intransitive* (Fig. 2d) [5]. If a cell array only contains formulas that do not reference the cell array itself, we say that it is intransitive, otherwise it is transitive. The need for this distinction will become clear later in Sects. 6 and 7 when we describe the algorithm and two of its extensions.

4.5   Array Formulas

When a user selects a cell area and enters a formula that returns an array, the elements of the array are distributed across the selected area. The cells in the area share the same singular formula expression but each cell refers only to part of the array.

5   Cost Model

Any static partitioning algorithm needs a cost model to produce well-balanced partitions. Specifically, we are concerned with two metrics: the cost of evaluating a cell and the cost of synchronizing groups of cells in the partition when it is run. We discuss these in turn.

5.1   Big-Step Cost Semantics

We have developed a concrete big-step cost semantics for Funcalc's formula language which we only briefly discuss here due to space limitations. We refer interested readers to the full details in our technical report [7]. The general judgement form $\sigma, \alpha \vdash e \Downarrow v, c$ states that given environment σ mapping cells to values and an environment α mapping cells to array formulas, the expression e may evaluate to some value v at cost c. The rule for the SUM built-in function is shown below. The cost is given as integers that effectively describe the number of operations needed to evaluate an expression but we intend to use more precise costs in the future e.g. obtained from profiling.

$$\frac{\sigma, \alpha \vdash e_1 \Downarrow v_1, c_1 \quad \ldots \quad \sigma, \alpha \vdash e_n \Downarrow v_n, c_n}{\sigma, \alpha \vdash \text{SUM}(e_1, \ldots, e_n) \Downarrow \sum_{i=1}^{n} v_i, 1 + \sum_{i=1}^{n} c_i} \text{ (sum)}$$

Rule (sum) states that if all its argument expressions evaluate to values at some cost, the function call may evaluate to the sum of those values. The total cost is the sum of costs of the individual function arguments plus one.

The big-step cost semantics has other uses. It may serve as a reliable, formal reference for implementations as it does for other functional programming languages; or used to guide other types of partitioning or parallelisation strategies such as off-loading work to a GPU [20]. We could also envision a refactoring tool that can identify and report bottlenecks or costly operations in spreadsheets.

5.2   Synchronization Cost

Sarkar's framework [17] targeted both shared-memory and distributed systems so their cost model had to accommodate different types of communication costs. Our algorithm targets shared-memory multicore architectures where the cost model must capture synchronization between threads. For simplicity, we use a constant cost for synchronization between threads based on benchmarking results. While this does not take memory latency and other hardware aspects into account, it is currently sufficient for generating partitions capable of accelerating spreadsheet computation. In the future, we intend to develop a more precise model based on the hardware and operating system.

6   Static Partitioning Algorithm

Sarkar [17] showed that finding the optimal partition is NP-complete in the strong sense and developed an approximate partitioning algorithm which was close to optimal in practice. In this section, we present a similar partitioning algorithm for spreadsheets. We first assign costs to all formula cells, then partition the spreadsheet by iteratively merging groups of cells and scheduling the computation of those groups. Afterwards, we introduce a preprocessing step in Sect. 6.3 that speeds up partitioning and a postprocessing step in Sect. 6.4 that applies an optimisation to sequential paths in the resultant partition.

6.1   Problem Formulation

We view a spreadsheet as a graph $G = (V, E)$ consisting of a set of formula cells $V = \{c_0, \ldots, c_n\}$ and a set of support edges $E \subset (V \times V)$. We can follow the edges in the opposite direction to follow cell dependencies. Inspired by Sarkar [17], we wish to partition V into an acyclic partition $P_f = \{\tau_0, \ldots, \tau_m\}$ consisting of disjoint, load-balanced groups τ_i where the cells in a group are a subset of V: $\text{CELLS}(\tau_i) \subseteq V$, all formula cells are contained in some τ: $\bigcup_{i=0}^{m} \text{CELLS}(\tau_i) = V$, and P_f minimizes an objective function F: $\arg\min F(P) = P_f$. Note that we do not require P_f to be optimal. The objective function F approximates the trade-off between parallelism and synchronization in a partition and is introduced in the next section. We can view a partition P as a condensation of the cell graph where subsets of cells have been assigned to some group τ_i and refer to this condensed graph as the τ-graph. Any partition P produced by the algorithm is required to be acyclic to ease scheduling but we defer a detailed discussion. We define the following operations on a group τ.

- $\text{CELLS}(\tau)$: The set of cells in τ.
- $\text{PRED}(\tau)$: The set of predecessors of τ.
- $\text{SUCC}(\tau)$: The set of successors of τ.
- $\text{TIME}(\tau)$: The estimated total time to recalculate each cell in $\text{CELLS}(\tau)$.
- $\text{SYNC}(\tau)$: The synchronization cost of τ.

The predecessors and successors are determined by the dependency and support edges of the cells in $\text{CELLS}(\tau)$.

6.2   Iterative, Greedy Group Merging

Starting from some initial partition, we now iteratively and greedily merge pairs of τ's as guided by the objective function F, until we reach the coarsest partition consisting of a single τ containing all cells with no parallelism but no synchronization overhead either. We select the intermediate partition that minimized F as the output of the algorithm. The objective function F is the maximum of the *critical path* term and the *overhead* term [17] as given by Eq. (3).

$$Sync(P) = \sum_{\tau \in P} (|\text{PRED}(\tau)| + |\text{SUCC}(\tau)|) \cdot Sync(\tau) \qquad (1)$$

$$Time(P) = \sum_{\tau \in P} \text{TIME}(\tau) \qquad (2)$$

$$F(P) = max \left(\frac{CPL(P)}{Time(P) \div N}, 1 + \frac{Sync(P)}{Time(P)} \right) \qquad (3)$$

The total synchronization cost of P in Eq. (1) is the number of predecessors and successors of each τ times its synchronization cost. The total time to execute P in Eq. (2) is the summation of the time taken to execute each $\tau \in P$, and is constant throughout partitioning since the amount of work in the partition remains constant but its distribution between τ's is not. Finally, the objective function in Eq. (3) is the maximum of the *critical path* and *overhead* terms. The former term is the critical path length (denoted as CPL in the equation), i.e. the most expensive sequential path in the τ-graph, divided by the ideal parallel execution time of P given N total processors. The overhead term is the synchronization cost of P normalised by the time taken to execute P.

A fine partition with a critical path length close to the ideal execution time would have a critical path term close to one, but is likely to have dominant overhead term since many τ's need to synchronize. Conversely, a coarser partition may have a small overhead term as the coarseness of the partition means less groups need to synchronize, but a dominant critical path term since many τ's might have been merged into the critical path. In this way, the merging step uses F to balance the degree of parallelism versus the cost of synchronization.

When selecting two groups τ_1 and τ_2 to merge, we select τ_1 as the group with the largest synchronization cost in hopes of reducing the partition's overall synchronization cost [17]. We select τ_2 as the group that yields the smallest change in the critical path length if we were to merge it with τ_1. During iteration, we record $F(P)$ for each partition and return the partition P_f which minimized F as the output of the algorithm.

Acyclic Constraint. To keep all partitions acyclic, we impose an *acyclic constraint*[1] on each partition [17]. When two groups τ_1 and τ_2 are selected for a merge, we also merge any τ that lies on a path between τ_1 and τ_2, and thus outside the *convex subgraph* defined by τ_1 and τ_2.

---

[1] Originally referred to as the *convexity constraint* in [17] as it relates to convex subgraphs.

Definition 1. *A subgraph H of a directed graph G is convex if for every pair of vertices $a, b \in H$, any path between a and b is fully contained in H.*

For example, if there is a path $\tau_1 \to \tau \to \tau_2$ and we did not merge τ as well, we would introduce a cycle in the τ-graph. Intuitively, the acyclic constraint prohibits τ's from spawning and waiting for work (a loop between two groups), and fork-join parallelism where the fork e.g. happens at τ_1 and the join at τ_2. While this may remove some parallelism from the partition, it greatly simplifies scheduling.

6.3   Cell Array Preprocessing

In a preprocessing step, we assign each cell array to its own τ in the initial partition so we can later exploit any internal parallelism. This has two advantages. First, it decreases the number of groups that need to be considered for merging, lowering the partitioning time. Second, the algorithm initially needs to determine the predecessors and successors of each τ, which is necessary for computing the synchronization cost of a partition and keeping track of dependencies when merging. Instead of querying each cell in a potentially large cell array in some τ, we can in most cases query only its four corner cells to quickly find predecessors in $\mathrm{PRED}(\tau)$ that also contain cell arrays. Due to the complementary nature of the support and dependency graphs, this also establishes that τ is a successor of each such $\tau_p \in \mathrm{PRED}(\tau)$. In other cases, we conservatively query each cell.

The preprocessing step can be said to be optimistic as many real-world spreadsheets contain large cell arrays that refer to other cell arrays, so we expect that the preprocessing will usually succeed. Most of our benchmark spreadsheets fall into this category.

Determining Reachability. Consider the two single-column cell arrays spanned by cell areas B1:B255 and C1:C255 respectively in Fig. 3a. The top and bottom cell references of the blue cell array in column B can both reach only constants in column A and so we cannot conclude anything about the dependencies of the remaining cells in the cell array since a subset of them might be able to reach some other cell array. The top and bottom cells of the red cell array in column C can both reach the blue cell array in column B and we conclude that all the cells in the range C2:C254 can also reach the blue cell array by virtue of the identical relative cell references shared by the cells. If the top and bottom cells of column C's cell array could reach different τ's, as in Fig. 3b, we cannot conclude anything about the other cells in the cell array and instead query each cell.

We can similarly analyse array formulas which is straight forward since their cells share a single formula expression. Due to space limitations, we omit their analysis here.

We exclude any corners whose cell references are transitive, i.e. all cells they refer to belong to the cell array itself. The rest of the analysis has three primary cases. In the first case, we handle cell references that are absolute in both

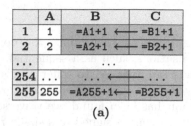

Fig. 3. Preprocessing of different cell arrays.

dimensions (e.g. A1). Every cell in the cell array depends on such a reference regardless of the relative position of the referring cell. Absolute cell areas referenced from the cell array must be fully enclosed in the reachable τ. If they are not, the other part of the cell area may belong to some τ_i which we will only discover by examining each cell in the referenced cell area.

In the second case, we observe that even cell references that are not fully absolute can be considered absolute in the context of a cell array as shown in Fig. 4. Since the cell array in column B refers to cell A1 using a row-absolute but column-relative reference, all cells in the cell array will always refer to that cell and it can be viewed as a constant. The same is true for row-relative, column-absolute references and single-row cell arrays.

	A	B
1	=PI()	
2		
3	6	=2*A$1*A3
4	2	=2*A$1*A4
5	...	...

Fig. 4. Spreadsheet calculating the circumference $2\pi r$ of various circle radii. Cell A1 holds the constant π which the cell array in column B refers to. Since the reference is row-absolute and column-relative, all cells in the cell array always refer to A1. This scenario occurs in the **building-design** spreadsheet.

The third and final case handles any other *relative* cell references. For each reference in the cell array's formula expression, we consider each unique pair of corners and examine what cells or areas they refer to. This is necessary since all pairs, even diagonally opposite corners, may refer to the same τ. For single-cell references, if both corners of a cell array in τ_i can reach cells belonging to the cell array of some τ_j, we add τ_j as a predecessor of τ_i. For cell areas, we require the same conditions but also require that the referenced cell areas are wholly contained in the reachable τ_i as for the second case. Any cells that are not part of a cell array, and thus not handled by this analysis, are put into their own initial τ. We are currently working on a formal version of the analysis.

6.4 Postprocessing

The algorithm is approximate and not guaranteed to produce the optimal partition [17] and may miss obvious optimisations, such as a sequential chain of dependencies in the τ-graph whose parts are assigned to different τ's. We could avoid unnecessary synchronization by instead assigning the entire chain to a single τ. Therefore, once the final partition has been found, we traverse the τ-graph to find such chains and ensure that they are assigned to a single τ.

6.5 Scheduling Partitions

The merging step of the algorithm leaves us with a final partition $P_f = \{\tau_0, \ldots, \tau_m\}$. Since P_f is acyclic, we can schedule the partition by first topologically sorting the τ-graph by its dependencies then create tasks using the Task Parallel Library (TPL) [15] to run each τ. We iterate through the topologically sorted list and either (1) mark a τ without dependencies as a *source* and create a task to execute it; (2) create a TPL continuation task that waits for *all* its dependent tasks to finish before starting. We then start every source task and wait for all tasks to complete. Each non-source task first checks if all its dependent tasks ran to normal completion. If not, it immediately stops and propagates any errors to its successors so that execution can quickly terminate.

7 Extensions

Cells within each τ are evaluated sequentially and the algorithm only parallelizes the execution of the τ-graph, disregarding any additional parallelism inside each τ. In this section, we present three extensions to the algorithm to remedy this: the first extension uses *nested parallelism* within cell arrays; the second extension uses our parallel spreadsheet interpreter [4] in each τ; the third extension uses the rewriting tool from [5] to rewrite cell arrays to calls to compiled higher-order functions that can also be executed in parallel.

7.1 Nested Cell Array Parallelism

This extension relies on the fact that spawning nested TPL tasks within a task will enqueue them in the current threadpool thread's local queue, circumventing the global queue and possibly reducing contention. However, we cannot necessarily spawn a task for each cell in the cell array since its references may be transitive [5].

In Fig. 2d on page 4, each reference in the formula of the cell array in column B refers to a cell in the same row but in column A. Since none of the relative cell references are transitive, we can easily spawn a task for each cell in the cell array, and because a τ is only executed when all its inputs are ready, its dependencies will already have been computed. In Fig. 2c, each cell reference refers transitively to a cell five rows below it. Blindly spawning tasks for each cell would not properly synchronize, but we can still parallelize some of the work by subdividing the cell array into subgroups of five which will not have any transitive references to themselves [5]. We then execute each subdivision in parallel in a lockstep fashion. Therefore, we must first perform an analysis of all cell arrays to determine if and how they can be executed in parallel, but do not currently parallelize transitive cell arrays.

7.2 Puncalc: A Parallel Interpreter for Spreadsheets

Unlike nested cell array parallelism, using our parallel spreadsheet interpreter does not require an additional analysis of cell arrays since the algorithm already ensures proper synchronization [4]. The interpreter follows the support graph in parallel in search of cells to compute, but this would mean that cells belonging to successor τ's might be evaluated prematurely. To avoid this, we disallow the interpreter from following support edges.

7.3 Rewriting Cell Arrays to Higher-Order Function Calls

Biermann et al. [5] analysed cell arrays and rewrote eligible ones to an array formula consisting of a call to a higher-order, compiled function based on patterns exhibited by the cell array's formulae. The higher-order, compiled functions are called *sheet-defined* functions and are a feature of Funcalc [18]. Users can define functions in cells which are then compiled to Common Intermediate Language (CIL) bytecode. Based on the cell array analysis, an expression might be rewritten to a `map` or `prefix` operation or not rewritten at all. This has led to good speed-ups, even with no parallelization and even for spreadsheets that contain little computation such as some from the EUSES corpus [11]. The spreadsheet is rewritten after being loaded from disk, so no change to the static partitioning algorithm is necessary since we already handle array formulas.

8 Results

8.1 Experimental Setup

To evaluate our algorithm, we adapted the spreadsheets from the LibreOffice Calc benchmark suite[2] to Funcalc. We partitioned all spreadsheets for each core configuration since the partitioning algorithm is dependent on the number of available cores (see Eq. (3) in Sect. 6.2).

Our test machine was an Intel Xeon E5-2680 v3 with two separate hardware chips with 12 2.5 GHz cores each and hyperthreading (48 logical cores total), running 64-bit Windows 10 and .NET 4.7.1. We initially performed three warm-up runs and ran each benchmark for two iterations. In each iteration, we ran the

---

[2] Available   unmodified   at   https://gerrit.libreoffice.org/gitweb?p=benchmark.git; a=tree.

benchmark ten times, for a total of 20 runs, and computed the average execution time.[3] We report the average of those two averages in Table 2. We disabled the TPL's heuristics for thread creation and destruction so that a thread was created per processor at start-up.

8.2 Discussion

Partitioning currently takes on the order of a few minutes where the dominating factor is applying the big-step cost rules to each cell. We could rectify this by caching and reusing the computed costs if cells are not modified between partitioning. This may inflate memory usage as the spreadsheets contain between 108 332 and 812 693 cells whose costs would need to be cached. It is also possible to save the partition alongside the spreadsheet data so that it can be loaded quickly next time without having to partition again. The partitioning itself is very fast primarily due to the cell array analysis discussed in Sect. 6.3 and the presence of large, dominating cell arrays as we discuss in a moment. There are five key observations to be made from Tables 1 and 2.

Observation 1. The benchmark spreadsheets contain large cell arrays that contain almost all formula cells.

Table 1 shows that all our benchmark spreadsheets are dominated by large, intransitive cell arrays which contain almost all formula cells. This aligns with the observations made by Dou et al. [9] that cell arrays are common structures in spreadsheets which has two implications. First, the preprocessing step successfully analyses most of the cell arrays. Second, the many large cell arrays means that there is a lot of parallel computation we can exploit with the three proposed extensions from Sect. 7.

Table 1. From left to right: The number of cell arrays in the LibreOffice Calc spreadsheets; the percentage of formulas contained in cell arrays; the average size of cell arrays; and the number of rewritten intransitive and transitive cell arrays. No transitive cell arrays are rewritten because none of the spreadsheets contain any.

Spreadsheet	Cell arrays	% of Formulas	Average size	Rewritten cell arrays
building-design	6	99.93%	18 042	6/0
energy-markets	76	99.99%	7032	76/0
grossprofit	9	99.94%	15 000	9/0
ground-water	12	100%	10 533	12/0
stock-history	22	99.97%	10 292	20/0
stocks-price	8	99.99%	101 578	8/0

---

[3] Raw data available at https://github.com/popular-parallel-programming/p3-results/tree/master/static-partitioning.

Table 2. Absolute running times in seconds for each configuration of cores for the base implementation and its three extensions. Speed-up is for parallel execution on 48 cores relative to normal sequential execution of Funcalc. Bold numbers denote the fastest execution for each spreadsheet. The standard deviation is within ±0.08 for all results, except for the base implementation running `stocks-price` on 16 cores with a standard deviation of ±0.18.

Spreadsheet	Sequential	x2	x4	x8	x16	x32	x48	Speed-up
Base implementation								
`building-design`	32.12	**30.72**	30.92	31.26	31.05	30.85	31.79	1.01x
`energy-markets`	168.16	157.08	95.75	66.51	**52.95**	75.45	139.41	1.21x
`grossprofit`	102.19	102.33	53.86	33.25	**32.59**	32.73	34.66	2.95x
`ground-water`	81.26	72.42	36.13	24.49	17.65	21.02	**17.30**	4.70x
`stock-history`	64.90	61.90	35.54	19.12	**17.20**	18.69	17.64	3.68x
`stocks-price`	102.74	**158.94**	171.10	169.56	174.53	168.10	172.34	0.60x
Nested cell array parallelism extension (Sect. 7.1)								
`building-design`	32.12	26.23	13.32	7.33	3.98	2.16	**1.62**	19.84x
`energy-markets`	168.16	156.68	95.84	66.67	**53.22**	89.35	200.28	0.84x
`grossprofit`	102.19	102.72	53.31	32.46	21.06	**17.16**	19.95	5.12x
`ground-water`	81.26	69.97	35.59	19.29	10.41	5.32	**3.71**	21.89x
`stock-history`	64.90	58.84	29.94	17.73	10.47	7.00	**6.17**	10.52x
`stocks-price`	102.74	130.46	166.70	164.37	**74.44**	145.48	166.87	0.62x
Puncalc extension (Sect. 7.2)								
`building-design`	32.12	31.97	16.12	8.86	4.82	2.68	**1.91**	16.81x
`energy-markets`	168.16	199.63	146.66	128.06	158.50	**90.95**	202.04	0.83x
`grossprofit`	102.19	106.70	55.22	33.48	21.57	**17.55**	20.25	5.05x
`ground-water`	81.26	80.47	41.22	22.81	12.17	6.26	**4.31**	18.87x
`stock-history`	64.90	59.05	29.97	17.81	10.92	7.12	**7.03**	9.24x
`stocks-price`	102.74	148.56	174.75	168.01	**65.26**	143.08	168.25	0.61x
Cell rewriting extension (Sect. 7.3)								
`building-design`	32.12	45.35	22.79	12.49	6.58	3.35	**2.39**	13.44x
`energy-markets`	168.16	206.16	150.10	99.84	**91.04**	335.60	400.26	0.42x
`grossprofit`	102.19	109.75	58.79	36.74	**26.56**	31.98	63.51	1.61x
`ground-water`	81.26	111.90	57.74	32.07	16.71	8.34	**5.79**	14.03x
`stock-history`	64.90	51.81	26.94	14.31	7.37	3.91	**2.72**	23.88x
`stocks-price`	102.74	149.98	91.09	66.45	**62.60**	205.99	239.11	0.43x

Observation 2. The performance of the base implementation shows that it is necessary to exploit the internal parallelism of cell arrays.

In Table 2, we get varying results for the base implementation but do get some speed-up, especially for the grossprofit, ground-water and stock-history spreadsheets. However, it is evident that we must also exploit the additional parallelism exposed by cell arrays when comparing these results with those of the three extensions.

Observation 3. The nested cell array extension produces the best overall speed-ups on 48 cores.

Out of the three extensions, the nested cell array parallelism extension gives the overall best speed-ups on 48 cores with a maximum speed-up of 21.89 for the ground-water spreadsheet.

Observation 4. The energy-markets, grossprofit and stocks-price spreadsheets have less predictable speed-ups and performance consistently peaks at 16 or 32 cores. Adding more cores seems to slow down recalculation.

Observation 4 applies to the base implementation and its three extensions with the exception of stocks-price for the base implementation where the best speed-up is achieved at 2 cores, although it is still slower than sequential execution. It is especially perplexing for energy-markets that contains ample parallelism since it consists of multiple independent cell arrays which is captured by partitioning. Likewise, stocks-price and grossprofit also contain some degree of parallelism.

The slowdown may stem from TPL scheduling and hardware. Our test machine has two separate chips of 12 physical cores each which may result in increasing amounts of off-chip communication. We still get approximately 1.3–3.0x speed-up for 16 and 32 cores for these spreadsheets which may be consistent with the above hardware observation since using more threads may increase off-chip communication.

One would also be inclined to suspect our simplified communication model since the amount of synchronization needed to execute a partition may outweigh the amount of parallelism in the spreadsheets in some cases.

In [4], we measured different structural properties of the spreadsheets but found no correlation with performance. Upon further investigation, the garbage collector was spending excessive amounts of time on generation zero and one collections which meant that less time was spent doing useful computation.[4] When inspecting the managed heap, memory usage stemmed partly from allocation of many small, ephemeral objects related to calling specific intrinsic Funcalc functions which were mostly used by the spreadsheets that exhibit poor performance. We also noticed memory usage related to TPL internals and task creation which may increase with the number of cores. The latter is likely caused by the fine granularity work distribution from parallelisation of cell arrays. We could chunk cell arrays based on the number of processors to create less tasks with a more

---

[4] We used the Windows Performance Monitor to monitor performance characteristics and WinDbg to inspect the managed heap.

sensible work distribution. One could also switch to manual thread management to circumvent TPL and task allocations. Finally, some object references might be retained when they should be garbage collected instead. We are currently working on identifying and rectifying these issues.

Observation 5. The cell rewriting extension achieves different speed-ups compared to the other extensions for some spreadsheets. The nested cell array and Puncalc extensions achieve similar speed-ups.

Table 1 shows that all intransitive cell arrays are rewritten except for two in the `stock-history` spreadsheet and that no transitive cell arrays exist in any of the spreadsheets. The results are quite different from the other two extensions. The `energy-markets` and `stocks-price` spreadsheets have even worse performance on 48 cores but their peak performance at 16 and 32 cores is comparable to the peak performances of the other two extensions. For the `ground-water` spreadsheet, we observe 14.03x speed-up as opposed to 21.89x and 18.87x for extension 1 and 2 respectively. The best speed-up out of all the results is 23.88 for 48 cores for the `stock-history` spreadsheet. We offer two explanations for these differences. First, more efficient and parallelizable sheet-defined functions may be generated for the `stock-history` spreadsheet. Second, Table 1 shows the average size of cell arrays is much larger in `stock-history` so more cells are rewritten that invoke generated bytecode instead of using the slower interpreter.

The two other extensions achieve similar speed-ups since their method of parallelization is similar. The nested cell array extension beats the Puncalc extension which is likely because it directly spawns tasks for each cell in the cell array while the Puncalc extension uses additional synchronization and a global shared work queue, as it is built to evaluate any kind of topology, not just cell arrays.

9   Conclusion

We have presented a static partitioning algorithm for spreadsheets that automatically identifies sufficient parallelism and achieves good speed-ups on a set of benchmark spreadsheets. A big-step cost semantics for the formula language of Funcalc was used to estimate the cost of cells. Finally, we extended the partitioning algorithm in three different ways to further accelerate computation.

While cell arrays are common structures in spreadsheets, they may not universally be so. We do not benchmark on spreadsheets that contain few or no cell arrays where the partitioning time and speed-up will likely be affected. In future work, we intend to benchmark large spreadsheets with these characteristics and ones with large, transitive cell arrays.

We have not compared any of our results to Excel or LibreOffice Calc and we do not believe this is particularly useful. Both Excel and LibreOffice Calc are intended for real-world use while Funcalc is primarily intended for research and has not been publicly distributed.

It would be interesting to capture hardware characteristics in the cost model to control the amount of parallelism if we suspect that execution may suffer if we use too many threads. It may also suffice to re-enable TPL's heuristics for thread creation or opt for manual thread management. Lastly, we acknowledge that our synchronization model may be too simplistic and it would be more meaningful to develop a model that takes hardware into account, e.g. based on benchmarks that compare on-chip versus off-chip synchronization. Another hardware aspect to consider is that memory bandwidth and cache hierarchies often limit scalability in NUMA systems which could also be incorporated into our synchronization cost model.

Acknowledgements. The author would like to thank Peter Sestoft and Florian Biermann for valuable insight and discussions during the development of this work, as well as Peter Sestoft and Holger Stadel Borum for proofreading.

References

1. Abraham, R., Erwig, M.: Inferring templates from spreadsheets. In: ICSE (2006)
2. Abramson, D., Sosic, R., Giddy, J., Hall, B.: Nimrod: a tool for performing parametrised simulations using distributed workstations. In: HPDC (1995)
3. Abramson, D., Roe, P., Kotler, L., Mather, D.: Activesheets: super-computing with spreadsheets. In: HPC (2001)
4. Biermann, F., Bock, A.A.: Puncalc: task-based parallelism and speculative reevaluation in spreadsheets. In: HLPP (2018)
5. Biermann, F., Dou, W., Sestoft, P.: Rewriting high-level spreadsheet structures into higher-order functional programs. In: Calimeri, F., Hamlen, K., Leone, N. (eds.) PADL 2018. LNCS, vol. 10702, pp. 20–35. Springer, Cham (2018). https://doi.org/10.1007/978-3-319-73305-0_2
6. Bock, A.A.: A literature review of spreadsheet technology. Technical report (2016). ISBN 978-87-7949-364-3
7. Bock, A.A., Bøgholm, T., Sestoft, P., Thomsen, B., Thomsen, L.L.: Concrete and abstract cost semantics for spreadsheets. Technical report (2018). ISBN 978-87-7949-369-8
8. Cann, D.: Retire Fortran? A debate rekindled. Commun. ACM **35**(8), 81–89 (1992)
9. Dou, W., Cheung, S.C., Wei, J.: Is spreadsheet ambiguity harmful? Detecting and repairing spreadsheet smells due to ambiguous computation. In: ICSE (2014)
10. EuSpRiG Horror Stories. http://eusprig.org/horror-stories.htm
11. Fisher, M., Rothermel, G.: The EUSES spreadsheet corpus: a shared resource for supporting experimentation with spreadsheet dependability mechanisms. In: SIGSOFT SEN (2005)
12. Hermans, F., Dig, D.: BumbleBee: a refactoring environment for spreadsheet formulas. In: SIGSOFT FSE (2014)
13. Hermans, F., Murphy-Hill, E.: Enron's spreadsheets and related emails: a dataset and analysis. In: ICSE (2015)
14. Hermans, F., Pinzger, M., van Deursen, A.: Supporting professional spreadsheet users by generating leveled dataflow diagrams. In: ICSE (2011)
15. Leijen, D., Schulte, W., Burckhardt, S.: The design of a task parallel library. SIGPLAN Not. **44**(10), 227–242 (2009)

16. Microsoft: HPC Services For Excel
17. Sarkar, V.: Partitioning and Scheduling Parallel Programs for Multiprocessors. Research Monographs In Parallel and Distributed Computing. MIT Press, Cambridge (1989)
18. Sestoft, P.: Spreadsheet Implementation Technology. MIT Press, Cambridge (2014)
19. Swidan, A., Hermans, F., Koesoemowidjojo, R.: Improving the performance of a large scale spreadsheet: a case study. In: SANER (2016)
20. Trudeau, J.: Collaboration and Open Source at AMD: LibreOffice. https:// developer.amd.com/collaboration-and-open-source-at-amd-libreoffice/
21. Wack, A.P.: Partitioning dependency graphs for concurrent execution: a parallel spreadsheet on a realistically modeled message passing environment. Ph.D. thesis, Newark, DE, USA (1996)

Author Index

Printed in the United States
By Bookmasters